CREATING THE BILL OF RIGHTS

Sponsored in part by the Virginia Commission on the Bicentennial of the United States Constitution

PROJECT STAFF

Charlene Bangs Bickford, *Co-editor and Director*

Kenneth R. Bowling, *Co-editor*

Helen E. Veit, *Associate editor*

William Charles diGiacomantonio, *Research Assistant*

Creating the

BILL *of* RIGHTS

The Documentary Record from the FIRST FEDERAL CONGRESS

HELEN E. VEIT

KENNETH R. BOWLING

CHARLENE BANGS BICKFORD

EDITORS

The Johns Hopkins University Press Baltimore and London

Printed in the United States of America on acid-free paper
06 05 04 03 02 01 00 99 98 97 7 6 5 4 3

The Johns Hopkins University Press
2715 North Charles Street
Baltimore, MD 21218-4319
The Johns Hopkins Press Ltd., London

Library of Congress Cataloging-in-Publication Data
Creating the Bill of Rights : the documentary record from the First Federal Congress / Helen E. Veit, Kenneth R. Bowling, Charlene Bangs Bickford, editors.
p. cm.
Includes bibliographical references and index.
ISBN 0-8018-4099-6 (alk. paper).—ISBN 0-8018-4100-3 (pbk. : alk. paper)
1. Civil rights—United States—History—Sources. 2. United States—Constitutional law—Amendments—1st-10th—History—Sources. Veit, Helen E. II. Bowling, Kenneth R. III. Bickford, Charlene Bangs.
KF4749.C74 1991
342.73′085—dc20
[347.30285] 90-38624

A catalog record for this book is available from the British Library.

Contents

Foreword

For the first century and a half after the Bill of Rights was added to the Constitution, those Amendments saw surprisingly little judicial use. Until the "constitutional revolution" of 1937, the Supreme Court seemed more concerned with the commerce clause and with the general contours of due process of law. After World War II, and especially with the advent of the Warren Court, the justices began to look, more and more, to the provisions of the Bill of Rights as such. By the time Americans were celebrating the Bill of Rights' bicentennial, nearly all of that document's guarantees had been held to apply, not only to federal action, but to the states as well.

Modern debate over "judicial activism" has brought a renewed interest in the origins of constitutional provisions. Whatever position one takes on the controversy over "original intention," no judge, lawyer, or scholar would want to venture forth uninformed on the views expressed during the adoption of constitutional language. The present volume is bound to enlarge our understanding of the Bill of Rights, as it makes available, with commentary, the views given voice in the First Congress as the Bill of Rights was taking shape.

The founders' generation often counseled a frequent recurrence to fundamental principles. It is fitting that, as Americans embark on the third century of their Constitution and Bill of Rights, nations long under authoritarian yoke look to American precedents and principles for inspiration. The voices of the First Congress speak not only to their posterity in this country, but also to peoples in other lands seeking to understand the precepts of ordered liberty.

A. E. Dick Howard
Chairman, Virginia Commission on the
Bicentennial of the United States Constitution

Introduction

At the 1787 Federal Convention in Philadelphia George Mason of Virginia and Elbridge Gerry of Massachusetts had proposed that the Constitution include a bill of rights to reassure the people that the vastly strengthened federal government would not oppress them and to secure individual rights for the long term. The convention refused unanimously—a critical error that almost proved fatal to ratification. Antifederalist Richard Henry Lee of Virginia unsuccessfully attempted to attach several amendments to the Constitution in September, before the Confederation Congress submitted it to the states for ratification. His recommendations extended beyond guarantees of personal liberty to changes in the structure and powers of the new federal government. Thus, at the very beginning of the ratification debate the word "amendment" acquired a double meaning. This ambiguity continued throughout. Support for amendments could mean a desire either to protect personal liberties or to make fundamental changes in the balance of power between the state and federal governments and in the structure of the federal government, or both.

As time passed, some participants in the debate over the Constitution sought to eliminate this confusion by replacing "amendment" with "bill" or "declaration of rights" for the former sense and "alteration" for the latter. Each of the last four states to ratify submitted its proposed amendments in two lists to reflect this distinction. In this introduction we use "amendment" to refer to both types and "alteration" and "bill of rights" or "rights related amendments" to distinguish between them.

Having failed to attach amendments in the Confederation Congress, Antifederalists demanded them from the ratifying conventions. Party leaders stressed the absence of a bill of rights similar to those in most state constitutions. Many Federalists considered the eloquent pleas of Antifederalist leaders for a bill of rights during the ratification campaign as merely a ruse to cover opposition to a Constitution that threatened their political bases by restricting state sovereignty. Federalists generally opposed amendments, arguing that the Constitution should be allowed a trial period for problems to emerge. They claimed that a bill of rights was unnecessary since most of the states had bills of rights, and the federal government created by the Constitution was limited and could not interfere with those rights. A federal bill of rights might even endanger liberties because it included only certain specified rights, leaving others unprotected, and implied that the federal government had the power to decide which rights to guarantee. Antifederalists believed the Federalists' arguments to be naive, since the Constitution made the federal government supreme over the states. They insisted that amendments should be one of the first matters taken up by Congress.

Delaware, New Jersey, Georgia, and Connecticut ratified without the issue of amendments creating much stir. In Pennsylvania, Antifederalists unsuccessfully urged the ratification convention to propose fifteen primarily rights related amendments in conjunction with its adoption. Although published by the minority, the proposals had no legal standing. But in February the Massachusetts convention became the first to adopt amendments, proposing for the consideration of Congress nine "amendments and alterations" that were basically the latter and did not include protections for the freedoms of press, speech, assembly, or religion. As in Pennsylvania, Maryland's convention rejected the efforts of its Antifederalists to adopt amendments and the minority then published them. Although many of the twenty-eight proposals were alterations, they included far more rights-related amendments than either those of Massachusetts or the Pennsylvania minority. The South Carolina convention recommended four alterations. Its decision to omit rights related amendments may have arisen from the warning of one member that bills of rights generally began with a statement that all men are born free and equal, which was not the case in South Carolina. When, at the end of June 1788, New Hampshire became the decisive ninth state to ratify, its convention adopted the nine Massachusetts amendments almost verbatim and added three more protecting personal liberties.

Four states remained out of the new Union. Each had large Antifederalist constituencies, perhaps majorities, and their conventions proposed fundamental alterations. Virginia proposed twenty alterations and a separate bill of rights consisting of twenty more items. Virginia Federalists had to accept these recommendations in return for unconditional ratification. Modeled on George Mason's 1776 Virginia Declaration of Rights, Virginia's proposal was the first to recommend a complete and integrated bill of rights. In July the New York convention called for twenty-two alterations and listed as consistent with the Constitution twenty-three rights and explanations. In addition, New York Federalists, in order to avert a conditional ratification or an outright rejection, bowed to Antifederalist demands for a circular letter to the state legislatures calling for a second federal convention to adopt amendments. Both Virginia and New York adopted resolutions calling for a second convention. (These are printed in Part III below.) In August the North Carolina convention added six of its own amendments to those of Virginia, insisted that these amendments be added to the Constitution prior to its ratification, provided for delegates to a second convention, and adjourned. Rhode Island Antifederalists defeated the Constitution in a freeholders' election and prevented the calling of a convention several times before the First Federal Congress.

The members of the state ratification conventions had proposed almost two hundred separate amendments, often as part of their official ratification document. Allowing for duplication among the proposals, about one hundred separate amendments emerged. Most called for changes in the structure and powers of the new federal government. One of these declared as a principle of the Constitution a distinct separation of powers among the judicial, executive, and legislative branches. Others, concerned with federalism, aimed at altering the balance of power in the new system in order to make the states more equal with the federal government. Some southern Antifederalists sought amendments to provide greater protection to sectional interests.

Amendments aimed at the judiciary proposed severe limitations on the jurisdiction of the federal courts; reliance on the state courts instead of establishing such inferior federal bodies as district and circuit courts; and appointment of presidential commissions to override unpopular supreme court decisions. Others sought to restrict the powers of the president by denying him a third term, establishing an accountable cabinet to advise him, and limiting his powers of pardon and command of American military forces in the field. Congress was also a target. Proposed amendments would have restricted its power to regulate state militias and federal elections, to exercise exclusive jurisdiction over the capital city, to adopt direct taxes and excises, to maintain a standing army in peacetime, and to pass commercial laws. Most importantly, several states proposed that all powers not "expressly" or "clearly" delegated to Congress be reserved to the states.

Other amendments recommended by the states sought to provide protection at the federal level for certain traditional liberties claimed by Americans by virtue of their constitutional ancestry. Among these were the freedoms of speech, press, and religion; the rights to assemble, petition, and possess arms; and several provisions to protect Americans from arbitrary judges.

The first federal elections were held during the fall and winter of 1788–89. Several ratification conventions, including those of Virginia and Massachusetts, had instructed their delegations to the First Congress to devote every effort to obtaining amendments. Having failed to make changes before ratification, and being uncertain whether a second convention would be called, Antifederalist leaders attempted to develop a coordinated strategy to elect a sympathetic Congress. Pennsylvania Antifederalists held the first state-wide political party convention in American history for the purpose of adopting proposed amendments and selecting a slate of candidates to support them. Federalists saw an Antifederal leviathan poised to attack the ship of state and feared that Antifederalists might win a majority of the seats in the First Congress. George Washington lamented to Madison at the beginning of the elections that "to be shipwrecked in sight of the port would be the severest of all possible aggravations to our misery."[1]

Amendments became the only national issue during the election. All the Antifederalist candidates promised support for amendments, both alterations and rights related. In some cases, Federalist candidates pledged themselves to amendments, although usually remaining vague about which ones they might support. Despite their best efforts, Antifederalists did not fare well in the election. Americans, by virtue of a general willingness to try the new system, an expectation of amendments, and partisan election laws in some states, swept unanimous Federalist delegations into the First Congress from every ratifying state except Massachusetts, New York, Virginia, and South Carolina. Those four states sent ten Antifederalists to a fifty-nine-man House, while Virginia sent two Antifederalists to a twenty-two-man Senate.

The major contest—and the one given the most national attention—occurred during January and February of 1789 in the Virginia Piedmont, where James Madison ran against James Monroe, a moderate Antifederalist. Led by Antifederalist delegate Patrick Henry, the Virginia legislature had carefully constructed the congressional district to keep the nationally known and respected Madison out of the House of Representatives. Monroe advocated amendments to a sympathetic constituency which had been led to believe that Madison was "dogmatically attached to the Constitution in every clause, syllable and letter."[2]

Such an opinion about Madison had a firm foundation but failed to recognize the gradual shift in his thinking that had begun after he had condemned the proposed amendments of Massachusetts as a blemish and convincingly argued against a federal bill of rights in a letter to a Virginia

[1] 23 September 1788, *PJM* 11:262.
[2] James Madison to George Washington, 14 January 1789, ibid., p. 418.

political ally. In the Virginia convention, Madison had repeated the stock Federalist argument that a bill of rights was unnecessary if not dangerous, but in the end he gave tacit support to the convention's amendments even though he found many highly objectionable. The New York call for a second convention had alarmed Madison much more, but even as late as early August 1788 he still advocated a trial period of a few years for a consensus on the need for amendments to emerge. North Carolina's refusal to ratify without amendments and the Antifederalist resurgence as the autumn of 1788 approached converted him. It had taken him a year to accept the reality that a drastic political error of omission was made at the Federal Convention. At the end of September he informed Thomas Jefferson, then American minister to France, that "safeguards to liberty against which no objections can be raised" should be introduced in Congress.[3] "My own opinion has always been in favor of a bill of rights," he asserted a month later in a comprehensive letter to Jefferson, whose letters during the preceding year had helped to ease the transition by providing a sophisticated rationale. "At the same time," he continued,

> I have never thought the omission a material defect, nor been anxious to supply it even by *subsequent* amendment, for any other reason than that it is anxiously desired by others. I have favored it because I supposed it might be of use, and if properly executed could not be of disservice.[4]

In the election campaign, Madison stressed his support for personal liberties and declared in letters to influential constituents, publicly read around the district and printed in newspapers throughout the United States, that with the Constitution safely ratified, amendments could be considered. Specifically, he favored congressional action rather than a second convention as a means of approving amendments to safeguard all the "essential rights," to provide for the periodic increase of the House of Representatives, and to protect the people against nuisance appeals by the wealthy to a distant United States Supreme Court. "In a number of other particulars, alterations are eligible either on their own account, or on account of those who wish for them."[5] Although clearly refuting the allegation that he opposed any amendments, that statement was vague concerning the number and nature of the alterations he would support. Madison's effort was successful and he defeated Monroe, 1,308 to 972.

On 4 March 1789, the day on which the First Federal Congress was

---

[3] 21 September 1788, ibid., pp. 257–58.
[4] 17 October 1788, ibid., p. 297.
[5] To Thomas Mann Randolph, 13 January 1789, ibid., pp. 416–17.

scheduled to meet, an Antifederalist newspaper called on members of the First Congress to adopt amendments as their first order of business: "the interest of this new empire requires a union of sentiment, and Congress can do much that way, if the subject of amendments has that proper attention paid to it, which from its importance it naturally claims." But the Federalist press, having contributed to an election landslide, ridiculed the idea of amendments, especially alterations. An anonymous twenty-eight-part essay analyzing the state proposals concluded that "if we must have amendments, I pray for merely amusing amendments, a little frothy garnish."[6]

Congress achieved a quorum on 6 April and began the business of adopting legislation for raising revenue and organizing the executive and judicial branches outlined in the Constitution. True to his promise, Madison raised the issue of amendments to the House in May but postponed making a formal proposal. A month later he presented several amendments that he believed should be inserted directly into the text of the Constitution. Although he included a few alterations, most were related to personal rights. Relying heavily on the Virginia convention's bill of rights and therefore on George Mason's 1776 Virginia Declaration of Rights, Madison incorporated into his 8 June proposals most of the rights related amendments recommended by the states. Madison included two rights related proposals not recommended by any state: no person could be forced to give up private property without just compensation and *no state* could infringe the equal rights of conscience, freedom of the press, or trial by jury in criminal cases. The amendment on reserved powers that became the Tenth Amendment omitted the words "expressly" or "clearly." The omission of this limiting word gutted the amendment and left interpretation of the Constitution open to the doctrine of implied powers. Madison secured George Washington's support for amendments. In his inaugural address, the president asked Congress to consider them and provided a note of support for Madison's proposals.

Despite the fact that they held advanced civil libertarian views for their times, Federalists in Congress were less willing to consider amendments than Madison had expected. They believed that the first congressional election had demonstrated that Americans were satisfied with the new government, and that a debate on amendments would consume valuable time that should be devoted to more pressing matters. Several ridiculed

[6] [Philadelphia] *Freeman's Journal*, 4 March 1789; [Nicholas Collin], "Foreign Spectator," *Federal Gazette*, 21 October 1788–16 February 1789.

the value of paper declarations of rights. The handful of Antifederalists in Congress also expressed reluctance to consider amendments. They feared that the adoption of rights related amendments would close the door to consideration of amendments designed to rein in the federal government.

When describing Madison's proposals, both Federalists and Antifederalists turned to the popular ship of state metaphor. They called them "a tub to the whale," a literary allusion to Jonathan Swift's *Tale of a Tub* (1704). In his story, Swift described how sailors, encountering a whale that threatened to damage their ship, flung it "an empty tub by way of amusement" to divert it. Madison's contemporaries used the allusion to point out that he had proposed mostly rights related amendments rather than ones designed to change the structure or essence of the new government. The Antifederal leviathan would be diverted and the ship of state could sail away intact.

Madison bristled at the allusion, but agreed to postpone the debate on amendments in order to complete the revenue system. At last in August he persuaded the House to consider the question. Antifederalists proposed several structural amendments, but Federalists defeated them one by one. In response to the Federalist argument that Americans did not support amendments, Aedanus Burke of South Carolina pointedly denied the observation frequently heard in the House, "That this revolution or adoption of the new constitution was agreeable to the public mind, and that those who opposed it at first are now satisfied with it."[7] The debate became heated and is the first known instance of congressmen challenging each other to duels.

The respect in which Madison was held by his House colleagues gradually won support for the amendments from other Federalists, but at a price. Madison had to accept Roger Sherman of Connecticut's insistence that all amendments be placed at the end of the Constitution and not be woven into it. Thus, Americans owe to Sherman, who was actually an opponent of amending the Constitution, the existence of a separate group of Amendments known as the Bill of Rights.

Madison's colleagues also made several changes in his proposals. Perhaps most significant among these, they refused to accept his wish to add to the Constitution's preamble an eloquent statement, based in part on the Declaration of Independence, that all power comes from the people; that government should be exercised for their benefit, which he defined as "the enjoyment of life and liberty, with the right of acquiring and using

[7] See p. 204 below.

property, and generally of pursuing and obtaining happiness and safety";[8] and that the people retain the right to change a government whenever it was adverse to or inadequate for the purposes of its institution.

The Senate made further changes in the amendments passed by the House. Most significantly, it eliminated language that prohibited Congress from infringing the rights of conscience, declared separation of powers a principle of the U.S. Constitution, exempted from military service those with religious scruples, and forbade the states from abridging certain rights of Americans. Madison, unhappy with the changes made by the House, was even more displeased by what the Senate did.

Congress sent twelve Amendments to the states on 28 September 1789. Little is recorded about the ratification process within the states. The Antifederal leviathan had submerged and no new, unified opposition arose to replace it. Other issues, such as the assumption of the states' revolutionary war debts by the federal government and the location of the federal capital, captured public attention. Not until 15 December 1791 did enough states ratify ten Amendments, modifying the U. S. Constitution for the first time. (Admission of Vermont raised to eleven the number required; the three states which did not ratify the Amendments by 1791—Massachusetts, Connecticut, and Georgia—adopted them during the sesquicentennial of the Bill of Rights in 1939.)

Madison has a greater claim to being known as the father of the Bill of Rights than of the Constitution. Without his commitment there would have been no federal Bill of Rights in 1791. As he had predicted, the proposed Bill of Rights bolstered the Constitution and the Union created by it. North Carolina ratified in November 1789 and Rhode Island in May 1790. The Amendments satisfied most Americans with antifederal leanings and detached them from their leaders, who, especially in Virginia, remained dissatisfied with the Amendments. The opposition party that replaced the Antifederalists was led by Madison and Jefferson. The new party accepted the Constitution and challenged its interpretation rather than its essence. Alexander Hamilton, after a decade of violent party politics, reflected that Madison's Amendments met "scarcely any of the important objections which were urged, leaving the structure of the government and the mass and distribution of its powers where they were, [*and*] are too insignificant to be with any sensible man, a reason for being reconciled to the system if he thought it originally bad."[9] Significantly,

---

[8] See p. 11 below.

[9] "An Address to the Electors of the State of New-York" [21 March 1801], Harold C. Syrett and Jacob E. Cooke, eds., *The Papers of Alexander Hamilton*, 27 vols. (New York, 1961–79), 25:356.

the necessary eleventh state in 1791 was Virginia, the home of George Mason, whose language in the Virginia Declaration of Rights of 1776 so influenced the federal Bill of Rights; of James Madison, whose persistence in Congress resulted in the adoption of the Amendments soon known as the Bill of Rights; and of Thomas Jefferson, whose forward-looking perspective recognized that the true importance of a bill of rights was "the legal check which it puts into the hands of the judiciary." [10]

[10] See p. 218 below.

Editorial Method

This book brings together all of the significant documents related to the consideration by the First Federal Congress (1789–91) of the Constitutional Amendments that quickly became known as the Bill of Rights. Part I is a legislative history of the amendments' passage through Congress. Part II provides the extant House of Representatives debate on them. No Senate debate exists because the Senate met in secret. Part III contains relevant excerpts from significant letters to and from members of Congress. At the beginning of each part of the volume additional information is provided in order to make the documents more useful.

Documents in this volume have been transcribed literally with the following exceptions:

1. Superscript letters have been lowered.
2. Periods have been supplied at the end of any paragraph that either had no terminal punctuation or ended with some other mark, such as a dash.
3. Obvious typographical errors in printed documents and slips of the pen (such as word repetitions) have been silently corrected.
4. In cases where an opening or closing quotation mark was missing in the manuscript, the editors have provided these marks.
5. Capitalization was frequently a judgment call, but any word that was not clearly lower case was capitalized.
6. In official documents all crossed-out words and words inserted above the line were reproduced as written. Such authorial corrections were not retained in the letters.
7. Double punctuation (for example, both a period and a dash at the end of a sentence) has not been retained. The editors have chosen the form of punctuation that they believed fit best.
8. In the case of abbreviations that might have been difficult for the reader to interpret, the editors have expanded the abbreviation within brackets.
9. Readings of words that were unclear in the original have been placed in brackets. Torn or totally illegible sections are indicated by [*page torn*] or [*illegible*].

Acknowledgments

The Executive Director of the Virginia Commission on the Bicentennial of the United States Constitution, Timothy G. O'Rourke, deserves the credit for conceiving the idea for this volume and encouraging its production. We are most grateful for the financial subsidy provided by the Virginia Commission, chaired by Professor A. E. Dick Howard of the University of Virginia, for the First Federal Congress Project at the George Washington University to create the book and the Johns Hopkins University Press to publish it.

As always, we recognize the essential and continued longterm support for the First Federal Congress Project by our two sponsoring institutions, the National Historical Publications and Records Commission and The George Washington University. The staff of the NHPRC, particularly Executive Director Richard A. Jacobs, Assistant Director Roger Bruns, and Mary Giunta of the publications program, has encouraged all ventures, such as this one, which aim at distributing documentary sources to a wider audience.

The work on the debates that make up Part II was funded in part by several additional organizations and institutions: the AT&T Foundation, the Commission on the Bicentennial of the United States Constitution, the Federal Bar Council, the New York State Commission on the Bicentennial of the United States Constitution, and the United States Capitol Historical Society.

The Johns Hopkins University Press enthusiastically supported this project, and we would especially like to thank Jack Goellner, director of the press, Robert J. Brugger, acquisitions editor, Barbara Lamb, managing editor, James Johnston, production director, and Carol Zimmerman, our production editor.

We were ably assisted by two staff members of the First Federal Congress Project, William Charles diGiacomantonio and Kevin C. Ruffner who transcribed, proofread, and researched with great care. Our colleague at the Ratification of the Constitution Project at the University of Wisconsin, Gaspare J. Saladino, cheerfully and willingly provided us with research assistance.

Abbreviations

COWH	Committee of the Whole House
CtY	Yale University
DHFFC	*The Documentary History of the First Federal Congress* (Linda Grant DePauw, Charlene Bangs Bickford, and LaVonne Siegel Hauptman, eds., vols. 1–3, Washington, D.C., 1972–77; Charlene Bangs Bickford, Kenneth R. Bowling, and Helen E. Veit, eds., vols. 4–6 and 9, Washington, D.C., 1986–88)
DHROC	*The Documentary History of the Ratification of the Constitution* (Merrill Jensen, ed., vols. 1–3, Madison, Wis., 1976–78; John Kaminski, Gaspare Saladino, and Richard Leffler, eds., vols. 13–16, Madison, Wis., 1976–86)
DLC	Library of Congress
DNA	National Archives
GUS	*Gazette of the United States*
HJ	*House of Representatives Journal*, vol. III of the *DHFFC*
MB	Boston Public Library
MH	Harvard University Libraries
MHi	Massachusetts Historical Society
MSaE	Essex Institute, Salem, Massachusetts
MdHi	Maryland Historical Society, Baltimore
NHi	New York Historical Society
NN	Rare Books and Manuscripts Division, Astor, Lennox and Tilden Foundations, New York Public Library
NYDA	*The* [New York] *Daily Advertiser*
NYDG	*The New-York Daily Gazette*
PHC	Haverford College, Haverford, Pennsylvania
PHi	Historical Society of Pennsylvania, Philadelphia
PJM	*The Papers of James Madison* (Robert A. Rutland and Charles Hobson, eds., vols. 11–12, Charlottesville, Va., 1977–79)
PPAmP	American Philosophical Society
R-Ar	Rhode Island State Archives
RBkRm	Rare Book Room, Library of Congress

ScHi	South Carolina Historical Society, Charleston
ScU	University of South Carolina, Columbia
SLJ	*Senate Legislative Journal*, vol. I of the *DHFFC*
SR	Senate Records, National Archives
ViU	University of Virginia, Charlottesville

PART I

Legislative History

A complete legislative history of the progress of the Bill of Rights through both Houses of Congress, from James Madison's motion to consider amendments on 4 May 1789 through the signing of the enrolled Amendments by the Speaker of the House and the vice president on 28 September 1789 is presented below. Originally printed in volume IV of *The Documentary History of the First Federal Congress, 1789–1791*, this history provides the reader with the documents officially created or considered by the Congress during its legislative process. The editors' primary goal was to document, in the clearest possible form, the evolution of the Bill of Rights, rather than simply to reproduce the archive of available source material.

Following the first document (the Amendments as adopted and sent to the states for ratification) is a calendar tracing all substantive action proposed or taken concerning the amendments. Information in this outline came from several sources including: the *Senate Legislative Journal* and the *House of Representatives Journal* (volumes I and III of the *DHFFC*); the records of the Senate and House of Representatives in the National Archives; Thomas Lloyd's *Congressional Register*; and three newspapers published at the seat of government—the *Gazette of the United States*, *The* [New York] *Daily Advertiser*, and *The New-York Daily Gazette*. An italicized document title in the calendar indicates that the document is printed after the chronology. All information taken from sources other than the *SLJ* or *HJ* has been footnoted. We provide citations only to the first source, chronologically, that reports the motion or other action, unless two or more references have the earliest date of publication, are required for the full account, or contain conflicting versions.

Each document is followed by an unnumbered provenance footnote, which in some cases also contains the source for numbered footnote material. Numbered footnotes to documents, which usually record proposed or agreed upon amendments, represent actions taken after the document was created.

In presenting this legislative history we hope that readers can follow the evolution of the Bill of Rights quickly, easily, and in the depth desired.

Amendments to the Constitution

Amendments to the Constitution
September 28, 1789

The Conventions of a number of the States, having at the time of their adopting the Constitution, expressed a desire, in order to prevent misconstruction or abuse of its powers, that further declaratory and restrictive clauses should be added: And as extending the ground of public confidence in the Government, will best ensure the benificent ends of its institution

Resolved by the Senate and House of Representatives of the United States of America, in Congress assembled, two thirds of both Houses concurring, that the following Articles be proposed to the Legislatures of the several States, as amendments to the Constitution of the United States, all or any of which Articles, when ratified by three fourths of the said Legislatures, to be valid to all intents and purposes, as part of the said Constitution; vizt.

Articles in addition to, and amendment of the Constitution of the United States of America, proposed by Congress, and ratified by the Legislatures of the several States, pursuant to the fifth Article of the original Constitution.

Article the first. After the first enumeration required by the first Article of the Constitution, there shall be one Representative for every thirty thousand, until the number shall amount to one hundred, after which, the proportion shall be so regulated by Congress, that there shall be not less than one hundred Representatives, nor less than one Representative for every forty thousand persons, until the number of Representatives shall amount to two hundred, after which the proportion shall be so regulated by Congress, that there shall not be less than two hundred Representatives, nor more than one Representative for every fifty thousand persons.

Article the second. No law, varying the compensation for the services of the Senators and Representatives, shall take effect, until an election of Representatives shall have intervened.

Article the third. Congress shall make no law respecting an establishment of religion, or prohibiting the free exercise thereof; or abridging the freedom of speech, or of the press, or the right of the people peaceably to assemble, and to petition the Government for a redress of grievances.

ARTICLE THE FOURTH. A well regulated militia, being necessary to the security of a free State, the right of the people to keep and bear arms, shall not be infringed.

ARTICLE THE FIFTH. No Soldier shall, in time of peace be quartered in any House, without the consent of the owner, nor in time of war, but in a manner to be prescribed by law.

ARTICLE THE SIXTH. The right of the people to be secure in their persons, houses, papers, and effects, against unreasonable searches and seizures, shall not be violated, and no warrants shall issue, but upon probable cause, supported by oath or affirmation, and particularly describing the place to be searched and the persons or things to be seized.

ARTICLE THE SEVENTH. No person shall be held to answer for a capital, or otherwise infamous crime, unless on a presentment or indictment of [a] Grand Jury, except in cases arising in the land or naval forces, or in the militia, when in actual service in time of war or public danger; nor shall any person be subject for the same offence to be twice put in jeopardy of life or limb; nor shall be compelled in any criminal case to be a witness against himself, nor be deprived of life, liberty, or property, without due process of law; nor shall private property be taken for public use, without just compensation.

ARTICLE THE EIGHTH. In all criminal prosecutions, the accused shall enjoy the right to a speedy and public trial, by an impartial jury of the State and district wherein the crime shall have been committed; which district shall have been previously ascertained by law, and to be informed of the nature and cause of the accusation; to be confronted with the witnesses against him; to have compulsory process for obtaining witnesses in his favor, and to have the assistance of counsel for his defence.

ARTICLE THE NINTH. In suits at common law, where the value in controversy shall exceed twenty dollars, the right of trial by jury shall be preserved, and no fact tried by a jury, shall be otherwise re-examined in any Court of the United States, than according to the rules of the common law.

ARTICLE THE TENTH. Excessive bail shall not be required, nor excessive fines imposed, nor cruel and unusual punishments inflicted.

ARTICLE THE ELEVENTH. The enumeration in the Constitution, of certain rights, shall not be construed to deny or disparage others retained by the people.

ARTICLE THE TWELFTH. The powers not delegated to the United States by the Constitution, nor prohibited by it to the States, are reserved to the States respectively, or to the people.

FREDERICK AUGUSTUS MUHLENBERG
Speaker of the House of Representatives

JOHN ADAMS
Vice-President of the United States, and
President of the Senate

ATTEST,
JOHN BECKLEY, Clerk of the House of Representatives
SAM. A. OTIS Secretary of the Senate

Enrolled Resolutions, RG 11, DNA.

Calendar

Date	*House*	*Senate*
1789		
May 4	Motion by Madison, to debate the subject of Amendments to the Constitution on May 25, agreed to.[1]	
May 25	Motion by Madison, to postpone consideration of Amendments until June 8, agreed to.[2]	
June 8	Motion by Madison to debate Amendments in COWH; motion by Jackson to postpone until Mar. 1, 1790; Madison motion withdrawn in favor of motion to refer subject to select committee; latter motion withdrawn, and *Madison resolution* of Amendments to be incorporated into Constitution submitted; motion by Laurance to refer resolution to COWH; motion by Boudinot, to refer resolu-	

[1] *NYDG*, May 5. The *HJ* for this date records no action on this subject.
[2] *NYDG*, May 26. The *HJ* for this date records no action on this subject.

Date	House	Senate
1789		
	tion to select committee consisting of one member from each state, withdrawn; Laurance motion agreed to;[3] on a motion by Gerry, *Amendments* recommended by five of the ratifying states laid on the table.[4]	
July 21	Motion by Madison to debate resolution in COWH; motion by Ames, to discharge COWH and refer resolution and state Amendments to select committee, agreed to by a vote of 34–15; Vining, Madison, Baldwin, Sherman, Burke, Gilman, Clymer, Benson, Goodhue, Boudinot, and Gale appointed to committee; motion by Smith (S.C.?), that committee not be bound by state recommendations for Amendments, agreed to.[5]	
July 28	Vining presented *committee report,* which was read; on a motion by Gerry, 100 copies ordered printed.[6]	
Aug. 3	On a motion by Madison,[7] report referred to COWH for debate on Aug. 12.	

[3] *NYDA*, June 9; *GUS*, June 10.
[4] *NYDG*, June 9.
[5] *NYDG*, *GUS*, July 22; *CR*, July 21.
[6] *NYDG*, *GUS*, July 29.
[7] *NYDA*, Aug. 4.

Date	*House*	*Senate*
1789		
Aug. 13	Motion by Lee, to consider in COWH, debated and agreed to; first Amendment debated in COWH; question whether Amendments would be incorporated into or supplemental to the Constitution decided in favor of the former by defeat of *motion* by Sherman; question raised as to whether COWH agreement to amendments should be by two-thirds vote; chair's ruling in favor of a majority vote appealed and confirmed by House.[8]	
Aug. 14	First three Amendments debated in COWH, *amended,* and agreed to.[9]	
Aug. 15	Fourth and fifth Amendments debated in COWH, *amended,* and agreed to; motion by Ames, seconded by Sedgwick, to dismiss COWH, withdrawn; motion by Ames, to require two-thirds vote for actions regarding Amendments in COWH, tabled.[10]	
Aug. 17	Sixth through fourteenth Amendments debated in COWH, *amended,* and agreed to.[11]	

[8] *NYDA,* Aug. 14.
[9] *NYDA, GUS,* Aug. 15.
[10] *NYDA,* Aug. 17; *GUS,* Aug. 19; *CR,* Aug. 15.
[11] *NYDA,* Aug. 18; *GUS,* Aug. 19; *CR,* Aug. 17.

Date	*House*	*Senate*
1789		
Aug. 18	*Motion* by Gerry debated and disagreed to by a recorded vote on the previous question of 34–16; fifteenth through nineteenth Amendments debated in COWH, *amended,* and agreed to; Amendments reported to House; additional *Amendments* proposed by *Tucker* and motion to refer these to COWH disagreed to.[12]	
Aug. 19	Debated in House; motion by Sherman, to add Amendments to Constitution as a supplement, agreed to; first Amendment disagreed to; second Amendment debated; *amendment* proposed.[13]	
Aug. 20	Debated in House; second Amendment tabled; third through fourteenth Amendments agreed to with *amendments*.[14]	
Aug. 21	Debated in House; second and fifteenth through nineteenth Amendments agreed to with *amendments;* additional *Amendment* proposed by *Burke* and disagreed to by a recorded vote of 28–23.[15]	
Aug. 22	Debated in House; addi-	

[12] *NYDA, GUS,* Aug. 19; *CR,* Aug. 18.
[13] *NYDA,* Aug. 20; *GUS,* Aug. 22; *CR,* Aug. 19.
[14] *GUS,* Aug. 22; *CR,* Aug. 20.
[15] *NYDA, GUS,* Aug. 22; *CR,* Aug. 21.

Date	*House*	*Senate*
1789		
	tional *Amendment* proposed by *Tucker;* motions by Page and Gerry to refer to select committee; motion by Stone to table disagreed to; Partridge motion for previous question disagreed to; Tucker amendment disagreed to by a recorded vote of 39–9; additional *Amendments* proposed by *Tucker and Gerry* and disagreed to; *motion* by *Benson* referred (together with the amended Amendments) to Benson, Sherman, and Sedgwick to prepare an introduction to and arrangement of Articles of Amendment.[16]	
Aug. 24	Benson presented *resolution and Articles of Amendment,* which were agreed to.	
Aug. 25		Received, read, and ordered printed;[17] motion by Izard, seconded by Langdon,[18] to postpone to second session disagreed to.
Sept. 2		First Article debated, *amended,* and agreed to.
Sept. 3		Second and third Articles debated, *amended,* and agreed to; fourth Article debated and postponed.

[16] *NYDA,* Aug. 24; *GUS,* Aug. 26; *CR,* Aug. 22. The *CR* states that Gerry's motion was for consideration in the COWH.

[17] The order to print is noted on the printed resolution of August 24. According to Thomas Greenleaf's account in the Records of the Secretary of the Senate: Concerning printing, SR, DNA, 100 copies of this resolution were printed on August 26.

[18] Maclay, Aug. 25.

Date	*House*	*Senate*
1789		
Sept. 4		Fourth through eleventh Articles debated, *amended,* and agreed to.
Sept. 7		Twelfth through seventeenth Articles debated, *amended,* and agreed to, except the fourteenth and sixteenth, which were disagreed to; *additional Articles* disagreed to; preamble debated.
Sept. 8		Preamble debated, *amended,* and agreed to; *additional Articles* disagreed to.
Sept. 9		Articles debated, *amended,* renumbered, or disagreed to; Articles of Amendment agreed to with *amendments.*
Sept. 14	Senate amendments read; *Articles as agreed to by Senate* ordered printed.[19]	
Sept. 19	Debated.	
Sept. 21	Agreed to second, fourth, eighth, twelfth, thirteenth, sixteenth, eighteenth, nineteenth, twenty-fifth, and twenty-sixth amendments; disagreed to first, third, fifth, sixth, seventh, ninth, tenth, eleventh, fourteenth, fifteenth, seventeenth, twentieth, twenty-first, twenty-second, twenty-third, and twenty-fourth amendments; Madison, Sherman, and Vining ap-	Receded from third amendment; insisted on others disagreed to by House; Ellsworth, Carroll, and Paterson appointed to conference committee.

[19] *NYDA,* Sept. 15. The *HJ* for this date records no action on this subject.

Date	*House*	*Senate*
1789		
	pointed to conference committee.	
Sept. 24	Resolution agreed to, receding from disagreement to amendments insisted on by Senate and agreeing to *conference commitee report* with *amendments; amendments* to Article 8 agreed to by a recorded vote of 37–14, called for by Bland; *resolution* proposed by Madison and agreed to.[20]	Ellsworth presented conference committee report.
Sept. 25		Agreed to House resolution on report of conference committee.
Sept. 26		Agreed to House resolution of Sept. 24.
Sept. 28	Signed by speaker.	[Signed by vice president.]

[20] *GUS*, Sept. 26. The *HJ* for this date is in error in listing the third amendment of the Senate as the one accepted by the House.

Madison Resolution
June 8, 1789

Resolved, That the following amendments ought to be proposed by Congress to the legislatures of the states, to become, if ratified by three fourths thereof, part of the constitution of the United States.

First. That there be prefixed to the constitution a declaration—That all power is originally vested in, and consequently derived from the people.

That government is instituted, and ought to be exercised for the benefit of the people; which consists in the enjoyment of life and liberty, with the right of acquiring and using property, and generally of pursuing and obtaining happiness and safety.

That the people have an indubitable, unalienable, and indefeasible right to reform or change their government, whenever it be found adverse or inadequate to the purposes of its institution.

Secondly. That in article 1st, section 2, clause 3, these words be struck out, to wit, "The number of representatives shall not exceed one for every thirty thousand, but each state shall have at least one representative, and until such enumeration shall be made." And that in place thereof be inserted these words, to wit, "After the first actual enumeration, there shall be one representative for every thirty thousand, until the number shall amount to after which the proportion shall be so regulated by Congress, that the number shall never be less than nor more than but each state shall after the first enumeration, have at least two representatives; and prior thereto."

Thirdly. That in article 1st, section 6, clause 1, there be added to the end of the first sentence, these words, to wit: "But no law varying the compensation last ascertained shall operate before the next ensuing election of representatives."

Fourthly. That in article 1st, section 9, between clauses 3 and 4, be inserted these clauses, to wit: The civil rights of none shall be abridged on account of religious belief or worship, nor shall any national religion be established, nor shall the full and equal rights of conscience be in any manner, or on any pretext infringed.

The people shall not be deprived or abridged of their right to speak, to write, or to publish their sentiments; and the freedom of the press, as one of the great bulwarks of liberty, shall be inviolable.

The people shall not be restrained from peaceably assembling and consulting for their common good; nor from applying to the legislature by petitions, or remonstrances for redress of their grievances.

The right of the people to keep and bear arms shall not be infringed; a well armed, and well regulated militia being the best security of a free country: but no person religiously scrupulous of bearing arms, shall be compelled to render military service in person.

No soldier shall in time of peace be quartered in any house, without consent of the owner; nor at any time, but in a manner warranted by law.

No person shall be subject, except in cases of impeachment, to more than one punishment, or one trial for the same offence; nor shall be compelled to be a witness against himself: nor be deprived of life, liberty, or property without due process of law; nor be obliged to relinquish his property, where it may be necessary for public use, without a just compensation.

Excessive bail shall not be required, nor excessive fines imposed, nor cruel and unusual punishments inflicted.

The rights of the people to be secured in their persons, their houses, their papers, and their other property from all unreasonable searches and seizures, shall not be violated by warrants issued without probable cause, supported by oath or affirmation, or not particularly describing the places to be searched, or the persons or things to be seized.

In all criminal prosecutions, the accused shall enjoy the right to a speedy and public trial, to be informed of the cause and nature of the accusation, to be confronted with his accusers, and the witnesses against him; to have a compulsory process for obtaining witnesses in his favor; and to have the assistance of counsel for his defence.

The exceptions here or elsewhere in the constitution, made in favor of particular rights, shall not be so construed as to diminish the just importance of other rights retained by the people; or as to enlarge the powers delegated by the constitution; but either as actual limitations of such powers, or as inserted merely for greater caution.

Fifthly. That in article 1st, section 10, between clauses 1 and 2, be inserted this clause, to wit:

No state shall violate the equal rights of conscience, or the freedom of the press, or the trial by jury in criminal cases.

Sixthly. That article 3d, section 2, be annexed to the end of clause 2d, these words, to wit: but no appeal to such court shall be allowed where the value in controversy shall not amount to   dollars: nor shall any fact triable by jury, according to the course of common law, be otherwise re-examinable than may consist with the principles of common law.

Seventhly. That in article 3d, section 2, the third clause be struck out, and in its place be inserted the clauses following, to wit:

The trial of all crimes (except in cases of impeachments, and cases arising in the land or naval forces, or the militia when on actual service in time of war, or public danger,) shall be by an impartial jury of freeholders of the vicinage, with the requisite of unanimity for conviction, of the right of challenge, and other accustomed requisites; and in all crimes punishable with loss of life or member, presentment or indictment by a grand jury, shall be an essential preliminary, provided that in cases of crimes committed within any county which may be in possession of an enemy, or in which a general insurrection may prevail, the trial may by law be authorised in some other county of the same state, as near as may be to the seat of the offence.

In cases of crimes committed not within any county, the trial may by law be in such county as the laws shall have prescribed. In suits at common law between man and man, the trial by jury as one of the best securities to the rights of the people, ought to remain inviolate.

Eighthly. That immediately after article 6th, be inserted, as article 7th, the clauses following, to wit:

The powers delegated by this constitution, and appropriated to the departments to which they are respectively distributed: so that the legislative department shall never exercise the powers vested in the executive or judicial; nor the executive exercise the powers vested in the legislative or judicial; nor the judicial exercise the powers vested in the legislative or executive departments.

The powers not delegated by this constitution, nor prohibited by it to the states, are reserved to the states respectively.

Ninthly. That article 7th, be numbered as article 8th.

NYDA, June 12.

Amendments Proposed by the States
June 8, 1789

[AMENDMENTS PROPOSED BY THE MASSACHUSETTS CONVENTION
February 6, 1788]

FIRST, That it be explicitly declared that all Powers not expressly delegated by the aforesaid Constitution are reserved to the several States to be by them exercised.

SECONDLY, That there shall be one representative to every thirty thousand persons according to the Census mentioned in the Constitution until the whole number of the Representatives amounts to Two hundred.

THIRDLY, That Congress do not exercise the powers vested in them by the fourth Section of the first article, but in cases when a State shall neglect or refuse to make the regulations therein mentioned or shall make regulations subversive of the rights of the People to a free & equal representation in Congress agreeably to the Constitution.

FOURTHLY, That Congress do not lay direct Taxes but when the Monies arising from the Impost & Excise are insufficient for the publick exigencies nor then until Congress shall have first made a requisition upon the States to assess levy & pay their respective proportions of such Requisition agreeably to the Census fixed in the said Constitution; in such way & manner as the Legislature of the States shall think best, & in such case if any State shall neglect or refuse to pay its proportion pursuant to such requisition then Congress may assess & levy such State's proportion together with interest thereon at the rate of Six per cent per annum from the time of payment prescribed in such requisition.

FIFTHLY, That Congress erect no Company of Merchants with exclusive advantages of Commerce.

SIXTHLY, That no person shall be tried for any Crime by which he may incur an infamous punishment or loss of life until he be first indicted by a Grand Jury, except in such cases as may arise in the Government & regulation of the Land & Naval forces.

SEVENTHLY, The Supreme Judicial Federal Court shall have no jurisdiction of Causes between Citizens of different States unless the matter in dispute whether it concerns the realty or personalty be of the value of Three thousand dollars at the least. nor shall the Federal Judicial Powers extend to any actions between Citizens of different States where the matter in dispute whether it concerns the Realty or Personalty is not of the value of Fifteen hundred dollars at the least.

EIGHTHLY, In civil actions between Citizens of different States every issue of fact arising in Actions at common law shall be tried by a Jury if the parties or either of them request it.

NINTHLY, Congress shall at no time consent that any Person holding an office of trust or profit under the United States shall accept of a title of Nobility or any other title or office from any King, Prince or Foreign State.

[AMENDMENTS PROPOSED BY THE SOUTH CAROLINA CONVENTION MAY 23, 1788]

AND WHEREAS it is essential to the preservation of the rights reserved to the several states, and the freedom of the people under the operations of a General government that the right of prescribing the manner time and places of holding the Elections to the Federal Legislature, should be for ever inseperably annexed to the sovereignty of the several states. This convention doth declare that the same ought to remain to all posterity a perpetual and fundamental right in the local, exclusive of the interference of the General Government except in cases where the Legislatures of the States, shall refuse or neglect to perform and fulfil the same according to the tenor of the said Constitution.

THIS CONVENTION doth also declare that no Section or paragraph of the said Constitution warrants a Construction that the states do not retain every power not expressly relinquished by them and vested in the General Government of the Union.

RESOLVED that the general Government of the United States ought never to impose direct taxes, *but* where the monies arising from the duties, imposts and excise are insufficient for the public exigencies *nor then until* Congress shall have made a requisition upon the states to Assess levy and pay their respective proportions of such requisitions And in case any state shall neglect or refuse to pay its proportion pursuant to such requisition then Congress may assess and levy such state's proportion together with Interest thereon at the rate of six per centum per annum from the time of payment prescribed by such requisition.

RESOLVED that the third section of the Sixth Article ought to be amended by inserting the word "*other*" between the words "*no*" and "*religious.*"

[AMENDMENTS PROPOSED BY THE NEW HAMPSHIRE CONVENTION JUNE 21, 1788]

FIRST That it be Explicitly declared that all Powers not expressly & particularly Delegated by the aforesaid Constitution are reserved to the several States to be, by them Exercised.

SECONDLY, That there shall be one Representative to every Thirty thousand Persons according to the Census mentioned in the Constitution, untill the whole number of Representatives amount to Two hundred.

THIRDLY That Congress do not Exercise the Powers vested in them, by the fourth Section of the first Article, but in Cases when a State shall neglect or refuse to make the Regulations therein mentioned, or shall make regulations Subversive of the rights of the People to a free and equal Representation in CONGRESS. Nor shall Congress in any Case make regulations contrary to a free and equal Representation.

FOURTHLY That Congress do not lay direct Taxes but when the money arising from Impost, Excise and their other resources are insufficient for the Publick Exigencies; nor then, untill Congress shall have first made a Requisition upon the States, to Assess, Levy, & pay their respective proportions, of such requisition agreeably to the Census fixed in the said Constitution in such way & manner as the Legislature of the State shall think best and in such Case [if any] State shall neglect, then Congress may Assess & Levy such States proportion together with the Interest thereon at the rate of six ℘ Cent ℘ Annum from the Time of payment prescribed in such requisition.

FIFTHLY That Congress shall erect no Company of Merchants with exclusive advantages of Commerce.

SIXTHLY That no Person shall be Tryed for any Crime by which he may incur an Infamous Punishment, or loss of Life, untill he first be indicted by a Grand Jury except in such Cases as may arise in the Government and regulation of the Land & Naval Forces.

SEVENTHLY All Common Law Cases between Citizens of different States shall be commenced in the Common Law Courts of the respective States & no appeal shall be allowed to the Federal Court in such Cases unless the sum or value of the thing in Controversy amount to three Thousand Dollars.

EIGHTHLY In Civil Actions between Citizens of different States every Issue of Fact arising in Actions at Common Law shall be Tryed by Jury, if the Parties, or either of them request it.

NINTHLY Congress shall at no Time consent that any Person holding an Office of Trust or profit under the UNITED STATES shall accept any Title of Nobility or any other Title or Office from any King, Prince, or Foreign State.

TENTH,

That no standing Army shall be Kept up in time of Peace unless with the consent of three fourths of the Members of each branch of Congress, nor shall Soldiers in Time of Peace be Quartered upon private Houses without the consent of the Owners.

ELEVENTH

Congress shall make no Laws touching Religion, or to infringe the rights of Conscience.

TWELFTH

Congress shall never disarm any Citizen unless such as are or have been in Actual Rebellion.

[AMENDMENTS PROPOSED BY THE VIRGINIA CONVENTION
JUNE 27, 1788]

That there be a Declaration or Bill of Rights asserting and securing from encroachment the essential and unalienable Rights of the People in some such manner as the following:

FIRST, That there are certain natural rights of which men, when they form a social compact cannot deprive or divest their posterity, among which are the enjoyment of life and liberty, with the means of acquiring, possessing and protecting property, and pursuing and obtaining happiness and safety. SECOND. That all power is naturally vested in and consequently derived from the People; that Magistrates, therefore, are their trustees and agents and at all times amenable to them. THIRD, That Government ought to be instituted for the common benefit, protection and security of the People; and that the doctrine of non-resistance against arbitrary power and oppression is absurd slavish, and destructive of the good and happiness of mankind. FOURTH, That no man or set of Men are entitled to exclusive or seperate public emoluments or privileges from the community, but in consideration of public services; which not being descendible, neither ought the offices of Magistrate, Legislator or Judge, or any other public office to be hereditary. FIFTH, That the legislative, executive, and judiciary powers of Government should be seperate and distinct, and that the members of the two first may be restrained from oppression by feeling and participating the public burthens, they should, at fixt periods be reduced to a private station, return into the mass of the people; and the vacancies be supplied by certain and regular elections; in which all or any part of the former members to be eligible or ineligible, as the rules of the Constitution of Government, and the laws shall direct. SIXTH, That elections of representatives in the legislature ought to be free and frequent, and all men having sufficient evidence of permanent common interest with and attachment to the community ought to have the right of suffrage: and no aid, charge, tax or fee can be set, rated, or levied upon the people without their own consent, or that of their representatives so elected, nor can they be bound by any law to which they have not in like manner assented for the public good. SEVENTH, That all power of suspending laws or the execution of laws by any authority, without the consent of the representatives of the people in the legislature is injurious to their rights, and ought not to be exercised. EIGHTH, That in all capital and criminal prosecutions, a man hath a right to demand the cause and nature of his accusation, to be confronted with the accusers and witnesses, to call for evidence and be allowed counsel in his favor, and to a fair and speedy trial by an impartial Jury of his vicinage, without whose unanimous consent he cannot be found guilty, (except in the government of the land and naval forces) nor can he be compelled to give evidence against himself. NINTH. That no freeman ought to be taken imprisoned, or disseised of his freehold, liberties, privileges or franchises, or outlawed or exiled, or in any manner destroyed or deprived of his life, liberty or property but by the law of the land. TENTH. That every freeman restrained of his liberty is entitled to a remedy to enquire into the lawfulness thereof, and to remove the same, if unlawful, and that such remedy ought not to be denied nor delayed. ELEVENTH. That in controversies respecting property, and in suits between man and man, the ancient trial by Jury is one of the greatest Securities to the rights of the people, and ought to remain sacred and inviolable. TWELFTH. That every freeman ought to find a certain remedy by recourse to the laws for all injuries and wrongs he may receive in his person, property or character. He ought to obtain right and justice freely without sale, compleatly and without denial, promptly and without delay, and that all establishments or regulations contravening these rights, are oppressive and unjust. THIRTEENTH, That excessive Bail ought not be required, nor excessive fines imposed, nor cruel and unusual punishments inflicted. FOURTEENTH, That every freeman has a right to be secure from all unreasonable searches and siezures of his person, his papers and his property; all warrants, therefore, to search suspected places, or sieze any freeman, his papers or property, without information upon Oath (or affirmation of a person religiously scrupulous of taking an oath) of legal and sufficient cause, are grievous and oppressive; and all general Warrants to search suspected places, or to apprehend any suspected person, without specially naming or describing the place or person, are dangerous and ought not to be granted. FIFTEENTH, That the people have a right peaceably to assemble together to consult for the common good, or to instruct their Representatives; and that every freeman has a right to petition or apply to the legislature for redress of grievances. SIXTEENTH, That the people have a right to freedom of speech, and of writing and publishing their

Sentiments; but the freedom of the press is one of the greatest bulwarks of liberty and ought not to be violated. SEVENTEENTH, That the people have a right to keep and bear arms; that a well regulated Militia composed of the body of the people trained to arms is the proper, natural and safe defence of a free State. That standing armies in time of peace are dangerous to liberty, and therefore ought to be avoided, as far as the circumstances and protection of the Community will admit; and that in all cases the military should be under strict subordination to and governed by the Civil power. EIGHTEENTH, That no Soldier in time of peace ought to be quartered in any house without the consent of the owner, and in time of war in such manner only as the laws direct. NINETEENTH, That any person religiously scrupulous of bearing arms ought to be exempted upon payment of an equivalent to employ another to bear arms in his stead. TWENTIETH, That religion or the duty which we owe to our Creator, and the manner of discharging it can be directed only by reason and conviction, not by force or violence, and therefore all men have an equal, natural and unalienable right to the free exercise of religion according to the dictates of conscience, and that no particular religious sect or society ought to be favored or established by Law in preference to others.

AMENDMENTS TO THE BODY OF THE CONSTITUTION

FIRST, That each State in the Union shall respectively retain every power, jurisdiction and right which is not by this Constitution delegated to the Congress of the United States or to the departments of the Foederal Government. SECOND, That there shall be one representative for every thirty thousand, according to the Enumeration or Census mentioned in the Constitution, until the whole number of representatives amounts to two hundred; after which that number shall be continued or encreased as the Congress shall direct, upon the principles fixed by the Constitution by apportioning the Representatives of each State to some greater number of people from time to time as population encreases. THIRD, When Congress shall lay direct taxes or excises, they shall immediately inform the Executive power of each State of the quota of such state according to the Census herein directed, which is proposed to be thereby raised; And if the Legislature of any State shall pass a law which shall be effectual for raising such quota at the time required by Congress, the taxes and excises laid by Congress shall not be collected, in such State. FOURTH, That the members of the Senate and House of Representatives shall be ineligible to, and incapable of holding, any civil office under the authority of the United States, during the time for which they shall respectively be elected. FIFTH, That the Journals of the proceedings of the Senate and House of Representatives shall be published at least once in every year, except such parts thereof relating to treaties, alliances or military operations, as in their judgment require secrecy.

SIXTH, That a regular statement and account of the receipts and expenditures of all public money shall be published at least once in every year. SEVENTH, That no commercial treaty shall be ratified without the concurrence of two thirds of the whole number of the members of the Senate; and no Treaty ceding, contracting, restraining or suspending the territorial rights or claims of the United States, or any of them or their, or any of their rights or claims to fishing in the American Seas, or navigating the American rivers shall be but in cases of the most urgent and extreme necessity, nor shall any such treaty be ratified without the concurrence of three fourths of the whole number of the members of both houses respectively. EIGHTH, That no navigation law, or law regulating Commerce shall be passed without the consent of two thirds of the Members present in both houses. NINTH, That no standing army or regular troops shall be raised or kept up in time of peace, without the consent of two thirds of the members present in both houses. TENTH, That no soldier shall be inlisted for any longer term than four years, except in time of war, and then for no longer term than the continuance of the war. ELEVENTH, That each State respectively shall have the power to provide for organizing, arming and disciplining it's own Militia, whensoever Congress shall omit or neglect to provide for the same. That the Militia shall not be subject to Martial Law, except when in actual service in time of war, invasion, or rebellion; and when not in the actual service of the United States, shall be subject only to such fines, penalties and punishments as shall be directed or inflicted by the laws of its own State. TWELFTH That the exclusive power of legislation given to Congress over the Foederal Town and it's adjacent District and other places purchased or to be purchased by Congress of any of the States shall extend only to such regulations as respect the police and good government thereof. THIRTEENTH, That no person shall be capable of being President of the United States for more than eight years in any term of sixteen years. FOURTEENTH That the judicial power of the United States shall be vested in one supreme Court, and in such courts of Admiralty as Congress may from time to time ordain and establish in any of the different States: The Judicial power shall extend to all cases in Law and Equity arising under treaties made, or which shall be made under the authority of the United States; to all cases affecting ambassadors other foreign ministers and consuls; to all cases of Admiralty and maritime jurisdiction; to controversies to which the United States shall be a party; to controversies between two or States, and between parties claiming lands under the grants of different States. In all cases affecting ambassadors, other foreign ministers and Consuls, and those in which a State shall be a party, the supreme court shall have original jurisdiction; in all other cases before mentioned the supreme Court shall have appellate jurisdiction as to matters of law only: except in cases of equity, and of admiralty and maritime jurisdiction, in which the Supreme Court shall have appellate jurisdiction both as to law and fact, with such exceptions and under such regulations as the Congress shall make. But the judicial power of the United States shall extend to no case where the cause of action shall have originated before the ratification of this Constitution; except in disputes between States about their Territory, disputes between persons claiming lands under the grants of different States, and suits for debts due to the United States. FIFTEENTH, That in criminal prosecutions no man shall be restrained in the exercise of the usual and accustomed right of challenging or excepting to the Jury. SIXTEENTH, That Congress shall not alter, modify or interfere in the times, places, or manner of holding elections for Senators and Representatives or either of them, except when the legislature of any State shall neglect, refuse or be disabled by invasion or rebellion to prescribe the same. SEVENTEENTH, That those clauses which declare that Congress shall not exercise certain powers be not interpreted in any manner whatsoever to extend the powers of Congress. But that they may be construed either as making exceptions to the specified powers where this shall be the case, or otherwise as inserted merely for greater caution. EIGHTEENTH, That the laws ascertaining the compensation to Senators and Representatives for their services be postponed in their operation, until after the election of Representatives immediately succeeding the passing thereof; that excepted, which shall first be passed on the Subject. NINETEENTH, That some Tribunal other than the Senate be provided for trying impeachments of Senators. TWENTIETH, That the Salary of a Judge shall not be encreased or diminished during his continuance in Office, otherwise than by general regulations of Salary which may take place on a revision of the subject at stated periods of not less than seven years to commence from the time such Salaries shall be first ascertained by Congress.

[AMENDMENTS PROPOSED BY THE NEW YORK CONVENTION
JULY 26, 1788]

That all power is originally vested in and consequently derived from the People, and that Government is instituted by them for their common Interest Protection and Security.

That the enjoyment of Life, Liberty and the pursuit of Happiness are essential rights which every Government ought to respect and preserve.

That the Powers of Government may be reassumed by the People, whensoever it shall become necessary to their Happiness; that every Power, Jurisdiction and Right, which is not by the said Constitution clearly delegated to the Congress of the United States, or the departments of the Government thereof, remains to the People of the several States, or to their respective State Governments to whom they may have granted the same; And that those Clauses in the said Constitution, which declare, that Congress shall not have or exercise certain Powers, do not imply that Congress is entitled to any Powers not given by the said Constitution; but such Clauses are to be construed either as exceptions to certain specified Powers, or as inserted merely for greater Caution.

That the People have an equal, natural and unalienable right, freely and peaceably to Exercise their Religion according to the dictates of Conscience, and that no Religious Sect or Society ought to be favoured or established by Law in preference of others.

That the People have a right to keep and bear Arms; that a well regulated Militia, including the body of the People *capable of bearing Arms,* is the proper, natural and safe defence of a free State;

That the Militia should not be subject to Martial Law, except in time of War, Rebellion or Insurrection.

That standing Armies in time of Peace are dangerous to Liberty, and ought not to be kept up, except in Cases of necessity; and that at all times, the Military should be under strict Subordination to the civil Power.

That in time of Peace no Soldier ought to be quartered in any House without the consent of the Owner, and in time of War only by the civil Magistrate in such manner as the Laws may direct.

That no Person ought to be taken imprisoned, or disseised of his freehold, or be exiled or deprived of his Privileges, Franchises, Life, Liberty or Property, but by due process of Law.

That no Person ought to be put twice in Jeopardy of Life or Limb for one and the same Offence, nor unless in case of impeachment, be punished more than once for the same Offence.

That every Person restrained of his Liberty is entitled to an enquiry into the lawfulness of such restraint, and to a removal thereof if unlawful, and that such enquiry and removal ought not to be denied or delayed, except when on account of Public Danger the Congress shall suspend the privilege of the Writ of Habeas Corpus.

That excessive Bail ought not to be required; nor excessive Fines imposed; nor Cruel or unusual Punishments inflicted.

That (except in the Government of the Land and Naval Forces, and of the Militia when in actual Service, and in cases of Impeachment) a Presentment or Indictment by a Grand Jury ought to be observed as a necessary preliminary to the trial of all Crimes cognizable by the Judiciary of the United States, and such Trial should be speedy, public, and by an impartial Jury of the County where the Crime was committed; and that no person can be found Guilty without the unanimous consent of such Jury. But in cases of Crimes not committed within any County of any of the United States, and in Cases of

Crimes committed within any County in which a general Insurrection may prevail, or which may be in the possession of a foreign Enemy, the enquiry and trial may be in such County as the Congress shall by Law direct; which County in the two Cases last mentioned should be as near as conveniently may be to that County in which the Crime may have been committed. And that in all Criminal Prosecutions, the Accused ought to be informed of the cause and nature of his Accusation, to be confronted with his accusers and the Witnesses against him, to have the means of producing his Witnesses, and the assistance of Council for his defence, and should not be compelled to give Evidence against himself.

That the trial by Jury in the extent that it obtains by the Common Law of England is one of the greatest securities to the rights of a free People, and ought to remain inviolate.

That every Freeman has a right to be secure from all unreasonable searches and seizures of his person his papers or his property, and therefore, that all Warrants to search suspected places or seize any Freeman his papers or property, without information upon Oath or Affirmation of sufficient cause, are grievous and oppressive; and that all general Warrants (or such in which the place or person suspected are not particularly designated) are dangerous and ought not to be granted.

That the People have a right peaceably to assemble together to consult for their common good, or to instruct their Representatives; and that every Person has a right to Petition or apply to the Legislature for redress of Grievances.

That the Freedom of the Press ought not to be violated or restrained.

That there should be once in four years an Election of the President and Vice President, so that no Officer who may be appointed by the Congress to act as President in case of the removal, death, resignation or inability of the President and Vice President can in any case continue to act beyond the termination of the period for which the last President and Vice President were elected.

That nothing contained in the said Constitution is to be construed to prevent the Legislature of any State from passing Laws at its discretion from time to time to divide such State into convenient Districts, and to apportion its Representatives to and amongst such Districts.

That the Prohibition contained in the said Constitution against *ex post facto* Laws, extends only to Laws concerning Crimes.

That all Appeals in Causes determineable according to the course of the common Law, ought to be by Writ of Error and not otherwise.

That the Judicial Power of the United States in cases in which a State may be a party, does not extend to criminal Prosecutions, or to authorize any Suit by any Person against a State.

That the Judicial Power of the United States as to Controversies between

Citizens of the same State claiming Lands under Grants of different States is not to be construed to extend to any other Controversies between them, except those which relate to such Lands, so claimed under Grants of different States.

That the Jurisdiction of the Supreme Court of the United States, or of any other Court to be instituted by the Congress, is not in any case to be encreased enlarged or extended by any Fiction Collusion or mere suggestion; And

That no Treaty is to be construed so to operate as to alter the Constitution of any State.

UNDER these impressions and declaring that the rights aforesaid cannot be abridged or violated, and that the Explanations aforesaid are consistent with the said Constitution, And in confidence that the Amendments which shall have been proposed to the said Constitution will receive an early and mature Consideration: WE the said Delegates, in the Name and in the behalf of the People of the State of New York DO by these presents Assent to and Ratify the said Constitution. IN full Confidence nevertheless that until a Convention shall be called and convened for proposing Amendments to the said Constitution, the Militia of this State will not be continued in Service out of this State for a longer term than six weeks without the Consent of the Legislature thereof; that the Congress will not make or alter any Regulation in this State respecting the times places and manner of holding Elections for Senators or Representatives unless the Legislature of this State shall neglect or refuse to make Laws or regulations for the purpose, or from any circumstance be incapable of making the same, and that in those cases such power will only be exercised until the Legislature of this State shall make provision in the Premises; that no Excise will be imposed on any Article of the Growth production or Manufacture of the United States, or any of them within this State, Ardent Spirits excepted; And that the Congress will not lay direct Taxes within this State, but when the Monies arising from the Impost and Excise shall be insufficient for the public Exigencies, nor then, until Congress shall first have made a Requisition upon this State to assess levy and pay the Amount of such Requisition made agreably to the Census fixed in the said Constitution in such way and manner as the Legislature of this State shall judge best, but that in such case, if the State shall neglect or refuse to pay its proportion pursuant to such Requisition, then the Congress may assess and levy this States proportion together with Interest at the Rate of six per Centum per Annum from the time at which the same was required to be paid.

AND the Convention do in the Name and Behalf of the People of the State of New York enjoin it upon their Representatives in the Congress, to Exert all their Influence, and use all reasonable means to Obtain a Ratification of the following Amendments to the said Constitution in the manner prescribed therein; and in all Laws to be passed by the Congress in the meantime to conform to the spirit of the said Amendments as far as the Constitution will admit.

That there shall be one Representative for every thirty thousand Inhabitants, according to the enumeration or Census mentioned in the Constitution, until the whole number of Representatives amounts to two hundred; after which that number shall be continued or encreased but not diminished, as Congress shall direct, and according to such ratio as the Congress shall fix, in conformity to the rule prescribed for the Apportionment of Representatives and direct Taxes.

That the Congress do not impose any Excise on any Article (except Ardent Spirits) of the Growth production or Manufacture of the United States, or any of them.

That Congress do not lay direct Taxes but when the Monies arising from the Impost and Excise shall be insufficient for the Public Exigencies, nor then until Congress shall first have made a Requisition upon the States to assess levy and pay their respective proportions of such Requisition, agreably to the Census fixed in the said Constitution, in such way and manner as the Legislatures of the respective States shall judge best; and in such Case, if any State shall neglect or refuse to pay its proportion pursuant to such Requisition, then Congress may assess and levy such States proportion, together with Interest at the rate of six per Centum per Annum, from the time of Payment prescribed in such Requisition.

That the Congress shall not make or alter any Regulation in any State respecting the times places and manner of holding Elections for Senators or Representatives, unless the Legislature of such State shall neglect or refuse to make Laws or Regulations for the purpose, or from any circumstance be incapable of making the same; and then only until the Legislature of such State shall make provision in the premises; provided that Congress may prescribe the time for the Election of Representatives.

That no Persons except natural born Citizens, or such as were Citizens on or before the fourth day of July one thousand seven hundred and seventy six, or such as held Commissions under the United States during the War, and have at any time since the fourth day of July one thousand seven hundred and seventy six become Citizens of one or other of the United States, and who shall be Freeholders, shall be eligible to the Places of President, Vice President, or Members of either House of the Congress of the United States.

That the Congress do not grant Monopolies or erect any Company with exclusive Advantages of Commerce.

That no standing Army or regular Troops shall be raised or kept up in time of peace, without the consent of two-thirds of the Senators and Representatives present, in each House.

That no Money be borrowed on the Credit of the United States without the Assent of two-thirds of the Senators and Representatives present in each House.

That the Congress shall not declare War without the concurrence of two-thirds of the Senators and Representatives present in each House.

That the Privilege of the *Habeas Corpus* shall not by any Law be suspended for a longer term than six Months, or until twenty days after the Meeting of the Congress next following the passing of the Act for such suspension.

That the Right of the Congress to exercise exclusive Legislation over such District, not exceeding ten Miles square, as may by cession of a particular State, and the acceptance of Congress, become the Seat of the Government of the United States, shall not be so exercised, as to exempt the Inhabitants of such District from paying the like Taxes Imposts Duties and Excises, as shall be imposed on the other Inhabitants of the State in which such District may be; and that no person shall be privileged within the said District from Arrest for Crimes committed, or Debts contracted out of the said District.

That the Right of exclusive Legislation with respect to such places as may be purchased for the Erection of Forts, Magazines, Arsenals, Dockyards and other needful Buildings, shall not authorize the Congress to make any Law to prevent the Laws of the States respectively in which they may be, from extending to such places in all civil and Criminal Matters, except as to such Persons as shall be in the Service of the United States; nor to them with respect to Crimes committed without such Places.

That the Compensation for the Senators and Representatives be ascertained by standing Laws; and that no alteration of the existing rate of Compensation shall operate for the Benefit of the Representatives, until after a subsequent Election shall have been had.

That the Journals of the Congress shall be published at least once a year, with the exception of such parts relating to Treaties or Military operations, as in the Judgment of either House shall require Secrecy; and that both Houses of Congress shall always keep their Doors Open during their Sessions, unless the Business may in their Opinion require Secrecy. That the yeas & nays shall be entered on the Journals whenever two Members in either House may require it.

That no Capitation Tax shall ever be laid by the Congress.

That no Person be eligible as a Senator for more than six years in any term of twelve years; and that the Legislatures of the respective States may recal their Senators or either of them, and elect others in their stead, to serve the remainder of the time for which the Senators so recalled were appointed.

That no Senator or Representative shall during the time for which he was elected be appointed to any Office under the Authority of the United States.

That the Authority given to the Executives of the States to fill the vacancies of Senators be abolished, and that such vacancies be filled by the respective Legislatures.

That the Power of Congress to pass uniform Laws concerning Bankruptcy shall only extend to Merchants and other Traders; and that the States respectively may pass Laws for the relief of other Insolvent Debtors.

That no Person shall be eligible to the Office of President of the United States a third time.

That the Executive shall not grant Pardons for Treason, unless with the Consent of the Congress; but may at his discretion grant Reprieves to persons convicted of Treason, until their Cases can be laid before the Congress.

That the President or person exercising his Powers for the time being, shall not command an Army in the Field in person, without the previous desire of the Congress.

That all Letters Patent, Commissions, Pardons, Writs and Process of the United States, shall run in the Name of *the People of the United States,* and be tested in the Name of the President of the United States, or the person exercising his powers for the time being, or the first Judge of the Court out of which the same shall issue, as the case may be.

That the Congress shall not constitute ordain or establish any Tribunals or Inferior Courts, with any other than Appellate Jurisdiction, except such as may be necessary for the Tryal of Causes of Admiralty and Maritime Jurisdiction, and for the Trial of Piracies and Felonies committed on the High Seas; and in all other Cases to which the Judicial Power of the United States extends, and in which the Supreme Court of the United States has not original Jurisdiction, the Causes shall be heard tried, and determined in some one of the State Courts, with the right of Appeal to the Supreme Court of the United States, or other proper Tribunal to be established for that purpose by the Congress, with such exceptions, and under such regulations as the Congress shall make.

That the Court for the Trial of Impeachments shall consist of the Senate, the Judges of the Supreme Court of the United States, and the first or Senior Judge for the time being, of the highest Court of general and ordinary common Law Jurisdiction in each State; that the Congress shall by standing Laws designate the Courts in the respective States answering this Description, and in States having no Courts exactly answering this Description, shall designate some other Court, preferring such if any there be, whose Judge or Judges may hold their places during good Behaviour—Provided that no more than one Judge, other than Judges of the Supreme Court of the United States, shall come from one State—That the Congress be authorized to pass Laws for compensating the said Judges for such Services and for compelling their Attendance—and that a Majority at least of the said Judges shall be requisite to constitute the said Court—that no person impeached shall sit as a Member thereof. That each Member shall previous to the entering upon any Trial take an Oath or Affirmation, honestly and impartially to hear and determine the Cause—and that a Majority of the Members present shall be necessary to a Conviction.

That persons aggrieved by any Judgment, Sentence or Decree of the Supreme Court of the United States, in any Cause in which that Court has original Jurisdiction, with such exceptions and under such Regulations as the Congress shall make concerning the same, shall upon application, have a Commission to be issued by the President of the United States, to such Men learned in the Law as he shall nominate, and by and with the Advice and consent of the Senate appoint, not less than seven, authorizing such Commissioners, or any seven or more of them, to correct the Errors in such Judgment or to review such Sentence and Decree, as the case may be, and to do Justice to the parties in the Premises.

That no Judge of the Supreme Court of the United States shall hold any other Office under the United States, or any of them.

That the Judicial Power of the United States shall extend to no Controversies respecting Land, unless it relate to Claims of Territory or Jurisdiction between States, or to Claims of Land between Individuals, or between States and Individuals under the Grants of different States.

That the Militia of any State shall not be compelled to serve without the limits of the State for a longer term than six weeks, without the Consent of the Legislature thereof.

That the words *without the Consent of the Congress* in the seventh Clause of the ninth Section of the first Article of the Constitution, be expunged.

That the Senators and Representatives and all Executive and Judicial Officers of the United States shall be bound by Oath or Affirmation not to infringe or violate the Constitutions or Rights of the respective States.

That the Legislatures of the respective States may make Provision by Law, that the Electors of the Election Districts to be by them appointed shall chuse a Citizen of the United States who shall have been an Inhabitant of such District for the Term of one year immediately preceeding the time of his Election, for one of the Representatives of such State.

Ratifications of the Constitution by the States, RG 11, DNA.

House Committee Report
July 28, 1789

[1] IN the introductory paragraph before the words, "*We the people,*" add, "Government being[1] intended for the benefit of the people, and the rightful establishment thereof being derived from their authority alone."[2]

[2] ART. 1, SEC. 2, PAR. 3—Strike out all between the words, "*direct*" and "*and until such,*" and instead thereof insert, "After the first enumeration there shall be one representative for every thirty[3] thousand until the number shall amount to one hundred; after which the proportion shall be so regulated by Congress that the number of Representatives shall never be less than one[4] hundred, nor more than one hundred and seventy-five,[5] but each State shall always have at least one Representative."[6]

---

[1] On August 14, the COWH disagreed to a motion by Gerry to insert "of right" at this point.

[2] On August 13, the COWH disagreed to a motion by Sherman to substitute the following for this paragraph:

> Resolved by the senate and house of representatives of the United States in congress assembled, That the following articles be proposed as amendments to the constitution: and when ratified by three fourths of the state legislatures shall become valid to all intents and purposes, as part of the same. (*CR,* Aug. 13)

On August 14, the COWH agreed to the first resolution by a vote of 27–23. The House disagreed to it on August 19.

[3] On August 14, the COWH disagreed to a motion by Ames to strike out "thirty" and insert "forty."

[4] On August 14, by a vote of 27–22, the COWH disagreed to a motion by Livermore to strike out "one" and insert "two." (*CR,* Aug. 14) The *NYDA,* Aug. 15, says the motion was made by Tucker and included a provision to strike out the remainder of the resolution.

[5] On August 14, a motion by Vining, to insert a clause to the effect "that where the number of inhabitants of any particular State, amounts to 45,000, they shall be entitled to two representatives," was disagreed to. On the same day, the COWH agreed to a motion by Sedgwick to strike out "one hundred and seventy-five" and insert "two hundred." (*GUS,* Aug. 19)

[6] On August 14, the COWH agreed to the second resolution by a vote of 27–22. On August 19, the House debated a motion by Ames,

> That after the first enumeration, there shall be one representative for every 30,000 inhabitants, till the number of members shall amount to 100; after which the number of members shall not increase till the number of inhabitants shall amount to four millions, after which the ratio of representation shall be one for every 40,000, till the number amounts to 200, beyond which number it shall not be increased till the number of inhabitant amounts to ten millions, when the ratio of representation shall be one for every fifty thousand. (*NYDA,* Aug. 20)

On August 20, the House tabled the Ames motion and five or six substitutes. On August 21, the House agreed to a substitute proposed by Smith (S.C.) as follows:

> After the first enumeration, required by the first article of the constitution, there shall be one representative for every 30,000, until the number shall amount to one hundred. After which, the proportion shall be so regulated by congress, that there shall be not less than one hundred representatives, nor less

[3] ART. 1, SEC. 6—Between the words "*United States,*" and "*shall in all cases,*" strike out "*they,*" and insert, "But no law varying the compensation shall take effect until an election of Representatives shall have intervened. The members."[7]

[4] ART. 1, SEC. 9—Between PAR. 2 and 3 insert, "No[8] religion shall be established by law, nor shall the equal rights of conscience be infringed."[9]

[5] "The freedom of speech, and of the press, and the right of the people peaceably to assemble and[10] consult for their common good,[11] and to apply to the government for redress of grievances, shall not be infringed."

[6] "A well regulated militia,[12] composed of the body of the people, being the best security of a free State, the right of the people to keep and bear arms shall not be infringed, but no person religiously scrupulous shall be compelled to bear arms."[13]

[7] "No soldier shall in time of peace be quartered in any house without

---

> than one representative for every 40,000 persons, until the number of representatives shall amount to two hundred; after which the proportion shall be so regulated by congress, that there shall not be less than two-hundred representatives, nor less than one representative for 50,000 persons. (*CR*, Aug. 21)

[7] The third resolution was agreed to by the COWH on August 14, by a vote of 27–20.

[8] On August 15, Madison made and withdrew a motion to insert "national" at this point.

[9] On August 15, by a vote of 31–20, the COWH agreed to a motion by Livermore to strike out this resolution and insert, "The Congress shall make no laws touching religion or infringing the rights of conscience." (*CR*, Aug. 15) On August 20, the House agreed to a motion by Ames to alter the resolution to read, "Congress shall make no law establishing religion, or to prevent the free exercise thereof; or to infringe the rights of conscience." (*GUS*, Aug. 22) The final House resolution substitutes "prohibiting" for "to prevent."

[10] On August 15, the COWH disagreed to Sedgwick's motion to strike out "assemble and."

[11] On August 15, by a vote of 41–10, the COWH disagreed to Tucker's motion to insert "to instruct their representatives" at this point.

[12] On August 17, a motion by Gerry to insert "trained to arms" at this point failed for want of a second.

[13] On August 17, Jackson made a motion in the COWH to insert "upon paying an equivalent to be established by law" at this point. On the suggestion of Smith (S.C.), Jackson proposed to change this phrase to, "No one, religiously scrupulous of bearing arms, shall be compelled to render military service in person, upon paying an equivalent." This was apparently superseded by Benson's motion to strike out "but no person" through "bear arms," which the COWH disagreed to, 24–22. On the same day, a motion by Burke to insert the following at this point was disagreed to, by a majority of 13:

> A standing army of regular troops in time of peace, is dangerous to public liberty, and such shall not be raised or kept up in time of peace but from necessity, and for the security of the people, nor then without the consent of two-thirds of the members present of both houses, and in all cases the military shall be subordinate to the civil authority. (*CR*, Aug. 17)

The House, on August 20, agreed to a motion to insert "in person" at this point.

the consent of the owner, nor in time of war but[14] in a manner to be prescribed by law."[15]

[8] "No person shall be subject, except in case of impeachment, to more than one trial or[16] one punishment for the same offence,[17] nor shall[18] be compelled to be a witness against himself, nor be deprived of life, liberty, or property without due process of law; nor shall private property be taken for public use without just compensation."

[9] "Excessive bail shall not be required, nor excessive fines imposed, nor cruel and unusual punishments inflicted."

[10] "The right of the people to be secure in their person, houses, papers and effects,[19] shall not be violated by warrants issuing,[20] without probable cause supported by oath or affirmation, and not[21] particularly describing the places to be searched, and the persons or things to be seized."

[11] "The enumeration in this Constitution of certain rights shall not be construed to deny or disparage[22] others retained by the people."

[12] ART. 1, SEC. 10, between the 1st and 2d PAR. insert, "No State shall infringe the equal rights of conscience, nor the freedom of speech, or of the press, nor of the right of trial by jury in criminal cases."[23]

[13] ART. 3, SEC. 2, add to the 2d PAR. "But no appeal to such court[24]

---

[14] On August 17, by a vote of 35–13, the COWH disagreed to a motion by Gerry to insert "by a civil magistrate" at this point.

[15] On August 17, by a majority of 16, the COWH disagreed to a motion by Sumter to strike out "in time of peace" and "nor in time of war" through "law."

[16] On August 17, the COWH disagreed to Benson's motion to strike out "one trial or."

[17] On August 17, the COWH disagreed to Partridge's motion to insert "by any law of the United States" at this point.

[18] On August 17, the COWH agreed to Laurance's motion to insert "in any criminal case" at this point.

[19] On August 17, the COWH agreed to a motion to insert "against unreasonable searches and seizures" at this point. *CR*, Aug. 17, says this motion was Gerry's; according to *NYDA*, Aug. 18, and *GUS*, Aug. 19, 22, it was Benson's.

[20] On August 17, the COWH disagreed to a motion to strike out "by warrants issuing" and insert "and no warrant shall issue." In the *CR*, Aug. 17, this motion is attributed to Benson; the *GUS*, Aug. 22, says it was Gerry's.

[21] On August 17, the COWH disagreed to Livermore's motion to strike out "and not."

[22] On August 17, a motion by Gerry to strike out "disparage" and insert "impair" failed for lack of a second.

[23] On August 17, the COWH disagreed to a motion by Tucker to strike out the twelfth resolution, and agreed to Livermore's motion to reword it as follows:

> The equal rights of conscience, the freedom of speech, or of the press, and the right of trial by jury in criminal cases shall not be infringed by any state. (*CR*, Aug. 17)

The final House resolution, however, retains the original negative wording.

[24] The final House wording substitutes "the Supreme Court of the United States" for "such court."

shall be allowed, where the value in controversy shall not amount to one[25] thousand dollars;[26] nor shall any fact, triable by a Jury according to the course of the common law, be otherwise re-examinable than according to the rules of common law."

[14] ART. 3, SEC. 2—Strike out the whole of the 3d paragraph, and insert—"In all criminal prosecutions the accused shall enjoy the right to a speedy and public trial, to be informed of the nature and cause of the accusation, to be confronted with the witnesses against him, to have compulsory process for obtaining witnesses in his favor, and to have the assistance of counsel for his defence."[27]

[15] "The trial of all crimes (except in cases of impeachment, and in cases arising in the land or naval forces, or in the militia, when in actual service in time of war or public danger[28]) shall be by an impartial jury of freeholders[29] of the vicinage,[30] with the requisite of unanimity for conviction, the right of challenge and other accustomed requisites; and no person shall be held to answer for a capital, or otherwise infamous crime, unless on a presentment or indictment by a Grand Jury; but if a crime be committed in a place in the possession of an enemy, or in which an insurrection may prevail, the indictment and trial may by law be authorized in some other place within the same State; and if it be committed in a place not within a State, the indictment and trial may be at such place or places as the law may have directed."[31]

[16] "In suits at common law the right of trial by jury shall be preserved."

[17] "Immediately after ART. 6, the following to be inserted as ART. 7."

---

[25] On August 17, the COWH disagreed to a motion by Sedgwick, seconded by Livermore, to strike out "one" and insert "three."

[26] On August 17, the COWH disagreed to a motion by Benson to strike out "But no appeal" through "dollars."

[27] On August 17, by a vote of 41–9, the COWH disagreed to Burke's motion to amend this resolution so as:

> to leave it in the power of the accused to put off their trial to the next session, provided he made appear to the court, that the evidence of the witnesses, for whom process was granted, but not served, was material to his defence. (*CR*, Aug. 17)

The COWH agreed to a motion by Livermore to insert into the resolution a clause providing for the "right of being tried in the state where the offence was committed." Also on August 17, Burke made and withdrew a motion providing that "no criminal prosecution should be had by way of information." (*CR*, Aug. 17)

[28] On August 21, the House disagreed to a motion by Gerry to strike out "public danger" and insert "foreign invasion."

[29] The final House wording omits "of freeholders."

[30] On August 18, the COWH disagreed to a motion by Burke to strike out "vicinage" and insert "district or county in which the offence has been committed."

[31] On August 18, the COWH disagreed to Burke's motion to insert "no criminal prosecution should be had by way of information" at this point. On August 21, the House agreed to a motion to strike out "and if it be committed" through the end of the resolution.

"The powers delegated by this Constitution to the government of the United States, shall be exercised as therein appropriated, so that the Legislative shall never exercise the powers vested in the Executive or the Judicial; nor the Executive the powers vested in the Legislative or Judicial; nor the Judicial the powers vested in the Legislative or Executive."[32]

[18] "The powers not[33] delegated by this Constitution, nor prohibited by it to the States, are reserved to the States respectively."[34]

[19] ART. 7 to be made ART. 8.[35]

Extract from the Journal,
JOHN BECKLEY, CLERK

[NEW-YORK, PRINTED BY THOMAS GREENLEAF.]

Broadside Collection, RBkRm, DLC. Except in cases of conflict or direct quotation, we have not listed specific citations in each of the footnotes because of their repetitiveness. They are from *NYDA*, Aug. 15–22; *GUS*, Aug. 15, 19, 22; and *CR*, Aug. 14–21, and may be found in the notes to the calendar.

[32] On August 21, the House disagreed to a motion to strike out the latter clause. (*NYDA*, Aug. 22)

[33] On August 18, the COWH disagreed to a motion by Tucker to insert "All powers being derived from the people" as an introduction to the clause and to insert "expressly" at this point. On August 21, by a recorded vote of 32–17, the House disagreed to a motion by Gerry to insert "expressly" at this point.

[34] On August 18, the COWH disagreed to a motion by Gerry, opposed by Carroll, to insert "or to the people" at this point. (*GUS*, Aug. 22) According to the *CR*, Aug. 18, this motion was made by Carroll and agreed to, but the final House version does not have this change. The *GUS*, Aug. 22, states that on August 21 the House agreed to a motion by Sherman to insert "government of the United" between "by it to the" and "States," and to insert "individual" after "reserved to the." The *CR*, Aug. 21, says that powers would have been reserved to the states "or the people." The final House resolution, however, retains the original wording.

[35] The final House resolutions omit this amendment.

Gerry Motion
August 18, 1789

That such of the amendments to the Constitution proposed by the several states, as are not in substance comprized in the report of the select committee appointed to consider amendments, be referred to a committee of the whole House; and that all the amendments which shall be agreed to by the committee last mentioned, be included in one report.

HJ, p. 151.

Tucker Amendments
August 18, 1789

ARTICLE 1. *section* 2. clause 2. At the end add these words, "nor shall any person be capable of serving as a representative more than six years in any term of eight years."

Clause 3. At the end add these words, "from and after the commencement of the year one thousand seven hundred and ninety-five, the election of senators for each state shall be annual; and no person shall be capable of serving as a senator more than five years in any term of six years."

Section 4. clause 1. Strike out the words, "But the Congress may at any time by law make or alter such regulations, except as to the places of choosing senators."

Section 5. clause 1. Amend the first part to read thus, "Each state shall be the judge (according to its own laws) of the elections of its senators and representatives to sit in Congress, and shall furnish them with sufficient credentials; but each House shall judge of the qualifications of its own members. A majority of said House shall constitute, &c."

Clause 2. Strike out these words, "and with the concurrence of two thirds expel a member;" and insert the word "and" after the word "proceedings."

Section 6. clause 2. Amend to read thus, "No person having been elected, and having taken his seat as a senator or representative, shall, during the time for which he was elected, be appointed to any civil office under the authority of the United States; and no person, &c."

Section 8. clause 1. At the end add these words, "No direct tax shall be laid, unless any state shall have neglected to furnish in due time its proportion of a previous requisition, in which case Congress may proceed to levy by direct taxation, within any state so neglecting, its proportion of such requisition, together with interest at the rate of six per cent. per annum, from the time it ought to have been furnished, and the charges of levying the same."

Clause 9. Strike out the words, "tribunals inferior to the supreme court," and insert the words, "courts of admiralty."

Clause 17. At the end add these words, "Provided that the Congress shall not have authority to make any law to prevent the laws of the states respectively in which such district or places may be, from extending to such district or places in all civil and criminal matters, in which any person without the limits of such district or places, shall be a party aggrieved."

Section 9. clause 7. Strike out the words, "without the consent of the Congress;" and amend to read thus, "shall accept of any present or emolument, or hold any office or title of any kind whatever, from any king, prince or foreign state; Provided, That this clause shall not be construed to affect the rights of those persons (during their own lives) who are now citizens of the United States, and hold foreign titles."

Section 10. clause 2. Amend the first sentence to read thus, "No state shall lay any duties on imports or exports, or any duty of tonnage, except such as shall be uniform in their operation on all foreign nations, and consistent with the existing treaties; and also uniform in their operation on the citizens of all the several states in the Union."

ARTICLE 2. *section 1.* clause 5. At the end add these words, "Nor shall any person be capable of holding the office of President of the United States, more than eight years in any term of twelve years."

Section 2. clause 1. Strike out the words, "be commander in chief," and insert, "have power to direct (agreeable to law) the operations."

Clause 3. At the end add these words, "He shall also have power to suspend from his office, for a time not exceeding twelve months, any officer whom he shall have reason to think unfit to be entrusted with the duties thereof; and Congress may by law provide for the absolute removal of officers found to be unfit for the trust reposed in them."

ARTICLE 3. *section 1.* From each sentence strike out the words, "inferior courts," and insert the words, "courts of admiralty."

Section 2. clause 1. Strike out the words, "between a state and citizens of another state, &c." to the end; and amend to read thus, "between a state and foreign states, and between citizens of the United States claiming the same lands under grants of different states."

ARTICLE 6. clause 3. Between the word, "no," and the word, "religious," insert the word, "other."

HJ, pp. 153–54.

Burke Amendment
August 21, 1789

Congress shall not alter, modify or interfere in the times, places or manner of holding elections of senators or representatives, except when any state shall refuse or neglect, or be unable by invasion or rebellion to make such election.[1]

HJ, p. 161.

[1] On August 21, a motion by Sedgwick, to amend the resolution "by giving the power to congress to alter the times, manner and places of holding elections, provided the states made improper ones," was disagreed to. (*CR*, Aug. 21)

Tucker Amendment
August 22, 1789

The Congress shall never impose direct taxes, but where the monies arising from the duties, imposts and excise, are insufficient for the public exigencies; nor then, until Congress shall have made a requisition upon the states, to assess, levy and pay their respective proportions of such requisitions: and in case any state shall neglect or refuse to pay its proportion, pursuant to such requisition, then Congress may assess and levy such state's proportion, together with interest thereon, at the rate of six per cent. per annum, from the time of payment prescribed by such requisition.

HJ, p. 163.

Tucker and Gerry Amendments
August 22, 1789

ARTICLE I. *section 8.* clause 9. Strike out the words, "tribunals inferior to the supreme court," and insert the words, "courts of admiralty."

In the third section of the sixth article, insert the word, "other," between the word "*no,*" and the word "religious."

That Congress erect no company of merchants with exclusive advantages of commerce.

Congress shall at no time consent that any person holding an office of trust or profit under the United States, shall accept of a title of nobility, or any other title or office from any king, prince, or foreign state.

HJ, p. 164. According to the *CR*, Aug. 22, the first two resolutions were introduced by Tucker and the last two by Gerry.

Benson Motion
August 22, 1789

Resolved by the house of representatives of the United States in Congress assembled, that the following amendments to the constitution of the United States having been agreed to by two thirds of both houses, be submitted to the legislatures of the several states; which when ratified in whole or in part by three fourths of said legislatures, shall be valid to all intents and purposes as parts of said constitution.

GUS, Aug. 26.

House Resolution and Articles of Amendment August 24, 1789

CONGRESS OF THE UNITED STATES
In the HOUSE *of* REPRESENTATIVES,

Monday, 24th August, 1789,

[1]RESOLVED, BY THE SENATE AND HOUSE OF REPRESENTATIVES OF THE UNITED STATES OF AMERICA IN CONGRESS ASSEMBLED, two thirds of both Houses deeming it necessary,[2] That the following Articles be proposed to the Legislatures of the several States, as Amendments to the Constitution of the United States, all or any of which Articles, when ratified by three fourths of the said Legislatures, to be valid to all intents and purposes as part of the said Constitution—Viz.

ARTICLES in addition to, and amendment of, the Constitution of the United States of America, proposed by Congress, and ratified by the Legislatures of the several States, pursuant to the fifth Article of the original Constitution.

ARTICLE THE FIRST.

After the first enumeration, required by the first Article of the Constitution, there shall be one Representative for every thirty thousand, until the number shall amount to one[3] hundred, after which the proportion shall be so regulated by Congress, that there shall be not less than one hundred Representatives, nor less than one Representative for every forty thousand persons, until the number of Representatives shall amount to two hundred, after which the proportion shall be so regulated by Congress, that there shall not be less than two hundred Representatives, nor less than one Representative for every fifty thousand persons.[4]

---

[1] On September 8, the Senate agreed to a motion to insert the following at this point:

> The Conventions of a number of the States having, at the time of their adopting the Constitution, expressed a desire, in order to prevent misconstruction or abuse of its powers, that further declaratory and restrictive clauses should be added, and as extending the grounds of public confidence in the Government, will best insure the beneficent ends of its institution.

[2] On September 8, the Senate agreed to a motion to strike out "deeming it necessary" and insert "concurring."

[3] On September 2, by a recorded vote of 12–6, the Senate disagreed to a motion to strike out "one" and insert "two."

[4] On September 2, the Senate agreed to a motion to strike out from the first "after which" through "persons" and insert the following:

> to which number one Representative shall be added for every subsequent increase of forty thousand, until the Representatives shall amount to two hundred, to which one Representative shall be added for every subsequent increase of sixty thousand persons.

ARTICLE THE SECOND.

No law varying the compensation to the members of Congress,[5] shall take effect, until an election of Representatives shall have intervened.

ARTICLE THE THIRD.

Congress shall make no law establishing religion[6] or prohibiting the free exercise thereof,[7] nor shall the rights of Conscience be infringed.[8]

ARTICLE THE FOURTH.

The Freedom of Speech, and of the Press,[9] and the right of the People peaceably to assemble, and consult for their common good,[10] and[11] to apply to the Government for a redress of grievances, shall not be infringed.[12]

ARTICLE THE FIFTH.

A well regulated militia, composed of the body of the People, being the best security of a free State, the right of the People to keep and bear arms, shall not be infringed, but no one religiously scrupulous of bearing arms, shall be compelled to render military service in person.[13]

---

[5] On September 3, the Senate agreed to a motion to strike out "to the members of Congress" and insert "for the Service of the Senate and House of Representatives of the United States."

[6] On September 3, the Senate disagreed to a motion to strike out "religion" and insert "any particular denomination of religion in preference to another." On September 9, the Senate agreed to a motion to strike out "religion" and insert "articles of faith or a mode of worship."

[7] On September 3, the Senate disagreed to a motion to strike out "religion" through "thereof" and insert "One Religious Sect or Society in preference to others."

[8] On September 3, the Senate disagreed to motions (a) to strike out Article 3; (b) to strike out Article 3 and insert "Congress shall not make any law, infringing the rights of conscience, or establishing any Religious Sect or Society"; and (c) to agree to Article 3 as passed by the House. On the same date, a motion to strike out "nor shall" through "infringed" was agreed to.

On September 9, the Senate agreed to amend Article 3 to read as follows:

> Congress shall make no law establishing articles of faith or a mode of worship, or prohibiting the free exercise of religion, or abridging the freedom of speech, or the press, or the right of the people peaceably to assemble, and petition to the Government for the redress of grievances.

[9] On September 3, the Senate disagreed to a motion to insert "in as ample a manner as hath at any time been secured by the common law" at this point.

[10] On September 3, by a recorded vote of 14–2, the Senate disagreed to a motion to insert "to instruct their Representatives" at this point.

[11] On September 3, the Senate disagreed to a motion to strike out "and consult for their common good, and."

[12] On September 4, the Senate agreed to amend Article 4 to read as follows:

> Congress shall make no law, abridging the freedom of Speech, or of the Press, or the right of the People peaceably to assemble and consult for their common good, and to petition the Government for a redress of grievances.

On September 9, the Senate struck out Article 4, after incorporating its provisions into Article 3.

[13] On September 4, by a recorded vote of 9–6, the Senate disagreed to a motion to insert the following at this point:

> that standing armies, in time of peace, being dangerous to Liberty, should be avoided as far as the circumstances and protection of the community will

ARTICLE THE SIXTH.

No soldier shall, in time of peace, be quartered in any house without the consent of the owner, nor in time of war, but in a manner to be prescribed by law.

ARTICLE THE SEVENTH.

The right of the People to be secure in their persons, houses, papers and effects, against unreasonable searches and seizures, shall not be violated, and no warrants shall issue, but upon probable cause supported by oath or affirmation, and particularly describing the place to be searched, and the persons or things to be seized.

ARTICLE THE EIGHTH.

No person shall be subject, except in case of impeachment, to more than one trial, or one punishment[14] for the same offense, nor shall be compelled in any criminal case, to be a witness against himself, nor be deprived of life, liberty or property, without due process of law; nor shall private property be taken for public use without just compensation.

ARTICLE THE NINTH.

In all criminal prosecutions, the accused shall enjoy the right to a speedy and public trial, to be informed of the nature and cause of the accusation, to be confronted with the witnesses against him, to have compulsory process for obtaining witnesses in his favor, and to have the assistance of counsel for his defence.

ARTICLE THE TENTH.

The trial of all crimes (except in cases of impeachment, and in cases arising in the land or naval forces, or in the militia when in actual service in time of

---

> admit; and that in all cases the military should be under strict subordination to, and governed by the civil Power. That no standing army or regular troops shall be raised in time of peace, without the consent of two thirds of the Members present in both Houses, and that no soldier shall be inlisted for any longer term than the continuance of the war.

On September 4, the Senate agreed to amend Article 5 to read as follows:

> A well regulated militia, being the best security of a free state, the right of the people to keep and bear arms, shall not be infringed.

On September 9, the Senate replaced "the best" with "necessary to the." The *SLJ*, p. 167, omits both phrases, but the latter is included in Ellsworth's list. On the same day the Senate disagreed to a motion to insert "for the common defence" after "bear arms." This article and the following ones were then renumbered as articles 4 through 8.

[14] On September 4, the Senate struck out "except in case of impeachment, to more than one trial, or one punishment" and inserted "be twice put in jeopardy of life or limb by any public prosecution." On September 9, the Senate agreed to a motion to strike out "No person" through "punishment" and insert the following:

> No person shall be held to answer for a capital or otherwise infamous crime, unless on a presentment or indictment of a Grand Jury, except in cases arising in the land or naval forces, or in the militia, when in actual service, in time of war or public danger, nor shall any person be subject to be put in jeopardy of life or limb.

War or public danger) shall be by an impartial Jury of the Vicinage, with the requisite of unanimity for conviction, the right of challenge, and other accostomed requisites; and no person shall be held to answer for a capital, or otherways infamous crime, unless on a presentment or indictment by a Grand Jury; but if a crime be committed in a place in the possession of an enemy, or in which an insurrection may prevail, the indictment and trial may by law be authorised in some other place within the same State.[15]

ARTICLE THE ELEVENTH.

No appeal to the Supreme Court of the United States, shall be allowed, where the value in controversy shall not amount to one thousand dollars, nor shall any fact, triable by a Jury according to the course of the common law, be otherwise re-examinable, than according to the rules of common law.[16]

ARTICLE THE TWELFTH.

In suits at common law,[17] the right of trial by Jury shall be preserved.[18]

ARTICLE THE THIRTEENTH.

Excessive bail shall not be required, nor excessive fines imposed, nor cruel and unusual punishments inflicted.

---

[15] On September 4, the Senate struck out all of Article 10 except the following:

> No person shall be held to answer for a capital, or otherwise infamous crime, unless on a presentment or indictment by a Grand Jury.

On September 9, the Senate struck out Article 10, after partially incorporating it into Article 8. Otis noted, "8. & 10. united with an amendment." Also on September 9, by a recorded vote of 8–8, the Senate disagreed to a motion to restore "The trial" through "requisite."

[16] On September 4, the Senate disagreed to a motion to strike out Article 11 and insert the following:

> The Supreme Judicial Federal Court, shall have no jurisdiction of causes between citizens of different States, unless the matter in dispute, whether it concerns the realty or personalty, be of the value of three thousand dollars, at the least: Nor shall the Federal Judicial Powers extend to any actions between citizens of different States, where the matter in dispute, whether it concerns the realty or personalty is not of the value of fifteen hundred dollars, at the least—And no part, triable by a Jury according to the course of the common law, shall be otherwise re-examinable, than according to the rules of common law.

Also on September 4, the Senate agreed to amend Article 11 to read as follows:

> No fact, triable by a Jury according to the course of common law, shall be otherwise re-examinable in any court of the United States, than according to the rules of common law.

On September 9, the Senate struck out Article 11, after incorporating it into Article 8. Otis noted, "10th. and 11th incorporated."

[17] On September 7, the Senate inserted "where the consideration exceeds twenty dollars" at this point. Otis noted, "where the Value in controversy shall exceed twenty dollars"; this was the wording used in the final Senate amendments.

[18] On September 9, the Senate amended Article 12 to read as follows:

> In suits at common law, where the value in controversy shall exceed twenty dollars, the right of trial by Jury shall be preserved, and no fact tried by a Jury, shall be otherwise re-examined in any Court of the United States, than according to the rules of the common law.

This article was then renumbered as Article 9 and Article 13 became Article 10.

ARTICLE THE FOURTEENTH.

No State shall infringe the right of trial by Jury in criminal cases, nor the rights of conscience, nor the freedom of speech, or of the press.[19]

ARTICLE THE FIFTEENTH.

The enumeration in the Constitution of certain rights, shall not be construed to deny or disparage others retained by the people.

ARTICLE THE SIXTEENTH.

The powers delegated by the Constitution to the government of the United States, shall be exercised as therein appropriated, so that the Legislative shall never exercise the powers vested in the Executive or Judicial; nor the Executive the powers vested in the Legislative or Judicial; nor the Judicial the powers vested in the Legislative or Executive.[20]

ARTICLE THE SEVENTEENTH.

The powers not[21] delegated[22] by the Constitution, nor prohibited by it, to the States, are reserved to the States respectively.[23]

Teste,

JOHN BECKLEY, CLERK

In SENATE, *August* 25, 1789

Read and ordered to be printed for the consideration of the Senate.

Attest, SAMUEL A. OTIS, Secretary

NEW-YORK, PRINTED BY T. GREENLEAF, near the COFFEE-HOUSE.

House Resolutions, SR, DNA. The Senate amendments are printed in the *SLJ*, pp. 149–55, 158–64, and 166–68; many were noted on the document by Otis.

[19] On September 7, the Senate disagreed to Article 14, and Article 15 was renumbered as Article 11.

[20] On September 7, the Senate disagreed to Article 16.

[21] On September 7, the Senate disagreed to a motion to insert "expressly" at this point.

[22] On September 7, the Senate inserted "to the United States" at this point.

[23] On September 7, the Senate inserted "or to the people" at this point. On September 9, this article was renumbered as Article 12.

Additional Articles of Amendment September 7, 1789

That the general Government of the United States ought never to impose direct taxes but where the monies arising from the duties, impost, and excise, are insufficient for the public exigencies, nor then until Congress shall have made a requisition upon the States to assess, levy, and pay their respective proportions of such requisitions; and in case any State shall neglect or refuse to pay its proportion, pursuant to such requisition, then Congress may assess and levy such State's proportion, together with interest thereon at the rate of six per cent, per annum, from the time of payment prescribed by such requisition.

That the third section of the sixth Article of the Constitution of the United States, ought to be amended by inserting the word OTHER between the words "No" and "Religious."

SLJ, pp. 158–59.

That Congress shall not exercise the powers vested in them by the fourth section of the first article, but in cases when a State shall neglect or refuse to make regulations therein mentioned, or shall make regulations subversive of the rights of the people, to a free and equal representation in Congress, agreeably to the Constitution.

That Congress shall not erect any Company of Merchants with exclusive advantages of Commerce.

Congress shall, at no time, consent that any person, holding an office of trust or profit, under the United States, shall accept of a title of Nobility, or any other title or office, from any king, prince, or foreign State.

House Joint and Concurrent Resolutions, SR, DNA, hand of Dalton.

No person Indebted to the United States shall be Entitled to a Seat in either Branch of the Legislature.

House Joint and Concurrent Resolutions, SR, DNA, hand of Butler.

Additional Articles of Amendment September 8, 1789

That there are certain natural rights, of which men, when they form a social compact, cannot deprive or divest their posterity, among which are the enjoyment of life and liberty, with the means of acquiring, possessing, and protecting property, and pursuing and obtaining happiness and safety.

That all power is naturally vested in, and consequently derived from the people; that Magistrates, therefore, are their Trustees and Agents, and at all times amenable to them.

That Government ought to be instituted for the common benefit, protection, and security of the people; and that the doctrine of non-resistence against arbitrary power and oppression, is absurd, slavish, and destructive of the good and happiness of mankind.

That no man or set of men are entitled to exclusive or separate public emoluments or privileges from the community, but in consideration of public services, which not being descendible, neither ought the offices of Magistrate, Legislator, or Judge, or any other public Officer to be hereditary.

That the Legislative, Executive, and Judiciary Powers of Government should be separate and distinct, and that the members of the two first may be restrained from oppression by feeling and participating the public burthens, they should, at fixed periods, be reduced to a private station, return into the mass of the people, and the vacancies be supplied by certain and regular elections; in which all or any part of the former members to be eligible or ineligible, as the rules of the Constitution of Government, and the laws, shall direct.

That every freeman restrained of his liberty, is entitled to a remedy, to enquire into the lawfulness thereof and to remove the same, if unlawful, and that such remedy ought not to be denied nor delayed.

That every freeman ought to find a certain remedy by recourse to the laws, for all injuries and wrongs he may receive in his person, property, or character. He ought to obtain right and justice freely without sale, completely and without denial, promptly and without delay, and that all establishments or regulations contravening these rights, are oppressive and unjust.

That the members of the Senate and House of Representatives shall be ineligible to, and incapable of holding any civil office under the authority of the United States, during the time for which they shall respectively be elected.

That the journals of the proceedings of the Senate and House of Representatives shall be published, at least, once in every year, except such parts thereof relating to treaties, alliances, or military operations, as in their judgment require secrecy.

That a regular statement and account of the receipts and expenditures of all public money shall be published, at least, once in every year.

That no commercial Treaty shall be ratified without the concurrence of two thirds of the whole number of the members of the Senate; and no Treaty, ceding, contracting, restraining or suspending the territorial rights or claims of the United States, or any of them or their, or any of their rights or claims to fishing in the American Seas, or navigating the American Rivers, shall be but in cases of the most urgent and extreme necessity; nor shall any such treaty be ratified without the concurrence of three fourths of the whole number of the members of both Houses respectively.

That no navigation law, or law regulating commerce, shall be passed without the consent of two thirds of the members present in both Houses.

That no standing army or regular troops shall be raised or kept up in time of peace, without the consent of two thirds of the members present in both Houses.

That no soldier shall be enlisted for any longer term than four years, except in time of war, and then for no longer term than the continuance of the war.

That each State respectively shall have the power to provide for organizing, arming, and disciplining its own militia, whensoever Congress shall omit or neglect to provide for the same. That the militia shall not be subject to martial law, except when in actual service in time of war, invasion or rebellion; and when not in the actual service of the United States, shall be subject only to such fines, penalties, and punishments as shall be directed or inflicted by the laws of its own State.

That the exclusive power of Legislation given to Congress over the Federal Town, and its adjacent district, and other places purchased or to be purchased by Congress of any of the States, shall extend only to such regulations as respect the police and good Government thereof.

That no person shall be capable of being President of the United States, for more than eight years in any term of sixteen years.

That the Judicial Power of the United States shall be vested in one Supreme Court, and in such Courts of Admiralty as Congress may from time to time ordain and establish in any of the different States; The Judicial Powers shall extend to all cases in law and equity arising under treaties made, or which shall be made under the authority of the United States; to all cases affecting Ambassadors, other foreign Ministers and Consuls; to all cases of Admiralty and Maritime Jurisdiction; to controversies to which the United States shall be a party; to controversies between two or more States; and between parties claiming lands under the grants of different States. In all cases affecting Ambassadors, other foreign Ministers and Consuls, and those in which a State shall be a party, the Supreme Court shall have original jurisdiction; in all other cases before mentioned the Supreme Court shall have appellate jurisdiction as to matters of law only, except in cases of equity, and of Admiralty and Maritime Jurisdiction, in which the Supreme Court shall have appellate Jurisdiction, both as to law and fact, with such exceptions, and under such regulations as the Congress shall make. But the Judicial Power of the United States shall extend to no case where the cause of action shall have originated before the ratification of this Constitution; except in disputes between States about their Territory, disputes between persons claiming lands under the grants of different States, and suits for debts due to the United States.

That Congress shall not alter, modify, or interfere in the times, places, or manner of holding elections for Senators and Representatives, or either of them, except when the Legislature of any State shall neglect, refuse, or be disabled by invasion or rebellion, to prescribe the same.

That some tribunal, other than the Senate, be provided for trying impeachments of Senators.

That the salary of a Judge shall not be increased or diminished during his continuance in office, otherwise than by general regulations of salary, which may take place on a revision of the subject at stated periods of not less than seven years, to commence from the time such salaries shall be first ascertained by Congress.

SLJ, pp. 160–64.

Senate Amendments
September 9, 1789

United States of America

In the Senate

Wednesday 9th Sept. 1789

On the question to concur with the House of Representatives on their resolution of the 24th. of Augt. proposing amendments to the constitution of the United States, with the following amendments vizt. [1] to insert before the word "*resolved*" in the first clause—

The conventions of a number of the States having, at the time of their adopting the constitution, expressed a desire, in order to prevent misconstruction or abuse of its powers, that further declaratory & restrictive clauses should be added: And as extending the ground of publick confidence in the government will best ensure the benificent ends of its institution.

[2] To erase from the same clause the words "*deeming it necessary*" & insert—*concurring.*

[3] To erase from the ~~third~~ first article all that follows the word "*hundred*" in the 3d. line, & insert—*to which number one Representative shall be added for every subsequent increase of forty thousand, until the Representatives shall amount to two hundred; to which number one Representative shall be added for every subsequent increase of ~~forty~~ Sixty thousand persons.*

[4] To erase from the ~~sec.~~ 2d. article the words, "*to the members of Congress*" & insert, *for the Services of the Senators & Representatives.*

[5] To erase from the 3d. Article the word "*Religion*" & insert—*articles of faith or a mode of worship.*

[6] And to erase from the same article the words "*thereof, nor shall the rights of Conscience be infringed*" & insert—*of Religion; or abridging the freedom of speech, or of the press, or ~~of~~ the right of the people peaceably to assemble, & to petition to the government for a redress of grievances.*

[7] To erase the 4th. article, & the words "*Article the fourth.*"

[8] To erase the word "*fifth*"—& insert—*fourth*—& to erase from the fifth article the words, "*composed of the body of the people*"—the word "*best*"—& the words "*but no one religiously scrupulous of bearing arms shall be compelled to render military service in person*"—& insert after the word ~~the~~ ^"being"— in the first line—*necessary to.*

[9] To erase the word "*Sixth*" & insert *Fifth.*

[10] To erase the word "*Seventh*" & insert *Sixth.*

[11] To erase the word "*Eighth*" & insert *Seventh.*

[12] To insert in the ~~Eighth~~ 8th. article ~~af~~ after the word "*shall*" in the 1st. line—*be held to answer for a capital or otherwise infamous crime, unless on a presentment or indictment of a grand Jury, except in cases arising in the land or naval forces, or in the militia when in actual Service in time of War or publick danger; nor shall any person*—&

[13] To erase from the same article the words "*except in case of impeachment, to more than one trial or one punishment*" & insert—*to be twice put in jeopardy of life or limb.*

[14] To erase the word "*Ninth,*" & insert ~~the word~~ *Eighth.*

[15] To erase the 10th. article, & the words "*article the Tenth.*"

[16] To erase the 11th. article & the words "*Article the Eleventh.*"

[17] To ~~insert~~ erase the word "*twelfth*" & insert—*Ninth.*

[18] To insert in the twelfth article after the word "*law*," *where the value in* shall
controversy^ *exceed~~s~~ twenty dollars*—&

[19] To insert at the end of the same article—*And no fact tried by a Jury shall be otherwise rexamined, in any court of the United States, than according to the rules of the common law.*

[20] To erase the word "*Thirteenth*" & insert—*Tenth.*

[21] To erase the 14th. article & the words—"*article the fourteenth.*"

[22] To erase the word—"*Fifteenth*"—& insert *Eleventh.*

[23] To erase the 16th. article & the words "*Article the Sixteenth.*"

[24] To erase the word "*Seventeenth,*" & insert *Twelfth*—~~&~~

[25] To insert in the seventeenth article after the word "*delegated*"—*to the United States.* &

[26] To insert at the end of the Same article—*or to the people*;

~~It was resolved in~~

It passed in the affirmative, two thirds of the Senators present concurring.

The amendments, in the hand of Ellsworth, are in House Joint and Concurrent Resolutions, SR, DNA The heading, "United States of America," was written by Otis, who also noted "Mr. Ellsworth's drat. amend. Art. of Const. U.S.A. Sept. 89" at the end. We have added the numbers in brackets to show the correspondence between this list and the numbering of the Senate amendments in the *HJ*, p. 217.

Articles of Amendment, as Agreed to by the Senate September 14, 1789

The Conventions of a Number of the States having, at the Time of their adopting the Constitution, expressed a Desire, in Order to prevent misconstruction or abuse of its Powers, that further declaratory and restrictive Clauses should be added: And as extending the Ground of public Confidence in the Government, will best insure the beneficent ends of its Institution—

RESOLVED, BY THE SENATE AND HOUSE OF REPRESENTATIVES OF THE UNITED STATES OF AMERICA IN CONGRESS ASSEMBLED, two thirds of both Houses concurring, That the following articles be proposed to the Legislatures of the several States, as amendments to the Constitution of the United States, all or any of which articles, when ratified by three fourths of the said Legislatures, to be valid to all intents and purposes, as part of the said Constitution—Viz.

ARTICLES in addition to, and amendment of, the Constitution of the United States of America, proposed by Congress, and ratified by the Legislatures of the several States, pursuant to the fifth Article of the original Constitution.

ARTICLE THE FIRST.

After the first enumeration, required by the first article of the Constitution, there shall be one Representative for every thirty thousand, until the number shall amount to one hundred; to which number one Representative shall be added for every subsequent increase of forty thousand, until the Representatives shall amount to two hundred, to wh[ich numbe]r one Representative shall be added f[or every subsequent increase of six]ty thou[sand] persons.

ARTICLE THE SECOND.

No law, varying the compensation for the services of the Senators and Representatives, shall take effect, until an election of Representatives shall have intervened.

ARTICLE THE THIRD.

Congress shall make no law establishing articles of faith, or a mode of worship, or prohibiting the free exercise of religion, or abridging the freedom of speech, or of the press, or the right of the people peaceably to assemble, and to petition to the government for a redress of grievances.

ARTICLE THE FOURTH.

A well regulated militia, being necessary to the security of a free State, the right of the people to keep and bear arms, shall not be infringed.

ARTICLE THE FIFTH.

No soldier shall, in time of peace, be quartered in any house, without the consent of the owner, nor in time of war, but in a manner to be prescribed by law.

ARTICLE THE SIXTH.

The right of the people to be secure in their persons, houses, papers, and effects, against unreasonable searches and seizures, shall not be violated, and no warrants shall issue, but upon probable cause, supported by oath or affirmation, and particularly describing the place to be searched, and the persons or things to be seized.

ARTICLE THE SEVENTH.

No person shall be held to answer for a capital, or otherwise infamous crime, unless on a presentment or indictment of a Grand Jury, except in cases arising in the land or naval forces, or in the militia, when in actual service in time of war or public danger; nor shall any person be subject for the same offence to be twice put in jeopardy of life or limb; nor shall be compelled in any criminal case, to be a witness against himself, nor be deprived of life, liberty or property, without due process of law; nor shall private property be taken for public use without just compensation.

ARTICLE THE EIGHTH.

In all criminal prosecutions, the accused shall enjoy the right to a speedy and public trial, to be informed of the nature and cause of the accusation, to be confronted with the witnesses against him, to have compulsory process for obtaining witnesses in his favour, and to have the assistance of counsel for his defence.

ARTICLE THE NINTH.

In suits at common law, where the value in controversy shall exceed twenty dollars, the right of trial by Jury shall be preserved, and no fact, tried by a Jury, shall be otherwise re-examined in any court of the United States, than according to the rules of the common law.

ARTICLE THE TENTH.

Excessive bail shall not be required, nor excessive fines imposed, nor cruel and unusual punishments inflicted.

[ARTICLE THE ELE]VENTH.

The en[umeration in the Constitution of certain] rights, shall not be construed to deny or disparage others retained by the people.

ARTICLE THE TWELFTH.

The powers not delegated to the United States by the Constitution, nor prohibited by it to the States, are reserved to the States respectively, or to the people.

[NEW-YORK, PRINTED BY THOMAS GREENLEAF.]

The printed Articles are in House Joint and Concurrent Resolutions, SR, DNA. We supplied the words in brackets by comparing the articles as passed by the House with Ellsworth's list of Senate amendments. Otis wrote "ag." in the margin beside all the paragraphs except the first, third, and eighth articles, to note House and conference agreement with the Senate wording. The first, third, and eighth articles were lined out, indicating that they were amended in accordance with the conference committee report.

Conference Committee Report
September 24, 1789

The Committees of the two Houses appointd to confer on thier different votes on the Amendments proposed by the Senate to the Resolution proposing Amendments to the Constitution, and disagreed to by the House of Representatives, have had a conferrence, and have agreed that it will be proper for the House of Representatives to agree to the said Amendments proposed by the Senate, with an Amendment to their fifth Amendment, so that the third Article shall read as follows "Congress shall make no law *respecting an establishment of Religion,* or prohibiting the free exercise thereof; or abridging the freedom of Speech, or of the Press; or the right of the people peaceably to assemble and ~~to~~[1] petition the Government for a redress of

[1] The House restored the word "to."

grievancies;" And with an Amendment to the fourteenth Amendment proposed by the Senate, so that the eighth Article, as numbered in the Amendments proposed by the Senate, shall read as follows "In all criminal prosecutions, the accused shall enjoy the right to a speedy & publick trial *by an impartial jury of the*[2] *district wherein the crime shall have been committed, as the*[3] *district shall have been previously asscertained by law,* and to be informed of the nature and cause of the accusation; to be confronted with the witnesses against him; and[4] to have compulsory process for obtaining Witnesses ~~against~~
to
~~him~~ in his favour, &^have the assistance of counsel for his defence."

The Committees were also of Opinion that it would be proper for both Houses to agree to amend the first Article, by striking out the word "*less*" in the last line but one, and inserting in its place, the word "more," and accordingly recommend that the said Article be reconsidered for that purpose.

The report, in the hand of Ellsworth, is in House Resolutions, SR, DNA. The House amendments are included in the resolution printed in the *HJ*, p. 228. The last three amendments, to Article 8, were agreed to by a recorded vote of 37–14.

[2] The House inserted "state and" at this point.
[3] The House struck out "as the" and inserted "which."
[4] The House struck out "and."

House Resolution
September 24, 1789

RESOLVED, That the President of the United States be requested to transmit to the executives of the several states which have ratified the Constitution, copies of the amendments proposed by Congress to be added thereto; and like copies to the executives of the states of Rhode-Island and North-Carolina.

HJ, p. 229.

Recorded Votes

Below are all of the recorded votes on the subject of Amendments to the Constitution. The reader should consult the entries in the legislative history calendar for the dates indicated to determine the subjects of the votes.

18 August 1789

Ayes 16, Noes 34.

Ayes, Aedanus Burke (S.C.), Isaac Coles (Va.), William Floyd (N.Y.), Elbridge Gerry (Mass.), Samuel Griffin (Va.), Jonathan Grout (Mass.), John Hathorn (N.Y.), Samuel Livermore (N.H.), John Page (Va.), Josiah Parker (Va.), Jeremiah Van Rensselaer (N.Y.), Roger Sherman (Conn.), Michael Jenifer Stone (Md.), Jonathan Sturges (Conn.), Thomas Sumter (S.C.), and Thomas Tudor Tucker (S.C.).

Noes, Fisher Ames (Mass.), Abraham Baldwin (Ga.), Egbert Benson (N.Y.), Elias Boudinot (N.J.), John Brown (Va.), Lambert Cadwalader (N.J.), Daniel Carroll (Md.), George Clymer (Penn.), Thomas Fitzsimons (Penn.), Abiel Foster (N.H.), Nicholas Gilman (N.H.), Benjamin Goodhue (Mass.), Thomas Hartley (Penn.), Daniel Hiester (Penn.), Benjamin Huntington (Conn.), John Laurance (N.Y.), Richard Bland Lee (Va.), James Madison, (Va.), Andrew Moore (Va.), Peter Muhlenberg (Penn.), George Partridge (Mass.), James Schureman (N.J.), Thomas Scott (Penn.), Theodore Sedgwick (Mass.), Joshua Seney (Md.), Peter Silvester (N.Y.), Thomas Sinnickson (N.J.), William Smith (Md.), William Smith (S.C.), George Thatcher (Mass.), Jonathan Trumbull (Conn.), John Vining (Del.), Jeremiah Wadsworth (Conn.), and Henry Wynkoop (Penn.).

21 August 1789
(on adding "expressly")

Ayes 17, Noes 32.

Ayes, Burke, Coles, Floyd, Gerry, Grout, Hathorn, James Jackson (Ga.), Livermore, Page, Parker, Partridge, Van Rensselaer, Smith (S.C.), Stone, Sumter, Thatcher, and Tucker.

Noes, Ames, Benson, Boudinot, Brown, Cadwalader, Carroll, Clymer, Fitzsimons, Foster, George Gale (Md.), Gilman, Goodhue, Hartley, Hiester, Laurance, Lee, Madison, Moore, Muhlenberg, Schureman, Scott, Sedgwick, Seney, Sherman, Silvester, Sinnickson, Smith (Md.), Sturges, Trumbull, Vining, Wadsworth, and Wynkoop.

21 August 1789
(on elections)

Ayes 23, Noes 28.

Ayes, Burke, Coles, Floyd, Gerry, Griffin, Grout, Hathorn, Hiester, Jackson, Livermore, George Mathews (Ga.), Moore, Page, Parker, Partridge, Van Rensselaer, Seney, Silvester, Smith (S.C.), Stone, Sumter, Thatcher, and Tucker.

Noes, Ames, Benson, Boudinot, Brown, Cadwalader, Carroll, Clymer, Fitzsimons, Foster, Gale, Gilman, Goodhue, Hartley, Laurance, Lee, Madison, Muhlenberg, Schureman, Scott, Sedgwick, Sherman, Sinnickson, Smith (Md.), Sturges, Trumbull, Vining, Wadsworth, and Wynkoop.

22 August 1789

Ayes 9, Noes 39.

Ayes, Burke, Coles, Floyd, Grout, Hathorn, Livermore, Van Rensselaer, Sumter, and Tucker.

Noes, Ames, Benson, Brown, Cadwalader, Carroll, Clymer, Fitzsimons, Foster, Gale, Gerry, Gilman, Goodhue, Hartley, Hiester, Jackson, Laurance, Lee, Madison, Mathews, Moore, Muhlenberg, Page, Parker, Partridge, Schureman, Scott, Sedgwick, Seney, Sherman, Silvester, Sinnickson, Smith (Md.), Smith (S.C.), Stone, Sturges, Thatcher, Trumbull, Vining, and Wadsworth.

2 September 1789

Yeas 6, Noes 12.

Yeas, Tristram Dalton (Mass.), James Gunn (Ga.), William Grayson (Va.), Rufus King (N.Y.), Richard Henry Lee (Va.), Philip Schuyler (N.Y.).

Noes, Richard Bassett (Del.), Pierce Butler (S.C.), Charles Carroll (Md.), Oliver Ellsworth (Conn.), Jonathan Elmer (N.J.), John Henry (Md.), William S. Johnson (Conn.), Ralph Izard (S.C.), Robert Morris (Penn.), William Paterson (N.J.), George Read (Del.), Paine Wingate (N.H.).

3 September 1789

Yeas 2, Noes 14.

Yeas, Grayson, Lee.

Noes, Bassett, Carroll, Dalton, Ellsworth, Elmer, Gunn, Henry, Johnson, Izard, King, Morris, Paterson, Read, Wingate.

4 September 1789

Yeas 6, Noes 9.

Yeas, Butler, Gunn, Grayson, Henry, Lee, Wingate.

Nays, Carroll, Dalton, Ellsworth, Elmer, Johnson, King, Paterson, Read, Schuyler.

9 September 1789

Yeas 8, Noes 8.

Yeas, Bassett, Dalton, Grayson, Gunn, Henry, Lee, Paterson, Schuyler.

Nays, Carroll, Ellsworth, Johnson, Izard, King, Morris, Read, Wingate.

24 September 1789

Ayes 37, Noes 14.

Ayes, Ames, Baldwin, Benson, Boudinot, Brown, Cadwalader, Carroll, Clymer, Benjamin Contee (Md.), Fitzsimons, Foster, Gale, Gilman, Goodhue, Griffin, Hartley, Lee, George Leonard (Mass.), Madison, Moore, Muhlenberg, Parker, Partridge, Schureman, Scott, Seney, Sherman, Silvester, Sinnickson, Smith (Md.), Smith (S.C.), Stone, Thatcher, Trumbull, Vining, Alexander White (Va.), and Wynkoop.

Noes, Theodorick Bland (Va.), Burke, Coles, Floyd, Gerry, Grout, Hathorn, Jackson, Livermore, Mathews, Page, Van Rensselaer, Sumter, and Tucker.

PART II

Debates in the House of Representatives

At the beginning of its first session the House of Representatives began admitting the public to its debates. Three newspaper publishers and shorthand writer Thomas Lloyd, an individual entrepreneur who came to the seat of government with the declared intention of publishing the debates, made serious attempts at recreating portions of the debates for the news-hungry public. Lloyd supported his efforts to produce the most complete account of the happenings on the floor through subscriptions to his *Congressional Register*, which contained only the debates. John Fenno began publishing the *Gazette of the United States* specifically for the purpose of reporting on and supporting the new government. Francis Childs (joined in July 1789 by John Swaine) and Archibald McLean had already established *The* [New York] *Daily Advertiser* and *The New-York Daily Gazette* respectively. These papers reported the debates only sporadically at first but, eventually, probably in part because of Lloyd's long delays in publication, their accounts became more complete.

These reports should be regarded as the results of an effort to record the debates while facing some very difficult odds. Reporters attended the sessions alone, trying to keep up with the debate while coping with dim lighting, quill pens, and poor acoustics. Without any of the modern day aids such as guides picturing the members, an excellent sound system, a board that shows recorded votes, and videotapes of the sessions to review, the reporters struggled to put together a coherent picture of the proceedings—which may not have been coherent at all! Thus, the debates they published represent their best efforts, but are not a verbatim or complete transcript.

Most of the debates occurred in the Committee of the Whole House (COWH). Under House rules that still exist today, the House would go into a COWH to consider a subject. The Speaker would relinquish the chair to a member designated as the chair of the COWH. After debate, the COWH would report the results of its deliberations to the House, which would often debate the COWH's report in detail.

Accounts that are simply paraphrases of another account or that add no new information to other versions are omitted from this text. Only the portion of the day's debate dealing with amending the Constitution is included. The complete extant debates of the first session of the House of Representatives will be printed in volumes X and XI of the *DHFFC*, to be published in 1991.

May 1789

5 May 1789

The Daily Advertiser, 6 May 1789

Mr. BLAND presented to the house an application of the state of Virginia, requesting Congress to call a convention for the purpose of revising and amending the constitution.

Mr. BLAND observed, that this application was made with a view of obtaining amendments to the constitution in one of the two modes pointed out in the 5th article;[1] that copies of the application with an address had been sent to the several states, but that few of them seemed to have coincided with Virginia in opinion, and whether the apprehensions of the people of that state were well or ill founded,[2] time alone would determine. He wished that the paper might be referred to a committee of the whole house, and thought that it would be advisable to give it a consideration at the same time that the amendment to be moved by Mr. MADISON, of which he gave notice yesterday, should be brought forward.

Mr. BOUDINOT was opposed to the commitment: He wished to pay respect to the application of the state of Virginia, but he thought it ought to lie on the table for the information of the members, when a sufficient number of the states should according to the constitution join the appli-

---

[1]The Constitution's Article V establishes the procedure for making amendments:

> The Congress, whenever two thirds of both Houses shall deem it necessary, shall propose Amendments to this Constitution, or, on the Application of the Legislatures of two thirds of the several States, shall call a Convention for proposing Amendments, which, in either Case, shall be valid to all Intents and Purposes, as Part of this Constitution, when ratified by the Legislatures of three fourths of the several States, or by Conventions in three fourths thereof, as the one or the other Mode of Ratification may be proposed by the Congress;

[2]The *NYDA*, 8 May, stated that Bland had said "whether *those* States were right or wrong" rather than "whether . . . or ill founded."

cation, it would then be the proper time to commit it—at present it was premature.

Mr. BLAND hoped that an equal respect would be paid to the wishes of the state of Virginia as had been shown to the petitions of the artisans of New-York and others—He hoped that the house would pay Virginia the compliment of committing their application. He knew not whether other states would come forward or not, but if the house had this address before them when the general subject of amendments was taken up, it might have some proper influence in their decision, tho' it were not accompanied by other applications.

Mr. MADISON said the house ought to treat this subject with all due respect; but the mode of disposing of this application, ought to be consistent with the principles and spirit of the Constitution. Congress had no deliberative power with respect to a convention; for whenever two thirds of the states should apply, they were bound to call one; but till this concurrent application took place, they had no power whatever to enter into the subject—The best mode was to let it lie upon the table till a sufficient number of applications appeared.

Mr. BOUDINOT assured the gentlemen it was from no disrespect that he objected to the commitment—He would wish to express his respect for every state, particularly for Virginia; but he did not conceive it would be paying any respect to Virginia to commit their application to a body which had no power to deliberate or decide upon it.

Mr. BLAND replied, that the committing the application could not lay any obligation upon the house whatever as to its merits—and therefore it was no unconstitutional step—The matter might regularly come before the house, without its over passing the bounds prescribed by the constitution, or actually doing any thing to contravene its principles.

Mr. HUNTINGTON opposed the commitment, and was for having the paper lie on the table.

Mr. TUCKER said the provision in the constitution did not appear to him in the same point of view in which it struck the gentlemen—If two thirds of the states made application, Congress were obliged to comply; but if this should not happen, they were at liberty to exercise their discretion—He thought therefore it would be constitutional to take this up, and deliberate upon it—Great respect was due to the application of any state—if the states had this power, as they certainly had, they ought not to be disregarded—They ought to be carefully attended to.

Mr. GERRY conceived this question to be out of order. A gentleman,[3]

[3] James Madison.

he said, had yesterday informed the house that on the 4th Monday of this month, he should move the house to go into a committee on the 5th article of the constitution; but there was no order of the house to go into a committee on that day—He had no doubt but the gentleman would bring forward his motion, but he thought it at present not in order on the expectation of such a motion, to refer any thing to a committee of the whole which was not yet in existence—He conceived therefore that the proper mode of treating this application was to let it lie on the table till the 5th article of the constitution should be taken into consideration.

Mr. PAGE was opposed to the commitment—He thought it would be a proper respect to the application to enter it on the journal, and he was willing this should be done.

Mr. BLAND said he had no objection to any mode of treatment which was respectful—it was a standing order that the house should go each day into a committee of the whole on the state of the Union—To this committee he wished the application should be referred—And he thought it would be in their power to take the same at any time into consideration.

Mr. MADISON said he would consent to enter the paper on the journal, and to have the original on the files of the clerk's office—He therefore moved that the application be entered on the journal, and the original deposited in the office of the clerk.

Mr. WHITE seconded this motion, and the question being put, it was agreed to.

Gazette of the United States, 9 May 1789

In our last we stated, that Mr. BLAND had introduced the proceedings of the legislature of Virginia on the subject of Amendments—it may not be uninteresting to state the substance of the observations that occurred upon this business. On one hand it was observed, that the application of the State of Virginia was made with a view of obtaining amendments, agreeably to the 5th article of the Constitution: That although the address of Virginia had been transmitted to the several Legislatures, but few of them had thought proper to coincide with that State—That it would be giving the address due consideration, to refer it to a committee of the whole, to be taken up at the time assigned for the House to consider amendments, of which notice had been given yesterday—That the address was from a respectable State, and merited an equal compliment at least, with other applications that had already been referred to the committee—That although this address might stand alone, yet it might be of weight in the decisions of the committee—That it rested on the basis of its own merits, and could not in the nature of its operation, if committed, contravene the spirit of the Constitution—That as it was a standing rule of the House, that they should go into a committee of the whole every day, there appeared to be a propriety in the commitment.

In reply, it was observed—That although the application was undoubtedly from the most respectable quarter, yet it appeared to be more proper, that it should lie on the table for the information of the members—that when a sufficient number of similar applications should be made, it might constitutionally come before Congress—That it ought to be treated with due respect—but that Congress had no deliberative voice, with respect to calling a Convention, agreeably to the application—That when two thirds of the States should apply, they were bound to call one—That it would not be paying proper respect to Virginia, to commit the application to a body which was not competent to deliberate or decide upon it—That as the House had been led to consider the fourth Monday of the present month as the time assigned to go into the consideration of amendments, then would be a proper season to bring forward the application—That it would be paying proper respect to it, to enter it on the journals: This was therefore acceeded to with the addition, that it should be put upon the files in the Clerk's Office.

The Congressional Register, 5 May 1789

Mr. Bland presented to the house the application of the legislature of Virginia, dated 14th November 1788, for the immediate calling of a convention of deputies from the several states, with full power to take into their consideration the defects of the federal Constitution, that have been suggested by the state conventions, and report such amendments thereto, as they shall find best suited to promote our common interests, and secure to ourselves and our latest posterity the great and unalienable rights of mankind.

After this application was read,

Mr. Bland moved to refer it to a committee of the whole, on the state of the union—his motion was seconded by Mr. Parker.

Mr. BOUDINOT.

According to the terms of the constitution, the business cannot be taken up until a certain number of states have concurred in similar applications; certainly the house are disposed to pay a proper attention to the application of so respectable a state as Virginia, but if it is a business which we cannot interfere with in a constitutional manner, we had better let it go and remain on the files of the house until the proper number of applications come forward.

Mr. BLAND

Thought there could be no impropriety in referring any subject to a committee, but surely this deserved the serious and solemn consideration of Congress, he hoped no gentleman would oppose the compliment of referring it to a committee of the whole; beside, it would be a guide to the deliberations of the committee on the subject of amendments, which would shortly come before the house.

Mr. MADISON

Said he had no doubt but the house were inclined to treat the present application with respect, but he doubted the propriety of committing it, because it would seem to imply that the house had a right to deliberate upon the subject—this he believed was not the case until two-thirds of the state legislatures concurred in such application, and then it is out of the power of Congress to decline complying, the words of the constitution are express and positive relative to the agency Congress may have in case of applications of this nature. The Congress, wherever two-thirds of both houses shall deem it necessary, shall propose amendments to this constitution; or, on the application of the legislatures of two-thirds of the several states, shall call a convention for proposing amendments. From hence it must appear, that Congress have no deliberative power on this occasion. The most respectful and constitutional mode of performing our duty will be to let it be entered on the minutes, and remain upon the files of the house until similar applications come to hand from two-thirds of the states.

Mr. BOUDINOT

Hoped the gentlemen who desired the commitment of the application, would not suppose him wanting in respect to the state of Virginia, he entertained the most profound respect for her—but it was a principle of respect to order and propriety that he opposed the commitment upon; enough had been said to convince gentlemen that it was improper to commit—for what purpose can it be done? what can the committee report? the application is to call a new convention. Now in this case, there is nothing left for us to do, but to call one when two-thirds of the state legislatures apply for that purpose[4]—he hoped the gentleman would withdraw his motion for commitment.

[4]Thomas Lloyd's notes on this debate include among Boudinot's remarks a statement that if the application from Virginia had "contained a list of grievances or amendments" the House "could consider them." Lloyd's Notes, DLC.

Mr. Bland.

The application now before the committee contains a number of reasons why it is necessary to call a convention, by the 5th article of the constitution, Congress are obliged to order this convention when two-thirds of the legislatures apply for it; but how can these reasons be properly weighed, unless it be done in committee? therefore I hope the house will agree to refer it.

Mr. Huntington

Thought it proper to let the application remain on the table, it can be called up with others when enough are presented to make two-thirds of the whole states. There would be an evident impropriety in committing, because it would argue a right in the house to deliberate and consequently a power to procrastinate the measure applied for.

Mr. Tucker

Thought it not right to disregard the application of any state, and inferred, that the house had a right to consider every application that was made; if two-thirds had not applied, the subject might be taken into consideration, but if two-thirds had applied it precluded deliberation on the part of the house. He hoped the present application would be properly noticed.

Mr. Gerry.

The gentleman from Virginia (Mr. Madison) told us yesterday, that he meant to move the consideration of amendments on the 4th Monday of this month; he did not make such motion then, and may be prevented by accident, or some other cause, from carrying his intention into execution when the time he mentioned shall arrive; I think the subject however is introduced to the house, and perhaps it may consist with order to let the present application lie on the table until the business is taken up generally.

Mr. Page

Thought it the best way to enter the application at large upon the Journals, and do the same by all that came in, until sufficient were made to obtain their object. The original being deposited in the archives of Congress. He deemed this the proper mode of disposing of it, and what is in itself proper can never be construed into disrespect.

Mr. Bland

Acquiesced in this disposal of the application. Whereupon it was ordered to be entered at length on the Journals, and the original to be placed on the files of Congress.

June 1789

8 June 1789

The Daily Advertiser, 9 June 1789

Mr. Madison according to notice, this day moved the house to go into a committee of the whole, in order to take into consideration the subject of amendments, in pursuance of the 5th article of the constitution.

This motion was opposed by Mr. Jackson, Mr. Burke, &c. on the ground of its being improper to enter on such a subject till the government was perfectly organized and in operation. It was contended that the discussion of so important a business would take up so much time as to produce too much delay in the bills already before Congress for the establishment of the judiciary, the executive departments, and the revenue system. Mr. Jackson in particular, argued that an attempt at amendments would be entirely improper before the constitution had been tried, and experience had ascertained its defects. That all investigation now would be merely speculative and theoretical, and that it was no time now to try experiments.

Mr. Madison replied in a long and able speech, in which he enforced the propriety of entering, at an early period, into the subject of amendments. He had no design to propose any alterations which in the view of the most sanguine friends to the constitution could affect its main structure or principles, or do it any possible injury—His object was to quiet the mind of the people by giving them some early assurance of a disposition in the house to provide expressly against all encroachments on their liberties, and against the abuses to which the principles of the constitution were liable.

He then stated a number of amendments which he thought should be incorporated in the constitution, and enforced the propriety of each by various explanations and arguments.

The opposition the original motion received, induced him at last to withdraw it in order to propose, that a special committee should be appointed to consider and report what amendments it would be proper to adopt.

He afterwards waved this proposition, and offered to the house a resolution comprehending the amendments at large, together with a bill of rights, which he moved might be referred to the committee of the whole, when sitting on the state of the Union. This was carried.

Gazette of the United States, 10 June 1789

Mr. MADISON, agreeably to notice, moved that the House now form itself into a committee of the whole, upon the state of the Union, to take into consideration the subject of amendments agreeably to the 5th article of the Constitution.

Mr. SMITH (of South-Carolina) suggested the inexpediency of taking up the subject at the present moment, in a committee of the whole, while matters of the greatest importance and of immediate consequence were lying unfinished. The great business of the revenue appeared to him to claim a constant and uninterrupted attention till compleated—he moved therefore, that instead of referring the subject to a committee of the whole, a select committee should be raised, to take into consideration the amendments proposed by the several States.

Mr. JACKSON—I am opposed, Sir, to taking up the subject of amendments to the Constitution till we have had some experience of its good or bad qualities. The Constitution may be compared to a ship that has never yet put to sea—she is now laying in the dock—we have had no tryal as yet; we do not know how she may steer—what force of a helm she carries—we can not determine with any precision, whether she sails upon an even keel or no—Upon experiment she may prove faultless, or her defects may be very obvious—but the present is not the time for alterations. Very important and urgent business now requires the attention of this honorable body—business of such consequence as that of revenue, without which the constitution is of very little importance in itself considered. Should amendments now be taken up, it will be months perhaps before we can get through with them—mean time the important interests of our constituents are sacrificed. The State that I have the honor to represent, has ratified the Constitution without specifying any amendments, they are satisfied with it, in its present form; till experience shall point out its defects—I move therefore, Sir, that the consideration of the subject of amendments be postponed till the first day of March, 1790.

Mr. GOODHUE observed, that though he considered it as being premature to take up the subject of amendments at the present time; yet he could not conceive the propriety of postponing the matter to so long a period—it certainly was the general idea that amendments should be considered, and a regard to the wishes of our constituents required that they should be attended to as soon as public interest permitted.

Mr. BURKE made some objections of a similar import with those which fell from Mr. Goodhue—and thought that the subject of the revenue, was of the greatest importance to be immediately attended to.

Mr. MADISON observed, that the subject had been postponed from time to time—that the members might have opportunity more fully to make up their judgments upon it—a fortnight has elapsed since the first assigned period, and if the motion for a further distant period should be adopted, it would be construed into a design, to take no serious notice of the business—the propositions for amendments to the constitution came from various quarters, and those the most respectable, and therefore to give some degree of satisfaction, it seemed necessary, that Congress should as soon as possible, attend to the wishes of their constituents—He did not propose that a full investigation should *immediately* be gone into—but to quiet the apprehensions of a great many persons, respecting the securing certain rights, which it was supposed were not sufficiently guarded, he thought it necessary, that Congress should commence the enquiry, and place the matter in such a train as to inspire a reasonable hope and expectation, that full justice would eventually be done to so important a subject—He therefore renewed his motion for the House to go into a committee of the whole, that the investigation of the business might at least commence.

Mr. SHERMAN supposed, that taking up the subject of amendments at this time would alarm more persons than would have their apprehensions quieted thereby—He thought that the necessity of amendments would be best pointed out by the defects, which experience may discover in the constitution.

Mr. WHITE observed, that the subject of amendments was of very extensive importance—he supposed that the House could not, with any propriety, defer their consideration any longer; for although the Constitution had been so generally ratified, yet it was evident, that alterations and amendments were expected by perhaps a majority of the people at large.

Mr. SMITH (S.C.) then introduced a proposition, for the appointment of a select committee to take the business into consideration, and report.

Mr. PAGE was in favour of a committee of the whole, and urged the propriety of commencing the enquiry without any further delay, as a measure that would be productive of very happy consequences.

Mr. VINING was opposed to the measure for several reasons—the incompleteness of the revenue and judiciary systems; these, he urged, ought to be finished previous to a discussion of amendments: The judiciary system may provide a remedy for some of the defects complained of—and without giving the Constitution any operation, it was impossible to determine what were defects, or not—and what alterations were necessary. He further observed, that he conceived it necessary, previous to any discussion of the subject, that it should be ascertained whether two-thirds of the House and Senate were in favour of entering upon the business—he supposed that the voice of two thirds were as requisite to sanction the *expediency* of the measure, as they were to the *adoption* of amendments—He was fully of opinion, that experience alone, could ascertain the real qualities of the Constitution—The people are waiting with anxiety for the operation of the Government—What has Congress done? Have they passed a revenue law? Is not the revenue daily escaping us? Is it not of immense consequence to compleat the system? Let us not perplex ourselves, by introducing one weighty and important question after another, till some decisions are made: This mode of introducing one piece of business, before a former one is compleated, tends to confuse the mind, and incapacitate it from doing full justice to any subject—He hoped, therefore, that the House would not go into a committee of *the whole* upon this business.

Mr. MADISON conceded to the motion for chusing a select committee—He then observed, That he thought it would be attended with salutary effects, should Congress devote, at the present time, so much at least as one day to this business, to convince the world, that the friends of the Constitution were as firm friends to liberty as those who had opposed it: The advocates for amendments are numerous and respectable—some alteration of the Constitution lays with great weight upon their minds—they merit consideration. He urged the expediency of the measure, from the situation of Rhode-Island and North-Carolina—He had no doubt that it would conciliate them towards the Union, and induce them to unite, and again become branches of the great American Family. He was, he observed, in favour of sundry alterations, or amendments, to the Constitution—he supposed that they could be made without injury to the system—He did not wish a re-consideration of the whole—but supposed that alterations might be made, without effecting the essential principles of the Constitution, which would meet with universal approbation; these he would propose should be incorporated in the body of the Constitution. He then mentioned the several objections which had been made by several of the States, and by people at large: A bill of rights has been the great object contended for—but this was one of those amendments which he had not supposed very essential. The freedom of the press, and the rights of conscience, those choicest flowers in the prerogative of the people, are not guarded by the British Constitution: With respect to these, apprehensions had been entertained of their insecurity under the new Constitution; a bill of rights, therefore, to quiet the minds of people upon these points, may be salutary. He then adverted to the several bills of rights, which were annexed to the Constitutions of individual States; the great object of these was, to limit and qualify the powers of Government—to guard against the encroachments of the Executive. In the Federal Government, the Executive is the weakest—the great danger lies not in the Executive, but in the great body of the people—in the disposition which the majority always discovers, to bear down, and depress the minority.

In stating objections which had been made to affixing a bill of rights to the constitution, Mr. MADISON observed, that objections to a continental bill of rights applied equally to their adoption by the States—The objection to a bill of rights, from the powers delegated by the Constitution, being defined and limited, has weight, while the Government confines itself to those specified limits; but instances may occur, in which those limits may be exceeded, by virtue of a construction of that clause empowering Congress to make all necessary laws to carry the Constitution into execution—The article of general warrants may be instanced. It has been observed, that the Constitution does not repeal the State bills of rights; to this it may be replied, that some of the States are without any—and that articles contained in those that have them, are very improper, and infringe upon the rights of human nature, in several respects. It has been said, that bills of rights have been violated—but does it follow from thence that they do not produce salutary effects: This objection may be urged against every regulation whatever. From these, and other considerations, Mr. Madison inferred the expediency of a declaration of rights, to be incorporated in the Constitution.

Mr. MADISON further observed, That the proportion of Representatives had been objected to—and particularly the discretionary power of diminishing the number. There is an impropriety in the Legislatures' determining their own compensation, with a power to vary its amount. The rights of conscience; liberty of the press and trial by jury, should be so secured, as to put it out of the power of the Legislature to infringe them. Fears respecting the judiciary system, should be entirely done away—and an express declaration made, that all rights not expressly given up, are retained. He wished, that a declaration upon these points might be attended to—and if the Constitution can be made better in the view of its most sanguine supporters, by making some alterations in it, we shall not act the part of wise men not to do it—He therefore moved for the appointment of a committee, to propose amendments, which should be laid before the Legislatures of the several States, agreeably to the 5th article of the Constitution.

Mr. JACKSON observed, That the Hon. Gentleman's ingenious detail, so far from convincing him of the expediency of bringing forward the subject of amendments at this time, had confirmed him in the contrary opinion: The prospect which such a discussion opened, was wide and extensive, and would preclude other business, of much greater moment, at the present juncture—He differed widely from the Gentleman, with regard to bills of rights—several of the States had no such bills—Rhode-Island had none—there, liberty was carried to excess, and licentiousness triumphed—In some States, which had such a nominal security, the encroachments upon the rights of the people had been most complained of. The press, Mr. Jackson observed, is unboundedly free—a recent instance of which the House had witnessed in an attack upon one of its members[5]—A bill of rights is a mere *ignis fatuus*,[6] amusing by appearances, and leading often to dangerous conclusions. I repeat it, Sir, the present is not the time to bring forward amendments—they must be speculative and theoretical in the very nature of things, and may themselves be the subjects of future amendments. This consideration points out in the clearest manner, the propriety of waiting the result of experiment, to determine the merits of the Constitution: To that let us refer the subject, and not waste our time in useless speculations.

Mr. GERRY thought it unnecessary to go into a committee of the whole upon this subject at the present moment. He did not think such a step necessary to satisfy the people, who are fully sensible that Congress is now engaged in the great objects of the government—he wished however, that as early a day as possible, might be assigned, that the mode of another convention might not be thought of—in which we might lose the most essential parts of the constitution—he observed, that he was not a blind admirer of the system, there were defects as well as beauties in it—but as it was now become the constitution of the Union, he conceived, that the salvation of the country depended upon its establishment, amended or not. He was further in favor of an early day, on account of *North-Carolina* and *Rhode-Island*, as the accession of these States to the Union was very desirable, and good policy dictated that every proper step should be taken to expedite that event. He was opposed to referring the matter to a select committee—as derogatory to the dignity of the States—he

[5]Jackson referred to a letter from William Strachan that had appeared in the *NYDA* on 5 June.

[6]Fool's fire.

conceived the whole of the amendments proposed by the several conventions should come immediately before the House—The faith of Congress ought to be considered as pledged to take up this business upon the most extensive scale—He moved therefore, that all the various propositions for amendments should be referred to a committee of the whole, and that an early day be assigned to go into a full investigation of the subject—and proposed the first Monday in July.

Several other gentlemen spoke upon the subject, when

Mr. MADISON arose and withdrew his last motion for a select committee, and then submitted to the House a resolve comprizing a number of amendments to be incorporated in the constitution, these he read for the consideration of the House.

Mr. LIVERMORE was opposed to this resolve—he conceived it entirely improper for any individual member to propose any particular number of amendments, which do not take up the different amendments proposed by the several States.

Mr. PAGE and Mr. LEE severally rose to justify Mr. Madison, they thought themselves under great obligations to him, and conceived that the mode he had adopted was just and fair—and calculated to bring the attention of the House to a proper point in determining the subject.

Mr. MADISON observed, that it was necessary the subject should be brought forward in some form or other—after waiting a considerable time for others to do it—he had thought proper to propose the form, now submitted to the House—newspapers and pamphlets were the repositories of the several amendments—those were not the proper sources—the resolve is now before the House, and they may do what they think proper with it.

The Congressional Register, 8 June 1789

Mr. MADISON.

This day Mr. Speaker, is the day assigned for taking into consideration the subject of amendments to the constitution. As I considered myself bound in honor and in duty to do what I have done on this subject, I shall proceed to bring the amendments before you as soon as possible, and advocate them until they shall be finally adopted or rejected by a constitutional majority of this house. With a view of drawing your attention to this important object, I shall move, that this house do now resolve itself into a committee of the whole, on the state of the union, by which an opportunity will be given, to bring forward some propositions which I have strong hopes, will meet the unanimous approbation of this house, after the fullest discussion and most serious regard. I therefore move you, that the house now go into a committee on this business.

Mr. SMITH [*S.C.?*]

Was not inclined to interrupt the measures which the public were so anxiously expecting, by going into a committee of the whole at this time. He observed there were two modes of introducing this business to the house: One by appointing a select committee to take into consideration the several amendments proposed by the state conventions; this he thought the most likely way to shorten the business. The other was, that the gentleman should lay his propositions on the table, for the consideration of the members; that they should be printed, and taken up for discussion at a future day. Either of these modes would enable the house to enter upon the business better prepared than could be the case by a sudden transition from other important concerns to which their minds were strongly bent. He therefore hoped the honorable gentleman would consent to bring the subject forward in one of those ways, in preference to going into a committee of the whole. For, said he, it must appear extremely impolitic to go into the consideration of amending the government, before it is organized, before it has begun to operate; certainly upon reflection it must appear to be premature. I wish, therefore, gentlemen will consent to the delay: for the business which lies in an unfinished state—I mean particularly the collection bill—is necessary to be passed; else all we have hitherto done is of no effect. If we go into the discussion of this subject, it will take us three weeks or a month; and during all this time every other business must be suspended, because we cannot proceed with either accuracy or dispatch when the mind is perpetually shifted from one subject to another.

Mr. JACKSON.

I am of opinion we ought not to be in a hurry with respect to altering the constitution. For my part I have no idea of speculating in this serious manner on theory; if I agree to alterations in the mode of administering this government, I shall like to stand on the sure ground of experience, and not be treading air. What experience have we had of the good or bad qualities of this constitution? Can any gentleman affirm to me one proposition that is a certain and absolute amendment? I deny that he can. Our constitution, sir, is like a vessel just launched, and lying at the wharf, she is untried, you can hardly discover any one of her properties; it is not known how she will answer her helm, or lay her course; whether she will bear in safety the precious freight to be deposited in her hold. But, in this state, will the prudent merchant attempt alterations? Will he employ two thousand workmen to tear off the planking and take asunder the frame? He certainly will not. Let us gentlemen, fit out our vessel, set up her masts, and expand her sails, and be guided by the experiment in our alterations. If she sails upon an uneven keel, let us right her by adding weight where it is wanting. In this way, we may remedy her defects to the satisfaction of all concerned; but if we proceed now to make alterations, we may deface a beauty, or deform a well proportioned piece of workmanship; in short, Mr. Speaker, I am not for amendments at this time, but if gentlemen should think it a subject deserving of attention, they will surely not neglect the more important business, which is now unfinished before them. Without we pass the collection bill, we can get no revenue, and without revenue the wheels of government cannot move. I am against taking up the subject at present, and shall therefore be totally against the amendments, if the government is not organized, that I may see whether it is grievous or not.

When the propriety of making amendments shall be obvious from experience, I trust there will be virtue enough in my country to make them. Much has been said by the opponents to this constitution, respecting the insecurity of jury trials, that great bulwark of personal safety; all their objections may be done away, by proper regulations on this point, and I do not fear but such regulations will take place. The bill is now before the senate, and a proper attention is shewn to this business. Indeed I cannot conceive how it could be opposed; I think an almost omnipotent emperor would not be hardy enough to set himself against it. Then why should we fear a power which cannot be improperly exercised.

We have proceeded to make some regulations under the constitution, but have met with no inaccuracy unless it may be said, that the clause respecting "vessels bound to or from one state be obliged to enter, clear, or pay duties in another," is somewhat obscure, yet there is not sufficient, I trust, in any gentleman's opinion to induce an amendment. But let me ask what will be the consequence of taking up this subject? are we going to finish it in an hour? I believe not; it will take us more than a day, a week, a month—it will take a year to complete it! and will it be doing our duty to our country to neglect or delay putting the government in motion, when every thing depends upon its being speedily done?

Let the constitution have a fair trial, let it be examined by experience, discover by that test what its errors are, and then talk of amending; but to attempt it now is doing it at risk, which is certainly imprudent. I have the honor of coming from a state that ratified the constitution by the unanimous vote of a numerous convention: the people of Georgia have manifested their attachment to it, by adopting a state constitution framed upon the same plan as this. But although they are thus satisfied, I shall not be against such amendments as will gratify the inhabitants of other states, provided they are judged of by experience and not theory. For this reason I wish the consideration of the subject postponed until the first of March, 1790.

Mr. GOODHUE.

I believe it would be perfectly right in the gentleman who spoke last, to move a postponement to the time he has mentioned; because he is opposed to the consideration of amendments altogether. But I believe it will be proper to attend to the subject earlier; because it is the wish of many of our constituents that something should be added to the constitution to secure in a stronger manner their liberties from the inroads of power. Yet I think the present time premature; inasmuch as we have other business before us, which is incomplete, but essential to the public interest; when that is finished, I shall concur in taking up the subject of amendments.

Mr. BURKE

Thought amendments to the constitution necessary, but this was not the proper time to bring them forward; he wished the government completely organized before they entered upon this ground: The law for collecting the revenue was immediately necessary, the treasury department must be established; till these, and other important subjects were determined, he was against taking this up. He said it might interrupt the harmony of the house, which was necessary to be preserved to dispatch the great objects of legislation. He hoped it would be postponed for the present, and pledged himself to bring it forward again, if nobody else would.

Mr. MADISON.

The gentleman from Georgia (Mr. Jackson) is certainly right in his opposition to my motion for going into a committee of the whole, because he is unfriendly to the object I have in contemplation; but I cannot see that the gentlemen, who wish for amendments being proposed at the present session, stand on good ground when they object to the house going into committee on this business.

When I first hinted to the house my intention of calling their deliberations to this object, I mentioned the pressure of other important subjects, and submitted the propriety of postponing this till the more urgent business was dispatched; but finding that business not dispatched, when the order of the day for considering amendments arrived, I thought it a good reason for a farther delay, I moved the postponement accordingly. I am sorry the same reason still exists in some degree; but operates with less force when it is considered, that it is not now proposed to enter into a full and minute discussion of every part of the subject, but merely to bring it before the house, that our constituents may see we pay a proper attention to a subject they have much at heart; and if it does not give that full gratification which is to be wished, they will discover that it proceeds from the urgency of business of a very important nature. But if we continue to postpone from time to time, and refuse to let the subject come into view, it may occasion suspicions, which, though not well founded, may tend to inflame or prejudice the public mind, against our decisions: they may think we are not sincere in our desire to incorporate such amendments in the constitution as will secure those rights, which they consider as not sufficiently guarded. The applications for amendments come from a very respectable number of our constituents, and it is certainly proper for congress to consider the subject, in order to quiet that anxiety which prevails in the public mind: Indeed I think it would have been of advantage to the government, if it had been practicable to have made some propositions for amendments the first business we entered upon; it would stifle the voice of complaint, and make friends of many who doubted its merits. Our future measures would then have been more universally agreeable and better supported; but the justifiable anxiety to put the government in operation prevented that; it therefore remains for us to take it up as soon as possible. I wish then to commence the consideration at the present moment; I hold it to be my duty to unfold my ideas, and explain myself to the house in some form or other without delay. I only wish to introduce the great work, and as I said before I do not expect it will be decided immediately; but if some step is taken in the business it will give reason to believe that we may come at a final result. This will inspire a reasonable hope in the advocates for amendments, that full justice will be done to the important subject; and I have reason to believe their expectation will not be defeated. I hope the house will not decline my motion for going into a committee.

Mr. SHERMAN

I am willing that this matter should be brought before the house at a proper time. I suppose a number of gentlemen think it their duty to bring it forward; so that there is no apprehension it will be passed over in silence: Other gentlemen may be disposed to let the subject rest until the more important objects of government are attended to; and I should conclude from the nature of the case, that the people expect the latter of us in preference of altering the constitution; because they have ratified that instrument, in order that the government may begin to operate. If this was not their wish, they might as well have rejected the constitution, as North-Carolina has done, until the amendments took place. The state I have the honor to come from, adopted this system by a very great majority, because they wished for the government; but they desired no amendments. I suppose this was the case in other states; it will therefore be imprudent to neglect much more important concerns for this. The executive part of the government wants organization; the business of the revenue is incomplete, to say nothing of the judiciary business. Now, will gentlemen give up these points to go into a discussion of amendments when no advantage can arise from them? For my part, I question if any alteration which can be now proposed would be an amendment in the true sense of the word; but nevertheless I am willing to let the subject be introduced; if the gentleman only desires to go into committee for the purpose of receiving his propositions, I shall consent; but I have strong objections to being interrupted in completing the more important business; because I am well satisfied it will alarm the fears of twenty of our constituents where it will please one.

Mr. WHITE.

I hope the house will not spend much time on this subject till the more pressing business is dispatched, but, at the same time, I hope we shall not dismiss it altogether; because I think a majority of the people, who have ratified the constitution, did it under an expectation that congress would, at some convenient time, examine its texture, and point out where it was defective, in order that it might be judiciously amended. Whether, while we are without experience, amendments can be digested in such a manner as to give satisfaction to a constitutional majority of this house, I will not pretend to say, but I hope the subject may be considered with all convenient speed, I think it would tend to tranquilize the public mind; therefore I shall vote in favor of going into a committee of the whole, and after receiving the subject shall be content to refer it to a special committee to arrange and report. I fear if we refuse to take up the subject it will irritate many of our constituents, which I do not wish to do: If we cannot, after mature consideration, gratify their wishes, the cause of complaint will be lessened if not removed; but a doubt on this head will not be a good reason why we should refuse to enquire. I do not say this as it affects my immediate constituents, because I believe a majority of the district which elected me do not require alterations; but I know there are people in other parts who will not be satisfied unless some amendments are proposed.

Mr. SMITH (of South-Carolina)

Thought the gentleman who brought forward the subject had done his duty: He had supported his motion with ability and candor, and if he did not succeed he was not to blame. On considering what had been urged for going into a committee, he was induced to join the gentleman; but it would be merely to receive his propositions; after which he would move something to this effect: That however desirous this house may be to go into the consideration of amendments to the constitution, in order to establish the liberties of the people of America on the securest foundation;

yet the important and pressing business of the government, prevents their entering upon that subject at present.

Mr. PAGE.

My colleague tells you, he is ready to submit to the committee of the whole, his ideas on this subject; if no objection had been made to his motion, the whole business might have been finished before this. He has done me the honor of shewing me certain propositions which he has drawn up, they are very important, and I sincerely wish the house may receive them. After they are published, I think the people will wait with patience till we are at leisure to resume them: but it must be very disagreeable to them to have it postponed from time to time, in the manner it has been, for six weeks past, they will be tired out by a fruitless expectation. Putting myself into the place of those who favor amendments, I should suspect Congress did not mean seriously to enter upon the subject; that it was vain to expect redress from them; I should begin to turn my attention to the alternative contained in the fifth article, and think of joining the legislatures of those states which have applied for calling a new convention. How dangerous such an expedient would be, I need not mention, but I venture to affirm, that unless you take early notice of this subject, you will not have power to deliberate. The people will clamor for a new convention, they will not trust the house any longer; those therefore, who dread the assembling of a convention, will do well to acquiesce in the present motion, and lay the foundation of a most important work. I do not think we need consume more than half an hour in the committee of the whole; this is not so much time but we may conveniently spare it, considering the nature of the business. I do not wish to divert the attention of congress from the organization of the government, nor do I think it need be done, if we comply with the present motion.

Mr. VINING

I hope the house will not go into a committee of the whole. It strikes me that the great amendment which the government wants, is expedition in the dispatch of business. The wheels of the national machine cannot turn, until the impost and collection bill are perfected; these are the desiderata, which the public mind is anxiously expecting. It is well known, that all we have hitherto done, is tantamount to nothing, if we leave the business in its present state—true—but say gentlemen, let us go into committee, it will take up but a short time, yet may it not take a considerable proportion of our time? May it not be procrastinated into days, weeks, nay months itself? It is not the most facile subject that can come before the legislature of the union. Gentlemen's opinions do not run in a parallel on this topic; it may take up more time to unite or concenter them, than is now imagined; and what object is to be attained by going into a committee? If information is what we seek after, cannot that be obtained by the gentleman's laying his propositions on the table; they can be read, or they can be printed. But I have two other reasons for opposing this motion; the first is, the uncertainty with which we must decide on questions of amendment, founded merely on speculative theory; the second is a previous question—how far it is proper to take the subject of amendments into consideration, without the consent of two-thirds of both houses. I will submit it to gentlemen, whether the words of the constitution, "the congress whenever two-thirds of both houses shall deem necessary, shall propose amendments," do not bear my construction, that it is as requisite for two-thirds, to sanction the expediency of going into the measure at present, as it will be to determine the necessity of amending at all. I take it, that the fifth article admits of this construction, and think that two-thirds of the senate and house of representatives must concur in the expediency, as to the time and manner of amendments, before we can proceed to the consideration of the amendments themselves; for my part, I do not see the expediency of proposing amendments. I think, sir, the most likely way to quiet the perturbation of the public mind, will be to pass salutary laws; to give permanency and stability to constitutional regulations, founded on principles of equity, and adjusted by wisdom. Altho' hitherto we have done nothing to tranquilize that agitation which the adoption of the constitution threw some people into, yet, the storm has abated, and a calm succeeds. The people are not afraid of leaving the question of amendments, to the discussion of their representatives; but is this the juncture, for discussing it? What have congress done toward completing the business of their appointment? They have passed a law regulating certain oaths; they have passed the impost bill; but are not vessels daily arriving, and the revenue slipping thro' our fingers? is it better than madness in us to neglect the completion of the revenue system? Is the system of jurisprudence unnecessary? And here let me ask gentlemen, how they propose to amend that part of the constitution which embraces the judicial branch of government, when they do not know the regulations proposed by the senate, who are forming a bill on this subject.

If the honorable mover of the question before the house, does not think he discharges his duty without bringing his propositions before the house, let him take the mode I have mentioned, by which there will be little loss of time. He knows as well as any gentleman, the importance of completing the business on your table, and that it is best to finish one subject before the introduction of another; he will not, therefore, persist in a motion which tends to distract our minds, and incapacitates us from making a proper decision on any subject. Suppose every gentleman who desired alterations to be made in the constitution, was to submit his propositions also to a committee of the whole, what would be the consequence? We should have strings of them contradictory to each other, and necessarily engaged in a discussion that would consume too much of our precious time.

Though the state I represent had the honor of taking the lead in the adoption of this constitution, and did it by an unanimous vote; and although I have the strongest predilection for the present form of government; yet I am open to information, and willing to be convinced of its imperfections; if this is done, I shall chearfully assist in correcting them. But I cannot think this a proper time to enter upon the subject; because more important business is suspended; and for want of experience we are as likely to do injury by our prescriptions as good. I wish to see every proposition which comes from that worthy gentleman on the science of government; but I think it can be presented better by staying where we are than by going into committee, and therefore shall vote against his motion.

Mr. MADISON.

I am sorry to be accessory to the loss of a single moment of time by the house. If I had been indulged in my motion, and we had gone into a committee of the whole, I think we might have rose, and resumed the consideration of other business before this time; that is, so far as it depended on what I proposed to bring forward. As that mode seems not to give satisfaction, I will withdraw the motion, and move you, sir, that a select committee be appointed to consider and report such amendments as are proper for Congress to propose to the legislatures of the several States, conformably to the 5th article of the constitution. I will state my reasons why I think it proper to propose amendments; and state the amendments themselves, so far as I think they ought to be proposed. If I thought I could fulfill the duty which I owe to myself and my constituents, to let the subject pass over in silence, I most certainly should not trespass upon the indulgence of this house. But I cannot do this; and am therefore compelled to beg a patient hearing to what I have to lay before you. And I do most sincerely believe that if congress will devote but one day to this subject, so far as to satisfy the public that we do not disregard their wishes, it will have a salutary influence on the public councils, and prepare the way for a favorable reception of our future measures. It appears to me that this house is bound by every motive of prudence, not to let the first session pass over without proposing to the state legislatures some things to be incorporated into the constitution, as will render it as acceptable to the whole people of the United States, as it has been found acceptable to a majority of them. I wish, among other reasons why something should be done, that those who have been friendly to the adoption of this constitution, may have the opportunity of proving to those who were opposed to it, that they were as sincerely devoted to liberty and a republican government, as those who charged them with wishing the adoption of this constitution in order to lay the foundation of an aristocracy or despotism. It will be a desirable thing to extinguish from the bosom of every member of the community any apprehensions, that there are those among his countrymen who wish to deprive them of the liberty for which they valiantly fought and honorably bled. And if there are amendments desired, of such a nature as will not injure the constitution, and they can be ingrafted so as to give satisfaction to the doubting part of our fellow citizens; the friends of the federal government will evince that spirit of deference and concession for which they have hitherto been distinguished.

It cannot be a secret to the gentlemen in this house, that, notwithstanding the ratification of this system of government by eleven of the thirteen United States, in some cases unanimously, in others by large majorities; yet still there is a great number of our constituents who are dissatisfied with it; among whom are many respectable for their talents, their patriotism, and respectable for the jealousy they have for their liberty, which, though mistaken in its object, is laudable in its motive. There is a great body of the people falling under this description, who at present feel much inclined to join their support to the cause of federalism, if they were satisfied in this one point: We ought not to disregard their inclination, but, on principles of amity and moderation, conform to their wishes, and expressly declare the great rights of mankind secured under this constitution. The acquiescence which our fellow citizens shew under the government, calls upon us for a like return of moderation. But perhaps there is a stronger motive than this for our going into a consideration of the subject; it is to provide those securities for liberty which are required by a part of the community, I allude in a particular manner to those two states who have not thought fit to throw themselves into the bosom of the confederacy: it is a desirable thing, on our part as well as theirs, that a re-union should take place as soon as possible. I have no doubt, if we proceed to take those steps which would be prudent and requisite at this juncture, that in a short time we should see that disposition prevailing in those states that are not come in, that we have seen prevailing in those states which are.

But I will candidly acknowledge, that, over and above all these considerations, I do conceive that the constitution may be amended; that is to say, if all power is subject to abuse, that then it is possible the abuse of the powers of the general government may be guarded against in a more secure manner than is now done, while no one advantage, arising from the exercise of that power, shall be damaged or endangered by it. We have in this way something to gain, and, if we proceed with caution, nothing to lose; and in this case it is necessary to proceed with caution; for while we feel all these inducements to go into a revisal of the constitution, we must feel for the constitution itself, and make that revisal a moderate one. I should be unwilling to see a door opened for a re-consideration of the whole structure of the government, for a re-consideration of the principles and the substance of the powers given; because I doubt, if such a door was opened, if we should be very likely to stop at that point which would be safe to the government itself: But I do wish to see a door opened to consider, so far as to incorporate those provisions for the security of rights, against which I believe no serious objection has been made by any class of our constituents. Such as would be likely to meet with the concurrence of two-thirds of both houses, and the approbation of three-fourths of the state legislatures. I will not propose a single alteration which I do not wish to see take place, as intrinsically proper in itself, or proper because it is wished for by a respectable number of my fellow citizens; and therefore I shall not propose a single alteration but is likely to meet the concurrence required by the constitution.

There have been objections of various kinds made against the constitution: Some were levelled against its structure, because the president was without a council; because the senate, which is a legislative body, had judicial powers in trials on impeachments; and because the powers of that body were compounded in other respects, in a manner that did not correspond with a particular theory; because it grants more power than is supposed to be necessary for every good purpose; and controuls the ordinary powers of the state governments. I know some respectable characters who opposed this government on these grounds; but I believe that the great mass of the people who opposed it, disliked it because it did not contain effectual provision against encroachments on particular rights, and those safeguards which they have been long accustomed to have interposed between them and the magistrate who exercised the sovereign power: nor ought we to consider them safe, while a great number of our fellow citizens think these securities necessary.

It has been a fortunate thing that the objection to the government has been made on the ground I stated; because it will be practicable on that ground to obviate the objection, so far as to satisfy the public mind that their liberties will be perpetual, and this without endangering any part of the constitution, which is considered as essential to the existence of the government by those who promoted its adoption.

The amendments which have occurred to me, proper to be recommended by congress to the state legislatures, are these:[7]

The first of these amendments, relates to what may be called a bill of rights; I will own that I never considered this provision so essential to the federal constitution, as to make it improper to ratify it, until such an amendment was added; at the same time, I always conceived, that in a certain form and to a certain extent, such a provision was neither improper nor altogether useless. I am aware, that a great number of the most respectable friends to the government and champions for republican liberty, have thought such a provision, not only unnecessary, but even improper, nay, I believe some have gone so far as to think it even dangerous. Some policy has been made use of perhaps by gentlemen on both sides of the question: I acknowledge the ingenuity of those arguments which were drawn against the constitution, by a comparison with the policy of Great-Britain, in establishing a declaration of rights;[8] but there is too great a difference in the case to warrant the comparison: therefore the arguments drawn from that source, were in a great measure inapplicable. In the declaration of rights which that country has established, the truth is, they have gone no farther, than to raise a barrier against the power of the crown, the power of the legislature is left altogether indefinite. Altho' I know whenever the great rights, the trial by jury, freedom of the press, or liberty of conscience, came in question in that body, the invasion of them is resisted by able advocates, yet their Magna Charta[9] does not contain any one provision for the security of those rights, respecting which, the people of America are most alarmed. The freedom of the press and rights of conscience, those choicest privileges of the people, are unguarded in the British constitution.

But altho' the case may be widely different, and it may not be thought necessary to provide limits for the legislative power in that country, yet a different opinion prevails in the United States. The people of many states, have thought it necessary to raise barriers against power in all forms and departments of government, and I am inclined to believe, if once bills of rights are established in all the states as well as the federal constitution, we shall find that altho' some of them are rather unimportant, yet, upon the whole, they will have a salutary tendency.

---

[7]See pp. 11–14 above.
[8]The British Declaration of Rights, 1689.
[9]Magna Charta, 1215.

It may be said, in some instances they do no more than state the perfect equality of mankind, this to be sure is an absolute truth, yet it is not absolutely necessary to be inserted at the head of a constitution.

In some instances they assert those rights which are exercised by the people in forming and establishing a plan of government. In other instances, they specify those rights which are retained when particular powers are given up to be exercised by the legislature. In other instances, they specify positive rights, which may seem to result from the nature of the compact. Trial by jury cannot be considered as a natural right, but a right resulting from the social compact which regulates the action of the community, but is as essential to secure the liberty of the people as any one of the pre-existent rights of nature. In other instances they lay down dogmatic maxims with respect to the construction of the government; declaring, that the legislative, executive, and judicial branches shall be kept separate and distinct: Perhaps the best way of securing this in practice is to provide such checks, as will prevent the encroachment of the one upon the other.

But whatever may be the form which the several states have adopted in making declarations in favor of particular rights, the great object in view is to limit and qualify the powers of government, by excepting out of the grant of power those cases in which the government ought not to act, or to act only in a particular mode. They point these exceptions sometimes against the abuse of the executive power, sometimes against the legislative, and, in some cases, against the community itself; or, in other words, against the majority in favor of the minority.

In our government it is, perhaps, less necessary to guard against the abuse in the executive department than any other; because it is not the stronger branch of the system, but the weaker: It therefore must be levelled against the legislative, for it is the most powerful, and most likely to be abused, because it is under the least controul; hence, so far as a declaration of rights can tend to prevent the exercise of undue power, it cannot be doubted but such declaration is proper. But I confess that I do conceive, that in a government modified like this of the United States, the great danger lies rather in the abuse of the community than in the legislative body. The prescriptions in favor of liberty, ought to be levelled against that quarter where the greatest danger lies, namely, that which possesses the highest prerogative of power: But this is not found in either the executive or legislative departments of government, but in the body of the people, operating by the majority against the minority.

It may be thought all paper barriers against the power of the community, are too weak to be worthy of attention. I am sensible they are not so strong as to satisfy gentlemen of every description who have seen and examined thoroughly the texture of such a defence; yet, as they have a tendency to impress some degree of respect for them, to establish the public opinion in their favor, and rouse the attention of the whole community, it may be one mean to controul the majority from those acts to which they might be otherwise inclined.

It has been said by way of objection to a bill of rights, by many respectable gentlemen out of doors, and I find opposition on the same principles likely to be made by gentlemen on this floor, that they are unnecessary articles of a republican government, upon the presumption that the people have those rights in their own hands, and that is the proper place for them to rest. It would be a sufficient answer to say that this objection lies against such provisions under the state governments as well as under the general government; and there are, I believe, but few gentlemen who are inclined to push their theory so far as to say that a declaration of rights in those cases is either ineffectual or improper. It has been said that in the federal government they are unnecessary, because the powers are enumerated, and it follows that all that are not granted by the constitution are retained: that the constitution is a bill of powers, the great residuum being the rights of the people; and therefore a bill of rights cannot be so necessary as if the residuum was thrown into the hands of the government. I admit that these arguments are not entirely without foundation; but they are not conclusive to the extent which has been supposed. It is true the powers of the general government are circumscribed, they are directed to particular objects; but even if government keeps within those limits, it has certain discretionary powers with respect to the means, which may admit of abuse to a certain extent, in the same manner as the powers of the state governments under their constitutions may to an indefinite extent; because in the constitution of the United States there is a clause granting to Congress the power to make all laws which shall be necessary and proper for carrying into execution all the powers vested in the government of the United States, or in any department or officer thereof; this enables them to fulfil every purpose for which the government was established. Now, may not laws be considered necessary and proper by Congress, for it is them who are to judge of the necessity and propriety to accomplish those special purposes which they may have in contemplation, which laws in themselves are neither necessary or proper; as well as improper laws could be enacted by the state legislatures, for fulfilling the more extended objects of those governments. I will state an instance which I think in point, and proves that this might be the case. The general government has a right to pass all laws which shall be necessary to collect its revenue; the means for enforcing the collection are within the direction of the legislature: may not general warrants be considered necessary for this purpose, as well as for some purposes which it was supposed at the framing of their constitutions the state governments had in view. If there was reason for restraining the state governments from exercising this power, there is like reason for restraining the federal government.

It may be said, because it has been said, that a bill of rights is not necessary, because the establishment of this government has not repealed those declarations of rights which are added to the several state constitutions: that those rights of the people, which had been established by the most solemn act, could not be annihilated by a subsequent act of that people, who meant, and declared at the head of the instrument, that they ordained and established a new system, for the express purpose of securing to themselves and posterity the liberties they had gained by an arduous conflict.

I admit the force of this observation, but I do not look upon it to be conclusive. In the first place, it is too uncertain ground to leave this provision upon, if a provision is at all necessary to secure rights so important as many of those I have mentioned are conceived to be, by the public in general, as well as those in particular who opposed the adoption of this constitution. Beside some states have no bills of rights, there are others provided with very defective ones, and there are others whose bills of rights are not only defective, but absolutely improper; instead of securing some in the full extent which republican principles would require, they limit them too much to agree with the common ideas of liberty.

It has been objected also against a bill of rights, that, by enumerating particular exceptions to the grant of power, it would disparage those rights which were not placed in that enumeration, and it might follow by implication, that those rights which were not singled out, were intended to be assigned into the hands of the general government, and were consequently insecure. This is one of the most plausible arguments I have ever heard urged against the admission of a bill of rights into this system; but, I conceive, that may be guarded against. I have attempted it, as gentlemen may see by turning to the last clause of the 4th resolution.

It has been said, that it is unnecessary to load the constitution with this provision, because it was not found effectual in the constitution of the particular states. It is true, there are a few particular states in which some of the most valuable articles have not, at one time or other, been violated; but it does not follow but they may have, to a certain degree, a salutary effect against the abuse of power. If they are incorporated into the constitution, independent tribunals of justice will consider themselves in a peculiar manner the guardians of those rights; they will be an impenetrable bulwark against every assumption of power in the legislative or executive; they will be naturally led to resist every encroachment upon rights expressly stipulated for in the constitution by the declaration of rights. Beside this security, there is a great probability that such a declaration in the federal system would be inforced; because the state legislatures will jealously and closely watch the operations of this government, and be able to resist with more effect every assumption of power than any other power on earth can do; and the greatest opponents to a federal government admit the state legislatures to be sure guardians of the people's liberty. I conclude from this view of the subject, that it will be proper in itself, and highly politic, for the tranquility of the public mind, and the stability of the government, that we should offer something, in the form I have proposed, to be incorporated in the system of government, as a declaration of the rights of the people.

In the next place I wish to see that part of the constitution revised which declares, that the number of representatives shall not exceed the proportion of one for every thirty thousand persons, and allows one representative to every state which rates below that proportion. If we attend to the discussion of this subject, which has taken place in the state conventions, and even in the opinion of the friends to the constitution, an alteration here is proper. It is the sense of the people of America, that the number of representatives ought to be encreased, but particularly that it should not be left in the discretion of the government to diminish them, below that proportion which certainly is in the power of the legislature as the constitution now stands; and they may, as the population of the country encreases, increase the house of representatives to a very unwieldy degree. I confess I always thought this part of the constitution defective, though not dangerous; and that it ought to be particularly attended to whenever congress should go into the consideration of amendments.

There are several lesser cases enumerated in my proposition, in which I wish also to see some alteration take place. That article which leaves it in the power of the legislature to ascertain its own emolument is one to which I allude. I do not believe this is a power which, in the ordinary course of government, is likely to be abused, perhaps of all the powers granted, it is least likely to abuse; but there is a seeming impropriety in leaving any set of men without controul to put their hand into the public coffers, to take out money to put in their pockets; there is a seeming indecorum in such power, which leads me to propose a change. We have a guide to this alteration in several of the amendments which the different conventions have proposed. I have gone therefore so far as to fix it, that no law, varying the compensation, shall operate until there is a change in the legislature; in which case it cannot be for the particular benefit of those who are concerned in determining the value of the service.

I wish also, in revising the constitution, we may throw into that section, which interdicts the abuse of certain powers in the state legislatures, some other provisions of equal if not greater importance than those already made. The words, "No state shall pass any bill of attainder, ex post facto law, &c." were wise and proper restrictions in the constitution. I think there is more danger of those powers being abused by the state governments than by the government of the United States. The same may be said of other powers which they possess, if not controuled by the general principle, that laws are unconstitutional which infringe the rights of the community. I should therefore wish to extend this interdiction, and add, as I have stated in the 5th resolution, that no state shall violate the equal right of conscience, freedom of the press, or trial by jury in criminal cases; because it is proper that every government should be disarmed of powers which trench upon those particular rights. I know in some of the state constitutions the power of the government is controuled by such a declaration, but others are not. I cannot see any reason against obtaining even a double security on those points; and nothing can give a more sincere proof of the attachment of those who opposed this constitution to these great and important rights, than to see them join in obtaining the security I have now proposed; because it must be admitted, on all hands, that the state governments are as liable to attack these invaluable privileges as the general government is, and therefore ought to be as cautiously guarded against.

I think it will be proper, with respect to the judiciary powers, to satisfy the public mind on those points which I have mentioned. Great inconvenience has been apprehended to suitors from the distance they would be dragged to obtain justice in the supreme court of the United States, upon an appeal on an action for a small debt. To remedy this, declare, that no appeal shall be made unless the matter in controversy amounts to a particular sum: This, with the regulations respecting jury trials in criminal cases, and suits at common law, it is to be hoped will quiet and reconcile the minds of the people to that part of the constitution.

I find, from looking into the amendments proposed by the state conventions, that several are particularly anxious that it should be declared in the constitution, that the powers not therein delegated, should be reserved to the several states. Perhaps words which may define this more precisely, than the whole of the instrument now does, may be considered as superfluous. I admit they may be deemed unnecessary; but there can be no harm in making such a declaration, if gentlemen will allow that the fact is as stated, I am sure I understand it so, and do therefore propose it.

These are the points on which I wish to see a revision of the constitution take place. How far they will accord with the sense of this body, I cannot take upon me absolutely to determine; but I believe every gentleman will readily admit that nothing is in contemplation, so far as I have mentioned, that can endanger the beauty of the government in any one important feature, even in the eyes of its most sanguine admirers. I have proposed nothing that does not appear to me as proper in itself, or eligible as patronised by a respectable number of our fellow citizens; and if we can make the constitution better in the opinion of those who are opposed to it, without weakening its frame, or abridging its usefulness, in the judgment of those who are attached to it, we act the part of wise and liberal men to make such alterations as shall produce that effect.

Having done what I conceived was my duty, in bringing before this house the subject of amendments, and also stated such as I wish for and approve, and offered the reasons which occurred to me in their support; I shall content myself for the present with moving, that a committee be appointed to consider of and report such amendments as ought to be proposed by congress to the legislatures of the states, to become, if ratified by three-fourths thereof, part of the constitution of the United States. By agreeing to this motion, the subject may be going on in the committee, while other important business is proceeding to a conclusion in the house. I should advocate greater dispatch in the business of amendments, if I was not convinced of the absolute necessity there is of pursuing the organization of the government; because I think we should obtain the confidence of our fellow citizens, in proportion as we fortify the rights of the people against the encroachments of the government.

Mr. JACKSON.

The more I consider the subject of amendments, the more, mr. speaker, I am convinced it is improper. I revere the rights of my constituents as much as any gentleman in congress, yet, I am against inserting a declaration of rights in the constitution, and that upon some of the reasons referred to by the gentleman last up. If such an addition is not dangerous or improper, it is at least unnecessary: that is a sufficient reason for not entering into the subject at a time when there are urgent calls for our attention to important business. Let me ask gentlemen, what reason there is for the suspicions which are to be removed by this measure? Who are congress that such apprehensions should be entertained of them? Do we not belong to the mass of the people? Is there a single right but, if infringed, will affect us and our connections as much as any other person? Do we not return at the expiration of two years into private life, and is not this a security against encroachment? Are we not sent here to guard those rights which might be endangered, if the government was an aristocracy or despotism? View for a moment the situation of Rhode-Island

and, say whether the people's rights are more safe under state legislatures than under a government of limited powers? Their liberty is changed to licentiousness. But do gentlemen suppose bills of rights necessary to secure liberty? If they do, let them look at New-York, New-Jersey, Virginia,[10] South Carolina, and Georgia. Those states have no bills of rights, and are the liberty of the citizens less safe in those states, than in the other of the United States? I believe they are not.

There is a maxim in law, and it will apply to bills of rights, that when you enumerate exceptions, that the exceptions operate to the exclusion of all circumstances that are omitted; consequently, unless you except every right from the grant of power, those omitted are inferred to be resigned to the discretion of the government.

The gentleman endeavours to secure the liberty of the press; pray how is this in danger? There is no power given to congress to regulate this subject as they can commerce, or peace, or war. Has any transactions taken place to make us suppose such an amendment necessary? An honorable gentleman, a member of this house, has been attacked in the public news-papers, on account of sentiments delivered on this floor.[11] Have congress taken any notice of it? Have they ordered the writer before them, even for a breach of privilege, altho' the constitution provides that a member shall not be questioned in any place for any speech or debate in the house? No, these things are suffered to public view, and held up to the inspection of the world. These are principles which will always prevail; I am not afraid, nor are other members I believe, our conduct should meet the severest scrutiny. Where then is the necessity of taking measures to secure what neither is nor can be in danger?

I hold, mr. speaker, that the present is not a proper time for considering of amendments. The States of Rhode-Island and North-Carolina are not in the Union. As to the latter, we have every presumption that they will come in. But in Rhode-Island I think the antifederal interest yet prevails. I am sorry for it, particularly on account of the firm friends of the Union, who are kept without the embrace of the confederacy by their

[10] Eleven states had constitutions whose texts provided certain rights. Seven states—New Hampshire, Massachusetts, Pennsylvania, Delaware, Maryland, Virginia, and North Carolina—also had formal bills or declarations of rights. New York, New Jersey, South Carolina, and Georgia did not. Assertions that Virginia did not have a bill of rights were based on Francis Bailey's failure to include it in his *Constitutions of the Several Independent States of America*, printed in Philadelphia in 1781 by order of Congress and reprinted in Boston (1785) and New York (1786). Connecticut and Rhode Island continued to operate under their seventeenth century charters until well after the First Federal Congress; the legislature of the former adopted a bill of rights but it had no constitutional sanction (*DHROC* 2:421n, 8:340n).

[11] See n. 5 above.

countrymen. These persons are worthy of our patronage; and I wish they would apply to us for protection; they should have my consent to be taken into the Union upon such an application. I understand there are some important mercantile and manufacturing towns in that state, who ardently wish to live under the laws of the general government; if they were to come forward and request us to take measures for this purpose, I would give my sanction to any which are likely to bring about such an event.

But to return to my argument. It being the case that those states are not yet come into the Union, when they join us we shall have another list of amendments to consider, and another bill of rights to frame. Now, in my judgment, it is better to make but one work of it whenever we set about the business.

But in what a situation shall we be with respect to those foreign powers with whom we desire to be in treaty? They look upon us as a nation emerging into figure and importance: But what will be their opinion if they see us unable to retain the national advantages we have just gained? they will smile at our infantine efforts to obtain consequence, and treat us with the contempt we have hitherto borne by reason of the imbecility of our government. Can we expect to enter into a commercial competition with any of them, while our system is incomplete? and how long it will remain in such a situation, if we enter upon amendments, God only knows. Our instability will make us objects of scorn. We are not content with two revolutions in less than 14 years; we must enter upon a third, without necessity or propriety. Our faith will be like the punica fides of Carthage;[12] and we shall have none that will repose confidence in us. Why will gentlemen press us to propose amendments, while we are without experience? Can they assure themselves that the amendments, as they call them, will not want amendments as soon as they are adopted? I will not tax gentlemen with a desire of amusing the people; I believe they venerate their country too much for this; but what more can amendments lead to? That part of the constitution which is proposed to be altered, may be the most valuable part of the whole; and perhaps those who now clamour for alterations may ere long discover that they have marred a good government, and rendered their own liberties insecure. I again repeat it, this is not the time for bringing forward amendments; and, notwithstanding the honorable gentleman's ingenious arguments on that point, I am now more strongly persuaded it is wrong.

If we actually find the constitution bad upon experience, or the rights and privileges of the people in danger, I here pledge myself, to step for-

[12] Bad faith, even treachery: characteristics attributed to Carthage by Rome.

ward among the first friends of liberty to prevent the evil; and if nothing else will avail, I will draw my sword in the defence of freedom, and chearfully immolate at that shrine my property and my life. But how are we now proceeding? Why on nothing more than theoretical speculation, pursuing a mere ignis fatuus,[13] which may lead us into serious embarrassments. The imperfections of the government are now unknown; let it have a fair trial, and I will be bound they shew themselves; then we can tell where to apply the remedy, so as to secure the great object we are aiming at.

There are, Mr. Speaker, a number of important bills on the table which require dispatch, but I am afraid if we enter on this business, we shall not be able to attend to them for a long time. Look, sir, over the long list of amendments proposed by some of the adopting states, and say, when the house could get thro' the discussion; and I believe, sir, every one of those amendments will come before us. Gentlemen may feel themselves called by duty or inclination to propose them; how are we then to extricate ourselves from this labyrinth of business? certainly we shall lose much of our valuable time, without any advantage whatsoever. I hope therefore the gentleman will press us no further, he has done his duty, and acquitted himself of the obligation under which he lay. He may now accede to what I take to be the sense of the house, and let the business of amendments lay over until next spring, that will be soon enough to take it up to any good purpose.

Mr. GERRY.

I do not rise to go into the merits or demerits of the subject of amendments; nor shall I make any other observations on the motion for going into a committee of the whole, on the state of the union, which is now withdrawn, than merely to say, that, referring the subject to that committee, is treating it with the dignity its importance requires. But I consider it improper to take up this business at this time, when our attention is occupied by other important objects: We should dispatch the subjects now on the table, and let this lie over until a period of more leisure for discussion and attention. The gentleman from Virginia says it is necessary to go into a consideration of this subject, in order to satisfy the people. For my part I cannot be of his opinion. The people know we are employed in the organization of the government, and cannot expect that we should forego this business for any other. But I would not have it understood, that I am against entering upon amendments when the proper time arrives. I shall be glad to set about it as soon as possible, but I would not

[13] Fool's fire.

stay the operations of the government on this account. I think, with the gentleman from Delaware (Mr. Vining), that the great wheels of the political machine should first be set in motion; and with the gentleman from Georgia (Mr. Jackson), that the vessel ought to be got under way, lest she lays by the wharf till she beat off her rudder, and runs herself a wreck on shore.

I say, sir, I wish as early a day as possible may be assigned for taking up this business, in order to prevent the necessity which the states may think themselves under of calling a new convention. For I am not, sir, one of those blind admirers of this system, who think it all perfection; nor am I so blind as not to see its beauties. The truth is, it partakes of humanity; in it is blended virtue and vice, errors and excellence. But I think, if it is referred to a new convention, we run the risk of losing some of its best properties; this is a case I never wish to see. Whatever might have been my sentiments of the ratification of the constitution without amendments, my sense now is, that the salvation of America depends upon the establishment of this government, whether amended or not. If the constitution which is now ratified should not be supported, I despair of ever having a government of these United States.

I wish the subject to be considered early for another reason: There are two states not in the union; it would be a very desirable circumstance to gain them. I should therefore be in favor of such amendments as might tend to invite them and gain their confidence; good policy will dictate to us to expedite that event. Gentlemen say, that we shall not obtain the consent of two-thirds of both houses to amendments. Are gentlemen willing then to throw Rhode-Island and North Carolina into the situation of foreign nations? They have told you, that they cannot accede to the union unless certain amendments are made to the constitution; if you deny a compliance with their request in this particular, you refuse an accommodation to bring about that desirable event, and leave them detached from the union.

I have another reason for going early into this business: It is necessary to establish an energetic government. My idea of such a government is, that due deliberation be had in making laws, and efficiency in the execution. I hope in this country the latter may obtain without the dread of despotism: I would wish to see the execution of good laws irresistible. But from the view which we have already had of the disposition of the government, we seem really to be afraid to administer the powers with which we are invested lest we give offence. We appear afraid to exercise the constitutional powers of the government, which the welfare of the state requires, lest a jealousy of our powers be the consequence. What is the reason of this timidity? why, because we see a great body of our constituents opposed to the constitution as it now stands, who are apprehensive of the enormous powers of governments. But if this business is taken up, and it is thought proper to make amendments, it will remove this difficulty. Let us deal fairly and candidly with our constituents, and give the subject a full discussion; after that I have no doubt but the decision will be such as upon examination, we shall discover to be right. If it shall then appear proper and wise to reject the amendments, I dare to say the reasons for so doing, will bring conviction to the people out of doors, as well as it will to the members of this house; and they will acquiesce in the decision, though they may regret the disappointment of their fondest hopes for the security of the liberties of themselves and their posterity. Thus, and thus only, the government will have its due energy, and accomplish the end for which it was instituted.

I am against referring the subject to a select committee; because I conceive it would be disrespectful to those states which have proposed amendments. The conventions of the states consisted of the most wise and virtuous men of the community; they have ratified this constitution, in full confidence that their objections would at least be considered; and shall we, sir, preclude them by the appointment of a special committee, to consider of a few propositions brought forward by an individual gentleman. Is it in contemplation that the committee should have the subject at large before them, or that they should report upon the particular amendments just mentioned, as they think proper? And are we to be precluded from the consideration of any other amendments but those the committee may report? A select committee must be considered improper, because it is putting their judgments against that of the conventions who have proposed amendments; but if the committee are to consider the matter at large, they will be liable to this objection, that their report will be only waste of time: For if they do not bring forward the whole of the amendments recommended, individual members will consider themselves bound to bring them forward for the decision of the house. I would therefore submit, if gentlemen are determined to proceed in the business at this time, whether it is not better that it should go, in the first instance, to a committee of the whole, as first proposed by the gentleman from Virginia.

Some gentlemen consider it necessary to do this to satisfy our constituents: I think referring the business to a special committee will be attempting to amuse them with trifles. Our fellow citizens are possessed of too much discernment not to be able to discover the intention of congress by such procedure. It will be the duty of their representatives to tell them, if they were not able to discover it of themselves; they require the subject to be fairly considered, and if it be found to be improper to comply with their reasonable expectations tell them so. I hope there is no analogy between federal and punic faith; but unless congress shall candidly consider the amendments which have been proposed in confidence by the state conventions, federal faith will not be considered very different from the punica fides of Carthage.[14] The ratification of the constitution in several states would never have taken place, had they not been assured, that the objections would have been duly attended to by congress: And I believe many members of these conventions would never have voted for it, if they had not been persuaded that congress would notice them with that candor and attention which their importance requires. I will say nothing respecting the amendments themselves; they ought to stand or fall on their own merits. If any of them are eligible they will be adopted, if not, they will be rejected.

Mr. LIVERMORE

Was against this motion; not that he was against amendments at a proper time; it is enjoined on him to act a rational part in procuring certain amendments, and he meant to do so; but he could not say what amendments were requisite, until the government was organized. He supposed the judiciary law would contain certain regulations that would remove the anxiety of the people respecting such amendments as related thereto; because he thought much of the minutiae respecting suits between citizens of different states, &c. might be provided by law. He could not agree to make jury trials necessary on every occasion; they were not practiced even at this time, and there were some cases in which a cause could be better decided without a jury than with one.

In addition to the judiciary business, there is that which relates to the revenue. Gentlemen had let one opportunity go through their hands of getting a considerable supply from the impost on the spring importation. He reminded them of this: and would tell them now was the time to finish that business; for if they did not sow in seed time, they would be beggars in harvest. He was well satisfied in his own mind, that the people of America did not look for amendments at present; they never could imagine it to be the first work of Congress.

He wished the concurrence of the senate upon entering on this business, because if they opposed the measure, all the house did would be a mere waste of time; and there was some little difficulty on this point, because it required the consent of two-thirds of them as well as the house of representatives to agree to what was proper on this occasion. He said

[14] Bad faith, even treachery: characteristics attributed to Carthage by Rome.

moreover it would be better to refer the subject generally, if referred to them at all, than to take up the propositions of individual members.

Mr. SHERMAN.

I do not suppose the constitution to be perfect, nor do I imagine if congress and all the legislatures on the continent were to revise it, that their united labours would make it perfect. I do not expect any perfection on this side the grave in the works of man; but my opinion is, that we are not at present in circumstances to make it better. It is a wonder that there has been such unanimity in adopting it, considering the ordeal it had to undergo; and the unanimity which prevailed at its formation, is equally astonishing; amidst all the members from the twelve states present at the federal convention, there were only three who did not sign the instrument to attest their opinion of its goodness.[15] Of the eleven states who have received it, the majority have ratified it without proposing a single amendment; this circumstance leads me to suppose that we shall not be able to propose any alterations that are likely to be adopted by nine states; and gentlemen know before the alterations take effect, they must be agreed to by the legislatures of three-fourths of the states in the union. Those states that have not recommended alterations will hardly adopt them, unless it is clear that they tend to make the constitution better; now how this can be made out to their satisfaction I am yet to learn; they know of no defect from experience. It seems to be the opinion of gentlemen generally, that this is not the time for entering upon the discussion of amendments: our only question therefore is, how to get rid of the subject; now for my own part I would prefer to have it referred to a committee of the whole, rather than a special committee, and therefore shall not agree to the motion now before the house.

Mr. Gerry moved, that the business lie over until the 1st. day of July next, and that it be the order for that day.

Mr. SUMTER.

I consider the subject of amendments of such great importance to the Union, that I should be glad to see it undertaken in any manner. I am not, mr. speaker, disposed to sacrifice substance to form; therefore, whether the business shall originate in a committee of the whole, or in the house, is a matter of indifference to me, so that it be put in train. Although I am seriously inclined to give this subject a full discussion, yet I do not wish it to be fully entered into at present, but am willing it should

[15] Rhode Island did not attend the Federal Convention. Delegates Elbridge Gerry of Massachusetts and George Mason and Edmund Randolph of Virginia refused to sign the Constitution.

be postponed to a future day, when we shall have more leisure. With respect to referring to a select committee, I am rather against it; because I consider it as treating the applications of the state conventions rather slightly; and I presume it is the intention of the house to take those applications into consideration as well as any other; if it is not, I think it will give fresh cause for jealousy; it will rouse the alarm which is now suspended, and the people will become clamorous for amendments; they will decline any further application to Congress, and resort to the other alternative pointed out in the constitution. I hope, therefore, this house, when they do go into the business, will receive those propositions generally. This I apprehend will tend to tranquilize the public mind, and promote that harmony which ought to be kept up between those in the exercise of the powers of government, and those who have cloathed them with the authority, or in other words between Congress and the people. Without a harmony and confidence subsists between them, the measures of government will prove abortive, and we shall have still to lament that imbecility and weakness which has long marked our public councils.

Mr. VINING

Found himself in a delicate situation respecting the subject of amendments. He came from a small state, and therefore his sentiments would not be considered of so much weight as the sentiments of those gentlemen who spoke the sense of much larger states; besides his constituents had prejudged the question, by an unanimous adoption of the constitution, without suggesting any amendments thereto. His sense accorded with the declared sense of the state of Delaware, and he was doubly bound to object to amendments, which were either improper or unnecessary. But he had good reasons for opposing the consideration of even proper alterations at this time. He would ask the gentleman who pressed them, whether he would be responsible for the risk the government would run of being injured by an inter regnum? Proposing amendments at this time, is suspending the operations of government, and may be productive of its ruin.

He would not follow the gentleman in his arguments, tho' he supposed them all answerable, because he would not take up the time of the house; he contented himself with saying that a bill of rights was unnecessary in a government deriving all its powers from the people; and the constitution enforced the principle in the strongest manner by the practical declaration prefixed to that instrument; he alluded to the words, "We the people do ordain and establish."

There were many things mentioned by some of the state conventions which he would never agree to, on any conditions whatever; they changed the principles of the government, and were therefore obnoxious to its friends—the honorable gentleman from Virginia, had not touched upon any of them; he was glad of it, because he could by no means bear the idea of an alteration respecting them; he referred to the mode of obtaining direct taxes, judging of elections, &c.

He found he was not speaking to the question; he would therefore return to it and declare he was against committing it to a select committee; if it was to be committed at all, he preferred a committee of the whole, but hoped the subject would be postponed.

Mr. MADISON

Found himself unfortunate in not satisfying gentlemen with respect to the mode of introducing the business; he thought from the dignity and peculiarity of the subject that it ought to be referred to a committee of the whole; he had accordingly made that motion first, but finding himself not likely to succeed in that way he had changed his ground. Fearing again to be discomfited, he would change his mode, and move the propositions he had stated before, and the house might do what they thought proper with them. He accordingly moved the propositions by way of resolutions to be adopted by the house.

Mr. Livermore objected to these propositions, because they did not take up the amendments of the several states.

Mr. Page was much obliged to his colleague for bringing the subject forward in the manner he had done. He conceived it to be just and fair. What was to be done when the house would not refer it to a committee of any sort, but bring the question at once before them? He hoped it would be the means of bringing about a decision.

Mr. Laurance moved to refer Mr. Madison's motion to the committee of the whole on the state of the union.

Mr. Lee thought it ought to be taken up in that committee; and hoped his colleague would bring the propositions before the committee, when on the state of the union, as he had originally intended.

July 1789

21 July 1789

The Daily Advertiser, 22 July 1789

Mr. MADISON then moved that the house resolve itself into a committee, in order to take into consideration the subject of amendments to the constitution.

Several members suggesting that it would be more proper to refer the subject to a special committee, a motion was made in form, that a committee of one member from each state be appointed to take in consideration the motion of the 8th of June, Mr. Madison's motion, offering certain amendments, together with the amendments proposed by the conventions of the different states, and to report thereon.

Upon this motion a dissusive debate ensued, which turned altogether upon the point of expediency as to the mode; it being agreed that it would be proper for the house to take the subject into consideration. The principal argument in favor of the motion was drawn from the infinite embarrassments which would take place, if the subject in its present irregular and disordered state should come first before the whole house, and the great delay which it would occasion.

On the other hand it was chiefly contended, that the method proposed would not give satisfaction to the people; and that it would not facilitate the business, since the whole subject would, on the report of the committee lie open to the house.

The motion was however carried by a large majority; and the house proceeded to ballot for the committee,[16]

[16]The *GUS*, 22 July, reported that at this point a "motion was made, that the committee be instructed to report as expeditiously as possible—this was superceded by a motion for adjournment—which accordingly took place."

The New-York Daily Gazette, 22 July 1789

Mr. Madison moved the house to resolve itself into a committee of the whole on the state of the union, for the purpose of taking into consideration the subject of amendments to the Constitution, as ordered on his motion of the 8th ult. He thought the present a leisure moment, and was desirous of embracing the earliest opportunity for discussing and determining the same.

Mr. Ames thought the business would be expedited by referring it, in the first instance, to a select committee; for which reason he moved to discharge the committee of the whole from taking cognizance of the business, and to refer it to a select committee consisting of a member from each state.

This question drew on a long argument, in which the whole day was consumed; and, on the question, Mr. Ames's motion obtained.

Mr. Smith proposed that the committee should have the subject generally before them, without being bound by the amendments proposed by some of the adopting states, and to report what they deemed proper. This being agreed to, the house adjourned until 11 o'clock to-morrow.

The Congressional Register, 21 July 1789

Mr. MADISON

Begged the house to indulge him in the further consideration of amendments to the constitution, and as there appeared, in some degree, a moment of leisure, he would move to go into a committee of the whole on the subject, conformably to the order of the 8th of last month.

Mr. AMES

Hoped that the house would be induced, on mature reflection, to rescind their vote of going into committee on the business, and refer it to a select committee: It would certainly tend to facilitate the business. If they had the subject at large before a committee of the whole, he could not see where the business was likely to end. The amendments proposed were so various, that their discussion must inevitably occupy many days, and that at a time when they can be illy spared; whereas a select committee could go through and cull out those of the most material kind, without interrupting the principal business of the house. He therefore moved, that the committee of the whole be discharged, and the subject referred to a select committee.

Mr. SEDGWICK

Opposed the motion, for the reasons given by his colleague, observing that the members from the several states proposing amendments, would no doubt drag the house through the consideration of every one, whatever their fate might be after they were discussed, now gentlemen had only to reflect on this, and conceive the length of time the business would take up, if managed in this way.

Mr. WHITE

Thought no time would be saved by appointing a select committee. Every member would like to be satisfied with the reasons upon which the amendments offered by the select committee are grounded, consequently the train of argument which gentlemen have in contemplation to avoid, must be brought forward.

He did not presume to say the constitution was perfect, but it was such as had met with the approbation of wise and good men in the different states. Some of the proposed amendments were also of high value, but he did not expect they would be supported by two thirds of both houses, without undergoing a thorough investigation. He did not like to refer any business to a select committee, until the sense of the house had been expressed upon it, because it rather tended to retard than dispatch it, witness the collection bill which had cost them much time, but after all had to be deserted.

Mr. SHERMAN.

The provision for amendments made in the fifth article of the constitution, was intended to facilitate the adoption of those which experience should point out to be necessary. This constitution has been adopted by eleven states, a majority of those eleven have received it without expressing a wish for amendments; now, is it probable that three fourths of the eleven states will agree to amendments offered on mere speculative points, when the constitution has had no kind of trial whatever? It is hardly to be expected that they will: Consequently we shall lose our labour, and had better decline having any thing farther to do with it for the present.

But if the house are to go into a consideration, it had better be done in such a way as not to interfere much with the organization of the government.

Mr. PAGE

Hoped the business would proceed as heretofore directed: He thought it would be very agreeable to the majority of the union; he knew it would to his constituents, to find that the government meant to give every security to the rights and liberties of the people, and to examine carefully into the grounds of the apprehensions expressed by several of the state conventions; he thought they would be satisfied with the amendments brought forward by his colleague, when the subject was last before the house.

Mr. PARTRIDGE knew the subject must be taken up in some way or another, and preferred, for the sake of expedition, doing it by a select committee.

Mr. JACKSON

Was sorry to see the house were to be troubled any further on the subject—he looked upon it as a mere waste of time; but as he always chose the least of two evils, he acquiesced in the motion for referring it to a special committee.

Mr. GERRY

Asked whether the house had cognizance of the amendments proposed by the state conventions, if they had not, he would make a motion to bring them forward.

Mr. PAGE replied that such motion would be out of order, until the present question was determined.

A desultory conversation ensued, and it was questioned whether the subject generally was to be before the committee of the whole, or those specific propositions only which had already been introduced.

Mr. GERRY

Said that it was a matter of indifference how this question was understood, because no gentleman could pretend to deny another the privilege of bringing forward propositions conformable to his sentiments. If gentlemen, then, might bring forward resolutions to be added, or motions of amendment, there would be no time saved even by referring the subject to a special committee: But such procedure might tend to prejudice the house against an amendment neglected by the committee, and thereby induce them not to shew that attention to the state which proposed it that would be delicate and proper.

He wished gentlemen to consider the situation of the states—seven out of thirteen had thought the constitution very defective, yet five of them has adopted it with a perfect reliance on congress for its improvement: Now, what will these states feel if the subject is discussed in a select committee, and their recommendations totally neglected. The indelicacy of treating the application of five states in a manner different from other important subjects, will give no small occasion for disgust, which is a circumstance that this government ought carefully to avoid. If, then, the house could gain nothing by this manner of proceeding, he hoped they would not hesitate to adhere to their former vote for going into a committee of the whole. That they would gain nothing was pretty certain, for gentlemen must necessarily come forward with their amendments to the report when it was brought in. The members from Massachusetts were particularly instructed to press the amendments recommended by the convention of that state at all times, until they had been maturely considered by congress; the same duties were made incumbent on the members from some other states; consequently, any attempt to smother the business, or prevent a full investigation, must be nugatory, while the house paid a proper deference to their own rules and orders. He did not contend for going into a committee of the whole at the present moment; he would prefer a time of greater leisure than the present, from the business of organizing the government.

Mr. Ames

Answered the house, that he was no enemy to the consideration of amendment; but he had moved to rescind their former vote, in order to save time, which he was confident would be the consequence of referring it to a select committee.

He was sorry to have an intention avowed by his colleague, of considering every part of the frame of this constitution: It was the same as forming themselves into a convention of the United States; he did not stand for words, the thing would be the same in fact. He could not but express a degree of anxiety at seeing the system of government encounter another ordeal when it ought to be extending itself to furnish security to others. He apprehended, if the zeal of some gentlemen broke out on this occasion, that there would be no limits to the time necessary to discuss the subject; he was certain the session would not be long enough; perhaps they might be bounded by the period of their appointment, but he questioned it.

When gentlemen suppose themselves called upon to vent their ardor in some favorite pursuit, in securing to themselves and their posterity, the inestimable rights and liberties they have but just snatched from the hand of despotism; they are apt to carry their exertions to an extreme; but he hoped the subject itself would be limited, not that he objected to the consideration of the amendments proposed, indeed he should move himself for the consideration, by the committee, of those recommended by Massachusetts, if his colleagues omitted to do it; but he hoped gentlemen would not think of bringing in new amendments, such as were not recommended, but went to tear the frame of government into pieces.

He considered a select committee much better calculated to consider and arrange a complex business, than a committee of the whole; he thought they were like the senses to the soul, and on an occasion like the present, could be made equally useful.

If he recollected rightly the decision made by the house on the 8th of June, it was that certain specific amendments be referred to the committee of the whole; not that the subject generally be referred, and that amendments be made in the committee, that were never contemplated before; this public discussion, would be like a dissection of the constitution, it would be defacing its symmetry, laying bare its sinews and tendons, ripping up the whole form and tearing out its vitals; but is it presumable that such conduct would be attended with success; two thirds of both houses must agree in all these operations, before they can have effect. His opposition to going into the committee of the whole, did not arise from any fear that the constitution would suffer by a fair discussion in this, or any other house; but while such business was going on, the government was laid prostrate, and every artery ceased to beat. The unfair advantages that might be taken in such a situation, were easier apprehended than resisted: Wherefore, he wished to avoid the danger, by a more prudent line of conduct.

Mr. TUCKER

Would not say whether the discussion alluded to by the gentleman last up, would do good or harm, but he was certain it ought to take place no where but in a committee of the whole; the subject is of too much importance for a select committee. Now, suppose such a committee to be appointed, and that the amendments proposed by the several states, together with those brought forward by the gentleman from Virginia, are referred to them; after some consideration they report—but not one of the amendments proposed by either state—what is the inference? They have considered them, and as they were better capable than the house of considering them, the house ought to reject every proposition coming from the state conventions. Will this give satisfaction to the states who have required amendments? Very far from it. They will expect that their propositions shall be fully brought before the house, and regularly and fully considered; if indeed then they are rejected, it may be some satisfaction to them, to know that their applications have been treated with respect.

What I have said with respect to the propositions of the several states, may apply in some degree to the propositions brought forward by the gentleman (mr. Madison) from Virginia; the select committee may single out one or two, and reject the remainder, notwithstanding the vote of the house for considering them. The gentleman would have a right to complain, and every state would be justly disgusted.

Will it tend to reconcile to the government that great body of the people who are dissatisfied, who think themselves and all they hold most dear, unsafe under it? Without certain amendments are made, will it answer any one good purpose to slurr over this business, and reject the propositions without giving them a fair chance of a full discussion? I think not, mr. speaker. Both the senate and this house ought to treat the present subject with delicacy and impartiality.

The select committee will have it in their power so to keep this business back, that it may never again come before the house; this is an imprudent step for us to take—not that I would insinuate it is an event likely to take place, or which any gentleman has in contemplation. I give every gentleman credit for his declaration, and believe the honorable mover means to save time by this arrangement; but do not let us differ on this point; I would rather the business should lay over for a month, nay, for a whole session, than have it put into other hands, and passed over without investigation.

Mr. Gerry

Enquired of his colleague how it was possible that the house could be a federal convention without the senate, and when two thirds of both houses are to agree to the amendments? He would also be glad to find out how a committee were the same to the house as the senses to the soul? What, said he, can we neither see, hear, smell nor feel, without we employ a committee for the purpose? My colleague further tells us, that if we proceed in this way, we shall lay bare the sinews and tendons of the constitution; that we shall butcher it, and put it to death. Now what does this argument tend to prove? Why, sir, to my mind, nothing more nor less than this, that we ought to adopt the report of the committee, whatever that report may be, for we are to judge by the knowledge derived through our senses, and not to proceed on to commit murder. If these are arguments to induce the house to refer the subject to a select committee, they are arguments to engage to go further, and give into the hands of select committees the whole legislative power: But what is that was said respecting a public discussion? Are gentlemen afraid to meet the public ear on this topic? Do they wish to shut the gallery doors? Perhaps nothing would be attended with more dangerous consequences—No, sir, let us not be afraid of full and public investigation; let our means, like our conclusions, be justified; let our constituents see, hear, and judge for themselves.

The question on discharging the committee of the whole on the state of the union from proceeding on the subject of amendments, as referred to them, was put, and carried in the affirmative; the house divided, 34 for it, and 15 against it.

It was then ordered, that mr. Madison's motion, stating certain specific amendments, proper to be proposed by congress to the legislatures of the states, to become, if ratified by three-fourths thereof, part of the constitution of the United States, together with the amendments to the said constitution as proposed by the several states, be referred to a committee, to consist of a member from each state, with instruction to take the subject of amendments to the constitution of the United States, generally into their consideration, and to report thereupon to the house.

August 1789

13 August 1789

The Daily Advertiser, 14 August 1789

Mr. Lee moved that the house should resolve itself into a committee of the whole in order to take up the report of the special committee on the subject of amendments to the constitution. This motion was opposed by a number of members. It was objected that the period proposed for adjournment was approaching; that many subjects of present and pressing importance were still before the house undecided, that the government was not yet organized, particularly the judiciary had not been passed and thereby the laws which had been already enacted were without a sanction, and destitute of force; that the establishment of the judicial system as a part of the government itself, and to give effect to the revenue laws ought to precede all other matters of lengthy discussion. It was a subject which would require considerable time and a very deliberate attention; it was contended that one or the other of these great objects must be sacrificed for the present. That the present session would not be lengthy enough to do justice to both, and to transact such other business as was of immediate moment, such as the establishment of a land-office, &c. The disadvantage and absurdity of postponing the judicial was dwelt upon in a particular manner and set in its full light.

Mr. Madison, on the other hand contended warmly for taking up the subject of amendments as of the first consequence. He said it had been deferred some time, tho' brought forward at an early stage; it ought to have been one of the first objects of the legislature and he was convinced that if it passed over this session the people would be disappointed and alarmed. It was an indispensable duty due to the people of the United States that something should be done early to quiet their apprehensions.

The question on the motion of Mr. Lee being put was carried in the affirmative.

The house then went into a committee.

Mr. Boudinot in the chair—

The clerk then read the amendments proposed by the committee; the first of which is the following, viz. In the introductory paragraph of the constitution, before the words, "we the people," add "government being intended for the benefit of the people, and the rightful establishment thereof being derived from their authority alone."

Mr. SHERMAN rose and moved that this clause be struck out, and that a declaration similar in substance which he read in his place, and preceeding the amendment to be made, be annexed to the constitution; he grounded his motion on the propriety of making the amendments supplemental to the constitution and not incorporating them in the body of the instrument; he said it was his wish not to alter by authority of Congress, the original instrument itself, which was made by authority of the people; that this house had no right, and that it would be a measure full of difficulties; there was no right, because any alterations of the individual articles of the constitution was a repeal of the constitution; that the house had no possible power of repealing or if they had, the authority on which the house acted, from that moment ceased; and they had no right to make a new constitution or to do any act whatsoever. The original form of the constitution ought to remain inviolate and all amendments which the Congress were authorised to make were only legislative acts which ought to be detached from the constitution and be supplementary to it.

Mr. SHERMAN was supported by Mr. STONE, Mr. LIVERMORE, Mr. LAURANCE, and Mr. JACKSON, and opposed by Mr. MADISON, Mr. SMITH (S.C.), Mr. PAGE, Mr. GERRY, and several others. A long and animated debate ensued.

For the motion it was contended, that an alteration would be a destruction of the instrument; that the original constitution ordained and signed by its framers was lodged in the archives of Congress, and was the sacred constitution of the Union, that any alterations or additions, in the body of the work, would involve an absurdity; since it would render the signature of those characters false in fact, whose names were the evidence of the instrument; they would be made to subscribe a constitution they never made. It was wrong that the amendments should wear the complexion of being derived originally from the people: They were from another power, and this ought to appear. It was said that the mode of inserting amendments in the body of a law by way of amendment was unprecedented and inconvenient; that the universal usage was, when deficiencies were to be supplied or alterations or additions made, to do it by supplementary acts; and that when a contrary mode had been adopted, it was always considered that the amendments then incorporated were a total repeal of the first act; there had been instances of several obscure laws, for the convenience of the people, being condensed into one; but in all those cases the old laws were done away, and a new one formed from them. This principle was inadmissible with respect to the constitution, because it was a sacred act which could never be annulled, but by the power which gave it birth; many other arguments were suggested.

Mr. JACKSON said that we had precedents for the measure proposed in constitutions the most sacred as well as in laws: Magna Charta remained inviolate as it came from King John. The amendments which subsequent measures had produced were all supplementary; and did not touch the form of that sacred deposit of English liberty. The privileges of the people had been secured by a series of distinct charters. But the great charter had never been altered, though defects had been supplied, and additions made. The constitution of England was the same; but that constitution consisted of many independent parts, which had never been blended together.

Against the motion it was argued, that the simplicity of the constitution would be destroyed by such a supplemental act. Other additions and emendations might take place in course of years.

There might be amendments to the supplement, and the constitution would become complex and obscure and would consist of a long train of laws which might fill a volume. The people would not know where to find it. It was observed that as for the difficulty stated respecting the names of the subscribers to the constitution in the federal convention. They were, tho' respectable in themselves, of no consequence to the validity of the instrument which derived its force from the ratifications of the several states. It was shewn that many of the states which had ratified the constitution with the desire of amendments had used a language which indicated their idea of the nature of this business. They expressed that amendments ought to be inserted and introduced—Clearly implying that any supplementary laws were improper. Many other arguments were adduced to prove that the principles of the gentlemen went to prove that the amendments should not be considered as parts of the constitution, for if the constitution was a distinct instrument not to be altered or violated, then the amendments were not parts, and would not be considered as possessing equal authority. The amendments ought to be incorporated and then the people would have one constitution, otherwise they would have more than one. If in the original instrument there were any clauses which were inconsistent with the amendments, the government would be a government of opposite principles, both in force—Or if the principle of the amendments should be considered of inferior authority, as it must be upon the gentlemen's idea of the sacredness of the original, then amendments themselves were of no consequence and had better not be established. If the idea prevailed that the first constitution was of superior authority to the amendments, then certainly a clause in the amendments in alteration of one in the constitution would have no force at all. This was a direct mode therefore to defeat the salutary purpose of amendments by derogating from their dignity and authority.

The reasoning on both sides was much more copious and was very ingenious and interesting. The question at length was carried in the negative.

A doubt being suggested by a member, whether, as the constitution required a recommendation of amendments to be made by two thirds of each house it was not also necessary that two thirds of the committee of the whole House should agree in reporting amendments.

This question of order being referred to the chair was determined in the negative, viz. that a majority of the committee was sufficient in order to report amendments to the house. An appeal was then made from the opinion of the chair to the house, and the decision was confirmed.

Gazette of the United States, 15 August 1789

Mr. LEE moved that the House should resolve itself into a committee of the whole on the state of the Union, to take into consideration the report of the committee on amendments to the Constitution.

The immediate adoption of this motion was advocated by Mr. MADISON, Mr. PAGE, and Mr. HARTLEY—and opposed by Mr. SEDGWICK, Mr. SMITH (S.C.), Mr. GERRY, Mr. LAURANCE, and Mr. SHERMAN—The latter gentlemen generally observed, That there was a great variety of business before the house, which it is of the greatest importance should precede the consideration of all other—that it appears absurd to make alteration in a form of government, before it has an operative existence—that it is of the first consequence to compleat the judiciary bill—that without this and several other bills now pending in the house, we cannot carry one of the revenue laws into execution—not a breach of the laws of the United States can be punished—not a vessel can be seized—The discussion of the subject at this moment will obstruct the wheels of government, and throw every thing into confusion—mean time the United States are without law, and have no authority to punish a single crime. It was further said, that few, if any of the State assemblies are in session, and therefore it will unnecessarily consume the present time, which is so precious—that the people reposing full confidence in the justice, and wisdom of the House that this subject would have seasonable and due attention paid to it, are as anxious and solicitous to see the government in operation, as they are about amendments.

The Speakers against the motion severally expressed themselves in favor of taking up the subject as soon as the judicial, executive, and revenue departments were so far completed that it could with propriety be said that we had a government.

In support of the motion it was observed, That since the subject had first been introduced, so much time has elapsed, that if it is not now taken up, the people will be led to suppose, that it is the intention of Congress never to do any thing in the business—that the people are extremely anxious upon the subject—and nothing short of a conviction that those rights, which they conceive to be in danger as the Constitution now stands, will be placed in a state of greater security, will quiet their apprehensions—that the number of those in favor of amendments consisted of a large and respectable proportion of the citizens of the States—that the peace and tranquility of the Union depend upon a proper attention to their just expectations—that if those who are anxious for amendments, had been added to those who openly opposed the Constitution, it would have probably met a quite different fate—that except these amendments are made, the government will want the confidence of the people, and that energy which is necessary to its existence—that the same reasons for a postponement have repeatedly been assigned, and there is no prospect that a more convenient opportunity will offer. The question being put on the motion of Mr. LEE, it passed in the affirmative. The House accordingly formed into a committee of the whole.

Mr. BOUDINOT in the chair.

The report of the committee was then read—the first article of which is in these words, viz.

In the introductory paragraph of the Constitution, before the words "We the people," add, "Government being intended for the benefit of the People, and the rightful establishment thereof being derived from their authority alone."

Mr. SHERMAN: I am opposed to this mode of making amendments to the Constitution—and am for striking out from the report of the committee the first article entirely. I conceive that we cannot incorporate these amendments in the body of the Constitution. It would be mixing brass, iron, and clay—it would be as absurd as to incorporate an act in addition to an act, in the body of the act proposed to be amended or explained thereby—which I believe was never heard of before. I conceive that we have no right to do this, as the Constitution is an act of the people, and ought to remain entire—whereas the amendments will be the act of the several legislatures. Mr. Sherman then read a proposition which he moved should be substituted in place of the article in the report.

This being seconded, brought on an interesting debate—Whether the amendments should be incorporated in the body of the Constitution, or be made a distinct supplementary act.

Mr. MADISON supported the former, and said, that he did not coincide with the gentleman from Connecticut: I conceive, said he, that there is a propriety in incorporating the amendments in the Constitution itself, in the several places to which they belong—the system will in that case be uniform and entire—nor is this an uncommon thing to be done—It is true that acts are generally amended by additional acts; but this I believe may be imputed rather to indolence—this however is not always the case, for where there is a taste for political and legislative propriety it is otherwise—If these amendments are added to the Constitution by way of supplement, it will embarrass the people—It will be difficult for them to determine to what parts of the system they particularly refer—and at any rate will create unfavorable comparisons between the two parts of the instrument. If these amendments are adopted agreeably to the plan proposed, they will stand upon as good a foundation as the other parts of the Constitution—and will be sanctioned by equally as good authority. I am not however very solicitous about the mode, so long as the business is fully attended to.

Mr. SMITH, (S.C.) agreed with Mr. Madison—and read that clause in the Constitution which provides that alterations and amendments when agreed to, shall become *part* of the Constitution—from whence he inferred, that it was evidently the design of the framers of the system, that they should be incorporated—nor is the house at liberty to adopt any other mode. Mr. Smith cited the instance of South-Carolina, who instead of making acts in addition to acts, which had been found extremely perplexing, repealed their laws generally, in order to form a more simple and unembarrassing code.

Mr. LIVERMORE supported the motion of Mr. Sherman—He adverted to the custom and usage of the British legislature, and of the several State Assemblies, in forming laws and additional acts. We have no right, he observed, to make any alterations or interlopations in the instrument—it will be attended with difficulties in some future day.

Mr. VINING observed, that he thought the mode was not essential—he therefore adverted to the expediency of the motion—adding amendments, said he, will be attended with a variety of inconveniencies—it will distort the system—it will appear like a letter, which, carelessly wrote in haste, requires a postscript much longer than the original composition—This motion is founded upon the custom of amending acts by additional acts, to explain and amend preceding acts, a custom, which involves endless perplexities, and has nothing in reason to recommend it. I hope Sir, the motion will not obtain.

Mr. CLYMER advocated the motion: I wish Sir that the Constitution may forever remain in its original form, as a monument of the wisdom and patriotism of those who framed it.

Mr. STONE was in favor of Mr. Sherman's motion. If Sir, said he, the amendments are incorporated in the instrument, it will assert that which is not true—for this Constitution has been signed by the delegates from the several States as a true instrument—and therefore in this case we must go further, and say, that a constitution made at such a time was defective, and GEORGE WASHINGTON, and those other worthy characters who signed this instrument, cannot be said to have signed the Constitution. According to the observation of the gentleman from South-Carolina, respecting repealing laws to make a complete act, we must repeal the Constitution in order to make a new one—but will any gentleman say that this legislature has authority to do this? To incorporate these amendments, the Constitution must however be repealed in part, at least—The moment we prepare ourselves to do this, there is an end of the Constitution, and to the authority under which we act. Mr. Stone then replied particularly to the inference drawn by Mr. Smith from the passage which he had quoted from the Constitution, and observed, that the words could not imply any thing more than this, that such amendments, when adopted, agreeably to the mode pointed out, would be equally binding with the other parts of the system to which they do not specially refer.

Mr. GERRY enquired whether the mode could make any possible difference in the validity of the system, provided the sanction is the same—he conceived it could not—The constitution in my opinion, said he, has provided that amendments should be incorporated—the words are express, that they shall become "*part* of this constitution." The gentleman, (Mr. Stone) says we shall lose the names of the worthy gentlemen who subscribed the constitution—but I would ask, whether the names would be of any consequence, except the constitution had been ratified by the several States? or will the system be of no effect since it is ratified, if the names were now erased? If we adopt the mode proposed, we shall in all probability go on to make supplements to supplements, and thus involve the system in a maze of doubts and perplexities. It appears to me, that in order that the citizens of the United States may know what the constitution is, it is necessary that it be comprized in one uniform, entire system. If the amendments are incorporated, the people will have one constitution; but if they are added by way of supplement, they will have more than one: And if in the original system there should any clauses be found, which are inconsistent with the added amendments, the government will be compounded of opposite principles, both in force at the same time.

Upon the idea of gentlemen as to the sacredness of the original system, if amendments are made upon their plan, they will be considered in a point of light inferior to the original; in this view, amendments are of no consequence, and had better be omitted. This would tend to defeat the salutary purposes of amendments altogether, by derogating from their dignity and authority.

Mr. LAURANCE was in favor of the motion made by Mr. Sherman—he said, it appeared to him impossible to incorporate the amendments in the constitution without involving very great absurdities in the supposition—if they should be engrafted in the body of the constitution, it will make it speak a language different from what it originally did—What will become of the laws enacted under the instrument as it originally stood? Will they not be vitiated thereby? The ratifications of the several States had respect to the original system. It is true that a majority of them have proposed amendments, but this does not imply a necessity of altering the original, so as to make it a different system from that which was ratified. The mode proposed by the motion is agreeable to custom—it is the least liable to objection, and appears to me safe and proper.

Mr. BENSON observed, that this question was agitated in the select committee, and the result is contained in the report now under consideration—It should be remembered, that the ratifications of several of the States enjoin the alterations and amendments in this way; they propose that some words should be struck out, and the sentences altered—I do not conceive that incorporating the amendments can affect the validity of the original constitution—that will remain where it is, in the archives of Congress unaltered with all the names of the original subscribers. The amendments are provided for in that instrument, and the compleating those amendments is compleating the original system—the records of the legislature will inform how this was done; and for my part, I can see no difficulty in proceeding agreeable to the report of the committee.

Mr. PAGE said that he supposed that the committee of the whole is now acting upon the constitution as upon a bill—and they have a right, said he, to take up the subject paragraph by paragraph.

I am opposed to the amendment of the preamble of the constitution as proposed by the committee, as well as to the motion of the gentleman from Connecticut—I could wish therefore that we may not consume time in settling the meer form of conducting the business—but proceed, after rejecting the first amendment, to consider those that are subsequent in the report.

Mr. LIVERMORE replied to Mr. Page—he said, that with respect to the constitution, the committee stood upon quite different grounds from what they did when discussing a bill, and he contended that it is not in the power either of the legislature of the United States, or of all the legislatures upon the continent to alter the constitution, unless they were specially empowered by the people to do it.

Mr. JACKSON advocated the motion of Mr. Sherman—he said, if we repeal this constitution we shall perhaps the next year have to make another—and in that way the people will never be able to know whether they have a permanent constitution or not. The constitution in my opinion ought to remain sacred and inviolate—I will refer to the constitution of England—Magna Charta has remained as it was received from King John to the present day, and the Bill of Rights the same; and although the rights of the people in several respects have been more clearly ascertained and defined, those charters remain entire: A constitutional privilege has lately been established in the independency of the Judges, but no alteration in the constitution itself was thought proper. All the amendments are supplementary—the sacred deposit of English liberty remains untouched—their great charter remains unaltered, though defects have been supplied and additions made. The constitution of the United States has been made by the people; it is their own act, and they have a right to it. I hope we shall not do any thing to violate or mutilate it.

I therefore heartily join in the motion for striking out the words and adopting the mode proposed by the gentleman from Connecticut.

Several of the gentlemen spoke repeatedly upon the subject, but time will not admit of our enlarging further. The question on Mr. Sherman's motion being taken, it passed in the negative.

A doubt was then raised, whether it was necessary that the article in the constitution which requires that two thirds of the legislature should recommend amendments, should be attended to by the committee—this occasioned a debate—an appeal was made to the chairman, who determined that the business while before the committee, should be transacted in the usual manner by a majority—an appeal was made from this judgment to the house, and on the question, being put, whether the chairman's decision was in order, it passed in the affirmative.

The Congressional Register, 13 August 1789

Mr. LEE

Moved that the house now resolve itself into a committee of the whole, on the report of the committee of eleven, to whom it had been referred to take the subject of amendments to the constitution of the United States generally into their consideration.

Mr. PAGE

Hoped the house would agree to the motion of his colleague without hesitation, because he conceived it essentially necessary to proceed and finish the business as speedily as possible; for whatever might be the fact with respect to the security which the citizens of America had for their rights and liberties under the new constitution, yet unless they saw it in that light they would be uneasy, not to say dissatisfied.

He thought, likewise, that the business would be expedited by the simplicity and self-evidence which the propositions reported, possessed, as it was impossible that much debate could take place.

Mr. SEDGWICK

Was sorry that the motion was made, because he looked upon this as a very improper time to enter upon the consideration of a subject which would undoubtedly consume many days, and when they had so much other and more important business requiring immediate attention; he begged gentlemen to recollect that all they had hitherto done was of little or no effect, their impost and tonnage laws were but a dead letter.

Mr. MADISON

Did not think it was an improper time to proceed in this business; the house had already gone through with subjects of a less interesting nature; now, if the judiciary bill was of such vast importance, its consideration ought not to have been postponed for those purposes.

He would remind gentlemen that there were many who conceived amendments of some kind necessary and proper in themselves; while others who are not so well satisfied of the necessity and propriety, may think they are rendered expedient from some other consideration. Is it desirable to keep up a division among the people of the United States on a point in which they consider their most essential rights are concerned? If this is an object worthy the attention of such a numerous part of our constituents, why should we decline taking it into our consideration, and thereby promote that spirit of urbanity and unanimity which the government itself stands in need of for its more full support?

Already has the subject been delayed much more than could have been wished: If after having fixed a day for taking it into consideration, we should put it off again, a spirit of jealousy may be excited, and not allayed, without great inconvenience.

Mr. VINING.

Impressed by the anxiety which the honorable gentleman from Virginia had discovered for having the subject of amendments considered, had agreed, in his own mind, to wave for the present, the call he was well authorised to make, for the house to take into consideration the bill for establishing a land-office for the disposal of the vacant lands in the western territory; in point of time his motion had the priority, in point of importance every candid mind would acknowledge its preference, and he conceived the house was bound to pay attention to it as early as possible; as they had given leave for a bill to be brought in, they ought not to neglect proceeding onward with it.

Mr. SEDGWICK

Hoped the house would not consume their time in a lengthy discussion upon what business should be done first; he was of opinion that there were several matters before them of more importance than the present, and he believed the people abroad were neither anxious nor jealous about it; but if they were, they would be satisfied at the delay, when they were informed of the cause: He begged therefore that the question proposed by the gentleman from Virginia, (mr. Lee) might be put without further debate.

Mr. SMITH [*S.C.*]

Said that the judicial bill was entitled to the preference in point of order, and in point of propriety it deserved the first attention of the house; for his part he could not conceive the necessity of going into any alterations of the government until the government itself was perfected; the constitution establishes three branches to constitute a whole; the legislative and executive are now in existence; but the judicial is uncreated; while we remain in this state not a single part of the revenue system can operate; no breach of your laws can be punished; illicit trade cannot be prevented; greater harm will arise from delaying the establishment of the judicial system, than can possibly grow from a delay of the other subject. If gentlemen are willing to let it lie over to a period of greater leisure, I shall join them chearfully and candidly, said he, in a full discussion of that business.

An honorable gentleman from Virginia observed to us that these propositions were so self evident, that little or no debate could grow out of them; that may be his opinion, but truly, sir, it is not mine, for I think some of them are not self evident, and some of them will admit of lengthy discussion, and other some, I hope, may be rejected, while their place may be better supplied by others hereafter to be brought forward: Some members are pledged to support amendments, and will no doubt support them with all the arguments their fancy or ingenuity can suggest; viewing it in this light, is it to be expected that the discussion will be ended in less than a fortnight or three weeks, and let gentlemen consult their own feelings whether they have so much time now to spare.

Mr. Hartley

Thought the judicial system ought to be finished before any other business was entered upon, and was willing to consider of amendments to the constitution when the house was more disengaged, because he wished very much that the constitution was so modified as to give satisfaction to honest and candid minds, such would be satisfied with securing to themselves and their posterity, all those blessings of freedom which they are now possessed of; As to the artful and designing, who had clamored against the whole work, he had not the smallest desire to gratify them; he hoped and trusted their numbers were but few.

Mr. Gerry

Thought the discussion would take up more time than the house could now spare; he was therefore in favor of postponing the consideration of the subject, until the judicial bill, and the bill for registering and clearing vessels, and some other bills relating to the revenue business were gone through. He asked the gentleman from Virginia, if he conceived that the amendments in the report were all that were to be taken into consideration; he thought the community would be little more pleased with them than if they had omitted the subject altogether; besides, it was absurd to suppose that the members were obliged to confine their deliberations solely to those objects when it was very well known that the members from Massachusetts and New-Hampshire were bound to bring forward and support others; the members from other states may be inclined to do the same with respect to the amendments of their own conventions, this will inevitably produce a more copious debate than what the gentleman contemplates; upon these considerations it might be hoped that honorable gentlemen would no longer press the motion.

Mr. Laurance.

Had no objection to consider of amendments at a proper time, but did not think that the present was a proper time to enter upon them, nor did he suppose that gentlemen would be precluded from a full discussion of the whole subject whenever it was taken up: Gentlemen would find him ready to acquiesce in every thing that was proper, but he could not consent to let the great business of legislation stand still, and thereby incur an absolute evil in order to rid themselves of an imaginary one, for whether the subject of amendments was considered now or at a more distant period, appeared to his mind a matter of mere indifference: It may further be observed, that few, if any of the state assemblies, are now in session, consequently the business could not be completed even if congress had already done their part; but certainly the people in general are more anxious to see the government in operation than speculative amendments upon an untried constitution.

Mr. MADISON.

I beg leave to make one or two remarks more in consequence of the observations which have fell from the different sides of the house: Some gentlemen seem to think that additional propositions will be brought forward, whether they will or not I cannot pretend to say; but if they are, I presume they will be no impediment to our deciding upon those contained in the report. But gentlemen who introduce these propositions will see, that if they are to produce more copious debate than has hitherto taken place, they will consume a great part of the remainder of the session. I wish the subject well considered, but I do not wish to see any unnecessary waste of time, and gentlemen will please to remember that this subject has yet to go before the senate.

I admit, with the worthy gentleman who preceded me, that a great number of the community are solicitous to see the government carried into operation; but I believe that there is a considerable part also anxious to secure those rights which they are apprehensive are endangered by the present constitution; now, considering the full confidence they reposed at the time of its adoption in their future representatives, I think we ought to pursue the subject to effect. I confess it has always appeared to me in point of candor and good faith, as well as policy, to be incumbent on the first legislature of the United States, at their first session, to make such alterations in the constitution as will give satisfaction without injuring or destroying any of its vital principles.

I should not press the subject at this time, because I am well aware of the importance of the other business enumerated by the gentlemen who are adverse to the present motion, but, from an apprehension that if it is delayed until the other is gone through, that gentlemen's patience and application will be so harassed and fatigued as to oblige them to leave it an unfinished state, until the next session; beside, was the judicial bill even to pass now, it could not take effect until others were enacted, which probably at this time are not drawn up.

Mr. SMITH [*S.C.*].

The honorable gentleman has concluded his remarks by assigning the best reason in the world why we should go into a consideration of the judicial bill; he says that even if it was now passed, it would take some time before it could get into operation, he must admit it to be an essential part of the government, and as such ought not to remain a single instant in a state of torpidity.

Mr. FITZSIMONS

Wished the gentleman would suffer the question to be put, and not consume their time in arguing about what should be done: If a majority was not in favor of considering amendments they might proceed to some other business.

Mr. PAGE

Was positive the people would never support the government, unless their anxiety was removed; they in some instances, adopted it, in confidence of its being speedily amended; they will complain of being deceived, unless their expectations are fulfilled. So much time has elapsed since the subject was first brought forward, said he, that people will not think us serious, unless we now set about and complete it.

He begged gentlemen to consider the importance of the number of citizens, who were anxious for amendments; if these had been added to those who openly opposed the constitution, it possibly might have met a different fate. Can the government, under these circumstances, possess energy, as some gentlemen suppose? Is not the confidence of the people absolutely necessary to support it?

The question was now put, and carried in the affirmative. The house then resolved itself into a committee of the whole, and took the amendments under consideration. The first article run thus, "*In the introductory paragraph of the constitution, before the words* "WE THE PEOPLE," Add "Government being intended for the benefit of the people and the rightful establishment thereof, being derived from their authority alone."

Mr. SHERMAN.

I believe, mr. chairman, this is not the proper mode of amending the constitution. We ought not to interweave our propositions into the work itself, because it will be destructive of the whole fabric. We might as well endeavor to mix brass, iron and clay, as to incorporate such heterogeneous articles; the one contradictory to the other. Its absurdity will be discovered by comparing it with a law: would any legislature endeavor to introduce into a former act, a subsequent amendment, and let them stand so connected. When an alteration is made in an act, it is done by way of supplement; the latter act always repealing the former in every specified case of difference.

Beside this, sir, it is questionable, whether we have the right to propose amendments in this way. The constitution is the act of the people, and ought to remain entire. But the amendments will be the act of the state governments; again all the authority we possess, is derived from that instrument; if we mean to destroy the whole and establish a new constitution, we remove the basis on which we mean to build. For these reasons I will move to strike out that paragraph and substitute another.

The paragraph proposed, was to the following effect; Resolved by the senate and house of representatives of the United States in congress assembled, That the following articles be proposed as amendments to the constitution; and when ratified by three fourths of the state legislatures shall become valid to all intents and purposes, as part of the same.

Under this title, the amendments might come in nearly as stated in the report, only varying the phraseology so as to accommodate them to a supplementary form.

Mr. MADISON.

Form, sir, is always of less importance than the substance; but on this occasion, I admit that form is of some consequence, and it will be well for the house to pursue that, which upon reflection, shall appear to be the most eligible. Now it appears to me, that there is a neatness and propriety in incorporating the amendments into the constitution itself; in that case the system will remain uniform and entire; it will certainly be more simple, when the amendments are interwoven into those parts to which they naturally belong, than it will if they consist of separate and distinct parts; we shall then be able to determine its meaning without references or comparison; whereas, if they are supplementary, its meaning can only be ascertained by a comparison of the two instruments, which will be a very considerable embarrassment, it will be difficult to ascertain to what parts of the instrument the amendments particularly refer; they will create unfavorable comparisons, whereas if they are placed upon the footing here proposed, they will stand upon as good foundation as the original work.

Nor is it so uncommon a thing as gentlemen suppose, systematic men frequently take up the whole law, and with its amendments and alterations reduce it into one act. I am not, however, very solicitous about the form, provided the business is but well completed.

Mr. SMITH [*S.C.*]

Did not think the amendment proposed by the honorable gentleman from Connecticut was compatible with the constitution, which declared, that the amendments recommended by congress, and ratified by the legislatures of three fourths of the several states should be part of this constitution; in which case it would form one complete system; but according to the idea of the amendment, the instrument is to have five or six suits of improvements, such a mode seems more calculated to embarrass the people than any thing else, while nothing in his opinion was a juster cause of complaint than the difficulties of knowing the law, arising from legislative obscurities that might easily be avoided. He said that it had certainly been the custom in several of the state governments, to amend their laws by way of supplement; but South Carolina had been an instance of the contrary practice, in revising the old code; instead of making acts in addition to acts, which is always attended with perplexity, she has incorporated them, and brought them forward as a complete system, repealing the old. This is what he understood was intended to be done by the committee, the present copy of the constitution was to be done away, and a new one substituted in its stead.

Mr. TUCKER

Wished to know whether the deliberations of the committee were intended to be confined to the propositions on the table, if they were not, he should beg leave to bring before them the amendments proposed by South Carolina; he considered himself as instructed to bring them forward, and he meant to perform his duty by an early and prompt obedience. He wished to have the sense of the house on this point, whether he was in order to bring them forward.

Mr. LIVERMORE

Was clearly of opinion that whatever amendments were made to the constitution, that they ought to stand separate from the original instrument. We have no right, said he, to alter a clause, any otherwise than by a new proposition. We have well-established precedents for such a mode of procedure in the practice of the British parliament, and the state legislatures throughout America. I do not mean, however, to assert that there has been no instance of a repeal of a whole law on enacting another; but this has generally taken place on account of the complexity of the original, with its supplements. Were we a mere legislative body, no doubt it might be warrantable in us to pursue a similar method, but it is questionable whether it is possible for us, consistent with the oath we have taken, to attempt a repeal of the constitution of the United States, by making a new one to substitute in its place; the reason of this is grounded on a very simple consideration. It is by virtue of the present constitution, I presume, that we attempt to make another; now, if we proceed to the repeal of this, I cannot see upon what authority we shall erect another; if we destroy the base, the superstructure falls of course. At some future day it may be asked upon what authority we proceeded to raise and appropriate public monies, we suppose we do it in virtue of the present constitution; but it may be doubted whether we have a right to exercise any of its authorities, while it is suspended, as it will certainly be, from the time that two-thirds of both houses have agreed to submit it to the state legislatures; so that unless we mean to destroy the whole constitution, we ought to be careful how we attempt to amend it in the way proposed by the committee. From hence I presume it will be more prudent to adopt the mode proposed by the gentleman from Connecticut, than it will be to risk the destruction of the whole by proposing amendments in the manner recommended by the committee.

Mr. VINING

Disliked a supplementary form, and said it was a bad reason to urge the practice of former ages when there was a more convenient method of doing the business at hand; he had seen an act entitled an act to amend a supplement to an act entitled an act for altering part of act entitled an act for certain purposes therein mentioned. If gentlemen were disposed to run into such jargon in amending and altering the constitution, he could not help it; but he trusted they would adopt a plainness and simplicity of style on this and every other occasion, which should be easily understood. If the mode proposed by the gentleman from Connecticut was adopted, the system would be distorted, and like a careless written letter, have more matter attached to it in a postscript than was contained in the original composition.

The constitution being a great and important work, ought all to be brought into one view, and made as intelligible as possible.

Mr. CLYMER

Was of opinion with the gentleman from Connecticut, that the amendments ought not to be incorporated in the body of the work, which he hoped would remain a monument to justify those who made it; by a comparison, the world would discover the perfection of the original, and the superfluity of the amendments; he made this distinction because he did not conceive any of the amendments essential, but as they were solicited by his fellow citizens, and for that reason they were acquiesced in by others; he therefore wished the motion for throwing them into a supplementary form might be carried.

Mr. STONE.

It is not a matter of much consequence with respect to the preservation of the original instrument, whether the amendments are incorporated or made distinct; because the records will always shew the original form in which it stood. But in my opinion we ought to mark its progress with truth in every step we take. If the amendments are incorporated in the body of the work, it will appear, unless we refer to the archives of congress, that George Washington, and the other worthy characters who composed the convention, signed an instrument which they never had in contemplation. The one to which he affixed his signature purports to be adopted by the unanimous consent of the delegates from every state there assembled.

Now if we incorporate these amendments, we must undoubtedly go further, and say that the constitution so formed, was defective, and had need of alteration; we therefore purpose to repeal the old and substitute a new one in its place. From this consideration alone I think we ought not to pursue the line of conduct drawn for us by the committee. This perhaps is not the last amendment the constitution may receive, we ought therefore to be careful how we set a precedent which in dangerous and turbulent times may unhinge the whole.

With respect to the observations of the gentleman from South Carolina, I shall just remark, that we have no authority to repeal the whole constitution. The words refered to in that instrument, only authorise us to propose amendments to it, which, when properly ratified, are to become valid as a part of the same; but these can never be construed to empower us to make a new constitution.

For these reasons I would wish our expressions might be so guarded as to purport nothing but what we really have in view.

Mr. LIVERMORE.

The mode adopted by the committee, might be very proper provided congress had the forming of a constitution in contemplation; then they, or an individual member might propose to strike out a clause and insert another, as is done with respect to article 3, section 2. But certainly no gentleman, acquainted with legislative business, would pretend to alter and amend in this manner, a law already passed. He was convinced it could not be done properly in any other way than by the one proposed by the gentleman from Connecticut.

Mr. GERRY

Asked if the the mode could make any possible difference, provided the sanction was the same; or whether it would operate differently in any one instance? If it will not, we are disputing about form, and the question will turn on the expediency. Now one gentleman tells you, said he, that he is so attached to this instrument that he is unwilling to lose any part of it; therefore to gratify him, we may throw it into a supplementary form. But let me ask, will not this as effectually destroy some parts, as if the correction had been made by way of incorporation, or will posterity have a more favorable opinion of the original, because it has been amended by distinct acts? For my part I cannot see what advantage can accrue from adopting the motion of the honorable gentleman from Connecticut, unless it be to give every one the trouble of erasing out of his copy of the constitution certain words and sentences, and inserting others. But perhaps in our great veneration for the original composition, we may go farther, and pass an act to prohibit these interpolations, as it may injure the text.

All this, sir, I take to be trifling about matters of little consequence. The constitution has undoubtedly provided, that the amendments shall be incorporated, if I understand the import of the words, "and shall be valid to all intents and purposes, as part of the constitution." If it had said that the present form should be preserved, then it would be proper to propose the alterations by way of a supplement. One gentleman has said we shall loose the names that are now annexed to the instrument. They are names, sir, I admit, of high respect; but I would ask that gentleman, if they would give validity to the constitution if it was not ratified by the several states, or if their names was struck out, whether it would be of less force than it is at present? If he answers these questions in the negative, I shall consider it of no consequence whether the names are appended to it or not. But it will be time enough to discuss this point when a motion is made for striking them out.

If we proceed in the way proposed by the honorable gentleman from Connecticut, I presume the title of our first amendment will be, a supplement to the constitution of the United States; the next a supplement to the supplement, and so on, until we have supplements annexed five times in five years, wrapping up the constitution in a maze of perplexity; and as great an adept as that honorable gentleman is at finding out the truth, it will take him, I apprehend, a week or a fortnight's study to ascertain the true meaning of the constitution.

It is said, if the amendments are incorporated it will be a virtual repeal of the constitution; I say the effect will be the same in a supplementary way, consequently the objection goes for nothing, or it goes against making any amendments whatever.

It is said that the present form of the amendments is contrary to the 5th article: I will not undertake to define the extent of the word amendment, as it stands in the fifth article; but I suppose if we proposed to change the division of the powers given to the three branches of the government, and that proposition is accepted and ratified by three-fourths of the state legislatures, it will become as valid to all intents and purposes as any part of the constitution; but if it is the opinion of gentlemen that the original is to be kept sacred, amendments will be of no use, and had better be omitted; whereas, on the other hand, if they are to be received as equal in authority, we shall have five or six constitutions, perhaps differing in material points from each other, but all equally valid; so that they may require a man of science to determine what is or is not the constitution, this will certainly be attended with great inconvenience, as the several states are bound up not to make laws contradictory thereto, and all officers sworn to support it without knowing precisely what it is.

Mr. STONE

Asked the gentleman last up, how he meant to have the amendments incorporated? Was it intended to have the constitution republished, and the alterations inserted in their proper places? He did not see how it was practicable to propose amendments, without making out a new constitution, in the manner brought forward by the committee.

Mr. LAURANCE

Could not conceive how gentlemen meant to ingraft the amendments into the constitution: The original one executed by the convention at Philadelphia, was lodged in the archives of the late congress, it was impossible for this house to take and correct and interpolate that without making it speak a different language, this would be supposing several things which never were contemplated. But what, said he, would become of the acts of congress; they will certainly be vitiated, unless they are provided for, by an additional clause in the constitution.

What shall we say with respect to the ratifications of the several states; they adopted the original constitution, but they have not thereby enabled us to change the one form of government for another. It is true amendments were proposed by some of them, but it does not follow of necessity, that we should alter the form of the original which they have ratified. Amendments in this way are only proper in legislative business, while the bill is on its passage, as was justly observed before.

Mr. BENSON

Said, that this question had been agitated in the select committee, and determined in favor of the form, in which it was reported; he believed this decision was founded in a great degree upon the recommendation of the state conventions, who had proposed amendments in this very form; this pointed out the mode most agreeable to the people of America, and therefore the one most eligible for congress to pursue; it will likewise be the most convenient way. Suppose the amendments ratified by the several states; congress may order a number of copies to be printed, into which the alterations will be inserted, and the work stand perfect and entire.

I believe it never was contemplated by any gentlemen to alter the original constitution deposited in the archives of the union, that will remain there with the names of those who formed it, while the government has a being. But certainly there is convenience and propriety in completing the work in a way provided for in itself. The records of congress, and the several states, will mark the progress of the business, and nothing will appear to be done but what is actually performed.

Mr. MADISON.

The gentleman last up has left me but one remark to add, and that is, if we adopt the amendment, we shall so far unhinge the business as to occasion alterations in every article and clause of the report.

Mr. HARTLEY

Hoped the committee would not agree to the alteration, because it would perplex the business: He wished the propositions to be simple and entire, that the state legislatures might decide without hesitation, and every man know what was the ground on which he rested his political welfare. Besides, the consequent changes which the motion would induce, were such as he feared would take up some days if not weeks; and the time of the house was too precious to be squandered away in discussing mere matter of form.

Mr. PAGE

Was sorry to find the gentlemen stop at the preamble, he hoped they would proceed as soon as the obstruction was removed, and that would be when the motion was negatived.

He thought the best way to view this subject, was to look at the constitution as a bill on its passage through the house, and to consider and amend its defects article by article, for which reason he was for entering at once upon the main business; after that was gone through it would be time enough to arrange the materials with which the house intended to form the preamble.

Mr. LIVERMORE

Insisted, that neither this legislature nor all the legislatures in America were authorized to repeal a constitution; and that must be an inevitable consequence of an attempt to amend it in the way proposed by the committee, he would then submit to gentlemen, the propriety of the alteration. As to the difficulty which had been supposed in understanding supplemental laws; he thought but little of it; he imagined, there were things in the constitution more difficult to comprehend, than any thing he had yet seen in the amendments.

Mr. JACKSON.

I do not like to differ with gentlemen about form, but as so much had been said, I wish to give my opinion, it is this, that the original constitution ought to remain inviolate, and not be patched up from time to time, with various stuffs resembling Joseph's coat of many colors.[17]

Some gentlemen talk of repealing the present constitution, and adopting an improved one. If we have this power, we may go on from year to year, making new ones; and in this way we shall render the basis of the superstructure the most fluctuating thing imaginable, and the people will never know what the constitution is. As for the alteration proposed by the committee to prefix before "We the people," certain dogmas, I cannot agree to it; the words as they now stand speak as much as it is possible to speak, it is a practical recognition of the right of the people to ordain and establish governments, and is more expressive than any other mere paper declaration.

[17]Genesis 37:3.

But why will gentlemen contend for incorporating amendments into the constitution? They say that it is necessary for the people to have the whole before them in one view; have they precedent for this assertion? Look at the constitution of Great Britain, is that all contained in one instrument? It is well known, that *magna charta* was extorted by the barons from king John some centuries ago. Has that been altered since by the incorporation of amendments? Or does it speak the same language now, as it did at the time it was obtained? Sir, it is not altered a tittle from its original form. Yet there has been many amendments and improvements in the constitution of Britain since that period. In the subsequent reign of his son, the great charters were confirmed with some supplemental acts. Is the *habeas corpus* act, or the statute *De Tallagio non concedendo*[18] incorporated in magna charta? And yet there is not an Englishman but would spill the last drop of his blood in their defence; it is these, with some other acts of parliament and magna charta, that form the basis of English liberty. We have seen amendments to their constitution during the present reign, by establishing the independence of the judges, who are hereafter to be appointed during good behavior; formerly they were at the pleasure of the crown. But was this done by striking out and inserting other words in the great charter? No, sir, the constitution is composed of many distinct acts, but an Englishman would be ashamed to own that on this account he could not ascertain his own privileges or the authority of the government.

The constitution of the union has been ratified and established by the people, let their act remain inviolable; if any thing we can do has a tendency to improve it, let it be done, but without mutilating and defacing the original.

Mr. SHERMAN.

If I had looked upon this question as mere matter of form, I should not have brought it forward or troubled the committee with such a lengthy discussion. But, sir, I contend that amendments made in the way proposed by the committee are void: No gentleman ever knew an addition and alteration introduced into an existing law, and that any part of such law was left in force; but if it was improved or altered by a supplemental act, the original retained all its validity and importance in every case where the two were not incompatible. But if these observations alone should be thought insufficient to support my motion, I would desire

[18]The 1297 statute *De Tallagio non concedendo* placed limitations on the right of the English kings to levy arbitrary taxes. This right was finally surrendered by statute in 1340. The British Habeas Corpus Act was passed in 1679.

gentlemen to consider the authorities upon which the two constitutions are to stand. The original was established by the people at large by conventions chosen by them for the express purpose. The preamble to the constitution declares the act: But will it be a truth in ratifying the next constitution, which is to be done perhaps by the state legislatures, and not conventions chosen for the purpose. Will gentlemen say it is "We the people" in this case, certainly they cannot, for by the present constitution, we nor all the legislatures in the union together, do not possess the power of repealing it: All that is granted us by the 5th article is, that whenever we shall think it necessary, we may propose *amendments to the constitution*; not that we may propose to repeal the old, and substitute a new one.

Gentlemen say it would be convenient to have it in one instrument that people might see the whole at once; for my part I view no difficulty on this point. The amendments reported are a declaration of rights, the people are secure in them whether we declare them or not; the last amendment but one provides that the three branches of government shall each exercise its own rights, this is well secured already; and in short, I do not see that they lessen the force of any article in the constitution, if so, there can be little more difficulty in comprehending them whether they are combined in one, or stand distinct instruments.

Mr. SMITH [*S.C.*]

Read extracts from the amendments proposed by several of the state conventions at the time they ratified the constitution, from which he said it appeared that they were generally of opinion that the phraseology of the constitution ought to be altered; nor would this mode of proceeding repeal any part of the constitution but such as it touched, the remainder will be in force during the time of considering it and ever after.

As to the observations made by the honorable gentleman from Georgia, respecting the amendments made to the constitution of Great-Britain, they did not apply—the cases were nothing like similar, and consequently could not be drawn into precedent. The constitution of Britain is neither the magna charta of John, nor the Habeas Corpus act, nor all the charters put together; it is what the parliament wills; it is true there are rights granted to the subject that cannot be resumed, but the constitution or form of government may be altered by the authority of parliament, whose power is absolute without controul.

Mr. SENEY

Was afraid the house would consume more time than was at first apprehended in discussing the subject of amendments, if he was to infer any thing from what had now taken place: He hoped the question would soon be put and decided.

Mr. VINING

Was an enemy to unnecessary debate, but he conceived the question to be an important one, and was not displeased with the discussion that had taken place; he should, however, vote in favor of the most simple mode.

Mr. GERRY

The honorable gentleman from Connecticut, if I understand him right, says that the words, "We the people" cannot be retained if congress should propose amendments, and they be ratified by the state legislatures: Now if this is a fact, we ought most undoubtedly adopt his motion; because if we do not, we cannot obtain any amendment whatever. But upon what ground does the gentleman's position stand? The constitution of the United States was proposed by a convention met at Philadelphia, but with all its importance it did not possess as high authority as the president, senate, and house of representatives of the union: For that convention was not convened in consequence of any express will of the people, but an implied one, through their members in the state legislatures. The constitution derived no authority from the first convention; it was concurred in by conventions of the people, and that concurrence armed it with power, and invested it with dignity. Now the congress of the United States are expressly authorised by the sovereign and uncontrollable voice of the people, to propose amendments whenever two-thirds of both houses shall think fit: Now if this is the fact, the propositions of amendment will be found to originate with a higher authority than the original system. The conventions of the states respectively have agreed for the people, that the state legislatures shall be authorised to decide upon these amendments in the manner of a convention. If these acts of the state legislatures are not good because they are not specifically instructed by their constituents, neither were the acts calling the first and subsequent conventions.

Does he mean to put amendments on this ground, that after they have been ratified by the state legislatures they are not to have the same authority as the original instrument; if this is his meaning, let him avow it, and if it is well founded, we may save ourselves the trouble of proceeding in the business. But for my part I have no doubt but a ratification of the amendments, in any form, would be as valid as any part of the constitution. The legislatures are elected by the people; I know no difference between them and conventions, unless it be that the former will generally be composed of men of higher characters than may be expected in conventions; and in this case, the ratification by the legislatures would have the preference.

Now if it is clear that the effect will be the same in either mode, will gentlemen hesitate to approve the most simple and clear? It will undoubtedly be more agreeable to have it all brought into one instrument, than have to refer to five or six different acts.

Mr. SHERMAN.

The gentlemen who oppose the motion say we contend for matter of form; they think it nothing more; now we say we contend for substance, and therefore cannot agree to amendments in this way. If they are so desirous of having the business compleated, they had better sacrifice what they consider but a matter of indifference to get gentlemen to go more unanimously along with them in altering the constitution.

The question on mr. Sherman's motion was now put and lost.

Mr. LIVERMORE

Wished to know whether it was necessary, in order to carry a motion in committee, that two-thirds should agree.

Mr. HARTLEY

Mentioned that in Pennsylvania they had a council of censors who were authorised to call a convention to amend the constitution when it was thought necessary, but two-thirds were required for that purpose; he had been a member of that body, when they had examined the business in a committee of council, the majority made a report, which was lost for want of two-thirds to carry it through the council.

Some desultory conversation took place on this subject, when it was decided by the chairman of the committee, that a majority of the committee were sufficient to form a report.

An appeal being made from the opinion of the chair, it was, after some observations, confirmed by the committee, after which the committee rose and reported progress.

14 AUGUST 1789

The Daily Advertiser, 15 August 1789

The house went into a committee on the amendments to the Constitution.

Mr. TRUMBULL in the chair.

The first amendment was again read, which was to fix per to the introductory paragraph these words, "Government being intended for the benefit of the people and the rightful establishment thereof being derived from their authority alone."

Mr. GERRY objected to the phraseology of this clause; it might seem to imply that all Governments were instituted and intended for the benefit of the people, which was not true. Indeed most of the governments both of antient and modern times were calculated on very different principles. They had chiefly originated in fraud or in force; and were designed for the purpose of oppression and personal ambition. He wished to have nothing go out from this body as a maxim, which was false in fact or which was not clear in its construction. He moved to alter the clause, by inserting the words "of right."

This motion was negatived.

Mr. TUCKER objected to any amendments being made to the preamble of the constitution. This he said, was no part of the constitution, and the object was only to amend the constitution: The preamble was no more a subject of amendment than the letter of the President annexed to the constitution.[19]

Mr. SMITH (S.C.) in answer to Mr. TUCKER shewed that this amendment had been recommended by three states; and that it was proper it should be made.

Mr. TUCKER replied that he was not opposed to the principle, but thought this was an improper place to express it; it could be inserted with propriety in a bill of rights, if one should be agreed on, and in that form be prefixed to the constitution, but the preamble was not the place for it.

Others objected to the whole clause as it was unnecessary, since the words, "We the people" contained in itself the principle of the amendment fully. Mr. SHERMAN observed that if the constitution had been a grant from another power, it would be proper to express this principle; but as the right expressed in the amendment was natural and inherent in the people, it is unnecessary to give any reasons or any ground on which they made their constitution. It was the act of their own sovereign will. It was also said that it would injure the beauty of the preamble.

Mr. MADISON contended for the amendment—He saw no difficulty in associating the amendment with the preamble without injuring the propriety or sense of the paragraph. Though it was indisputable that the principle was on all hands acknowledged, and could itself derive no force from expressing, yet he thought it prudent to insert it as it had been recommended by three respectable states.

The question on adopting the amendment being put, was carried in the affirmative.

Second amendment; from Art. 1. Sec. 2. par. 3. strike out all between the word "direct" and "until such" and instead thereof insert, "after the

---

[19] Washington's letter of 17 September 1787, as president of the Federal Convention, transmitting the proposed Constitution to Congress, can be found in *DHROC* 1:305–6.

first enumeration, there shall be one representative for every thirty thousand, until the number shall amount to one hundred; after which the proportion shall be so regulated by Congress, that the number of representatives shall never be less than one hundred, nor more than one hundred and seventy five, but each state shall always have at least one representative."

Mr. VINING moved that a clause should be inserted in the paragraph, providing that when any one state possessed forty five thousand inhabitants, it should be entitled to two representatives.

This was negatived without a division.

Mr. AMES then moved to strike out the word "thirty" and insert "forty," so that the ratio of representation should be one for forty thousand—He went into a train of reasoning to prove the superior advantages of a small representation: He drew an argument, in the first place, from the satisfaction which the people universally expressed in the present representation, that their minds were reconciled to it, and were convinced that a more faithful and more prompt discharge of the business of the Union would take place in so small an assembly. Experience had taught them that all the information that was necessary both of a general and local nature, would be found in a body similar to the present. He suggested the importance of the expence of a numerous representation, as a capital burthen, which would soon become dissatisfactory to the people. According to the ratio of 1 to 30,000, the increase of the people would swell the representation to an enormous mass, whose support would be insufferable, and whose deliberations would be rendered almost impracticable. The present population would, on the first census, produce upwards of 100. The augmentation would be very rapid; it was therefore proper to fix the proportion immediately, so as to prevent these evils—He went very copiously into the usual arguments to prove that all numerous popular bodies are liable in proportion to their number, of fluctuations, fermentations and a factious spirit—By enlarging the representation, the government, he said, would depart from that choice of characters who could best represent the wisdom and the interest of the United States; and who would alone be able to support the importance and dignity of this branch of the legislature—Men would be introduced, more liable to improper influences, and more easy tools for designing leaders.

Mr. AMES said it appeared clear to him that as the whole number was increased, the individual consequence, the pride of character, and consequently the responsibility of each member. The responsibility would also be in some proportion to the number of the constituents. A representative of a large body of people would feel in a higher degree the weight imposed upon him, and he would be thereby the more interested to support a virtuous fame, and redouble his exertions for the public good.

Mr. Ames contended that the original design of those who proposed the amendments respecting representation, was not to obtain an increase beyond what the first census would give them; their intention was to fix a limitation, that it should not be in the power of Congress to diminish the representation at any time, below the point of security. Their object was certainly not augmentation.

Mr. Ames was much more ample in his arguments, but want of time obliges us rather to sketch the topics on which he dwelt, than pursue the connected chain of his ideas.

Mr. MADISON in reply, insisted that the principal design of these amendments was to conciliate the minds of the people, and prudence required that the opinion of the states who had proposed the important amendment in contemplation, should be attended to. He said it was a fact that some states had not confined themselves to limitation, but had proposed an increase of the number, he did not conceive it to be very necessary in this case to investigate the advantages or disadvantages of a numerous representation; he acknowledged that beyond a certain point the number might be inconvenient. That point was a matter yet of uncertainty. It was true that numerous bodies were liable to some abuses; but if on one hand they were prone to those evils which the gentlemen had mentioned they were on the other hand less susceptible of corruption.

He thought also that to fix the ratio at even 40,000 for one would not prevent the abuses which Mr. Ames apprehended; for before the second census should be taken it was probable that the increase of population would be so great as to make the body very large—There was little choice therefore with a view to futurity between one ratio or the other; but as this of 1 for 30,000 was the proportion contemplated and proposed by the states, it was most advisable to adopt it.

Mr. GERRY, Mr. SEDGWICK, Mr. LIVERMORE, Mr. JACKSON, Mr. SENEY opposed the amendment; and Mr. AMES replied to them largely—The question being taken, Mr. Ames's proposition was rejected.

Mr. TUCKER moved to strike out the first "one hundred" in the amendment, and to insert "two hundred" and then to strike out the rest of the paragraph—so that the representation should not be less than two hundred, nor should Congress have a discretion to fix any ratio of increase, but that such proportion should be adopted as to keep the representation fixed at two hundred.

After some debate, this motion was negatived.

Gazette of the United States, 19 August 1789

In COMMITTEE of the whole. The first article of the report being read, Mr. GERRY rose and objected to the sentence, "*Government being intended for the benefit of the people.*"

THIS, said he, holds up an idea, that all government is intended for the benefit of the people: This is not true—for if we examine, we shall find that not one government in fifty, is constituted upon this principle. Most of the governments, ancient or modern, owed their existence to either fraud, force or accident, and are designed for the purposes of oppression and personal ambition. I wish to have nothing go out from this body as a maxim, which is not true in fact. He moved to amend the clause by inserting the words "of right." This motion was negatived.

Mr. TUCKER observed, that the preamble is no part of the Constitution: The object is to amend the Constitution; The preamble is no more a part of it, than the letter of the President which is annexed to the Instrument—and I cannot see that the committee has any thing to do with it.

Mr. SUMTER moved that the consideration of the preamble should be postponed till the whole amendments are gone through, and then we shall know what introduction may be proper.

Mr. SMITH, (S.C.) observed, that the amendments proposed to the preamble, had been recommended by three States, which renders it proper.

Mr. PAGE said, that in his opinion the original preamble will not be altered for the better, by this amendment, and therefore I hope it will remain as it is.

Mr. SHERMAN said he was satisfied with the original clause: If the Constitution was a grant from another power it would be proper; but as the right is a natural and unalienable right, and inherent in the people, it is quite unnecessary to give any reasons for forming the Constitution. It is the act of their own sovereign will. The words "WE THE PEOPLE" contain in themselves the principle fully, and the alteration proposed will injure the preamble.

Mr. MADISON observed, that the proposed amendment is a truth, and I conceive there is a propriety in inserting it; besides several of the States have thought proper to mention the preamble in their ratifications, which renders it proper to be attended to. I can see no difficulty in associating the amendment with the preamble, without injuring the beauty or sense of the paragraph: The principle it is acknowledged on all hands is self evident, and can derive no force from this expression, still for the reason before suggested it may be prudent to insert it.

The question on this amendment was carried in the affirmative.

Second amendment: From art. 1, sec. II, par. 3, strike out all between the word "direct" and "until such," and instead thereof, insert "*after the first enumeration there shall be one representative for every thirty thousand, until the number shall amount to one hundred; after which, the proportion shall be so regulated by Congress, that the number of representatives shall never be less than one hundred, nor more than one hundred and seventy five; but each state shall always have at least one representative.*"

Mr. VINING: The duty which I owe to my constituents—my anxiety on the subject of amendments, and the justice, propriety, and policy of the measure, lead me to propose, after the words, "one hundred and seventy-five," to insert these words, "*that where the number of inhabitants of any particular State, amounts to* 45,000, *they shall be entitled to two representatives.*" This was negatived without a division.

Mr. AMES moved, that the word "thirty" should be struck out, and *forty* inserted—so that the ratio of representation should be one for forty thousand. I am induced, said he, to make this motion, because I think the present number sufficiently large for the purpose of legislation—that number which is found adequate to the object is to be prefered: The people it is presumed are universally satisfied with the present number, which falls short of what would, on this proposition, actually constitute the house, upon an exact apportionment upon the present supposed number of inhabitants: Experience has taught, that all the information necessary, both of a general and local nature, may be found in a body not more numerous than the present legislature: The expence of a numerous representation would soon become dissatisfactory to the people, and be considered as an intolerable burden: The ratio of one to every 30,000 will swell the representation to an enormous mass, whose support will be insufferable, and whose deliberations will be impracticable: The present population will on the first census produce upwards of 100—the augmentation will be very rapid: It therefore appears proper to fix the proportion immediately, to prevent these evils. By enlarging the representation, we lessen the chance of selecting the most competent characters, and of concentering the wisdom and abilities of the United States, which alone can support the importance and dignity of that branch in which the people are more peculiarly interested: The responsibility of any assembly, is in proportion to the number: In larger representations the weight, the consequence, and responsibility of individuals is diminished. Numerous representations engender parties, are subject to peculiar fermentations, delay the public business, and by encreasing the expence, lead the people to consider government rather a curse than a blessing. Tho parties may promote the public good, they often give rise to very alarming evils. Whether it is possible so to constitute a popular assembly as to banish or restrain to any considerable degree, a spirit of faction, is an important enquiry. This however is certain, that in proportion as the assembly is encreased, the opportunity for intrigue and cabal, to influence weak and unsuspicious characters, and to attach them to the views of ambitious men, is encreased. It may also be observed, that responsibility is in some proportion to the numbers represented. A representative of a large body of people will feel in a higher degree the weight of the charge he undertakes, and will thereby be more interested to support a virtuous fame, and redouble his exertions for the public good.

The people are not anxious to have a representation for every 30,000: This was not the object originally in view by those who proposed this amendment; their intention was to fix a limitation, so that the representation should not be diminished by Congress in any future time, below the point of security—their object was certainly not augmentation, for in proportion as the people multiply, the representation will encrease, and their influence will be diminished; this will lessen the controul of the people over them; increasing the number therefore beyond certain limits will expose the government to factions, will lessen the agency of the understanding, and augment that of the passions. Improper characters will more easily get elected. The number of suitable persons is not great in any country, of those, many will be indisposed to serve. The United States has as great a proportion of competent abilities perhaps as any country whatever. If however the representative body is unduly enlarged, the probability of inferior candidates being elected will rise. It has been asserted that so large a territory as the United States contain cannot remain united under one government, even if the administration was entrusted to men of consummate abilities, and incorruptible virtue; but this idea will receive additional force, if the chance of different characters being called to the administration is encreased.

Mr. AMES added many other observations, and concluded by saying, that from the foregoing reflections upon the subject, he was led to make the motion, conceiving it to be consonant to the ideas of the people, and that it would conduce to the dignity and security of the government, and the preservation of the rights, and privileges of the people.

Mr. MADISON said, he thought differently from the gentleman last speaking: The design of the amendments is to conciliate the minds of the people to the government—prudence requires that the opinion of those States who have proposed this important amendment should be attended to. It is a fact that some States have proposed an encrease of the number—several have mentioned 200—this renders it probable that they would not be satisfied with a less number. I do not think it necessary at this time to go into an accurate investigation of the advantages or disadvantages of a numerous representation; beyond a certain rule, the number might be inconvenient; that point is a matter of uncertainty. It is true that numerous bodies are liable to some abuses, but large assemblies are not so subject to corruption as smaller ones: If we fix the ratio at one for forty thousand, it will not prevent the abuses the gentleman apprehends, for before the second census shall be taken, it is probable that the population will be so encreased, as to make the representative body very large; there is therefore, with respect to futurity, but little choice between one ratio, or the other. I think it will be best to retain the 30,000, as attended with the least difficulty—it is the proportion contemplated by the States, and I hope therefore that this part of the report will be adopted.

Mr. SEDGWICK stated some particulars respecting instructions from the Commonwealth of Massachusetts, and said he hoped the article in the report of the committee would be adopted.

Mr. GERRY also replied to Mr. Ames: He controverted his calculations, and enforced the necessity of an ample and adequate representation. He observed, that the gentleman had said, "encreasing the number lessens the importance of the members;" but Sir, said Mr. Gerry, are we, in order to preserve our own dignity and importance, to sacrifice the liberties of the people? He asserted that small assemblies are more liable to fermentation than large; large representative assemblies will commonly be composed of a considerable proportion of the yeomanry of the country, who are found to be more dispassionate than persons elected from elevated walks of life.

Mr. LIVERMORE was opposed to the motion for 40,000.

Mr. AMES rose to justify the motives which induced him to make the motion: He made a copious reply, and among other observations said, that he had no idea of attempting any alterations of the Constitution which would injure or weaken the system: The amendments it is to be expected will improve and make it better; this he conceived would be the case by the alteration he proposed.

Mr. JACKSON said, that what he had expected, had taken place. It is now proposed, by way of amendment to the Constitution, to restrict the number of the representative body to one for every 40,000 inhabitants. In support of the argument, the gentleman says, that in a small assembly the abilities of the best men may be brought as it were to a focus: If this argument has any weight in it, why not trust one person? One representative to 30,000 has been complained of—one to 40,000 would certainly be less competent to doing justice to his constituents. The motion for striking out 30,000, in order to insert 40,000, was negatived.

Mr. SEDGWICK moved, that the words "one hundred and seventy-five" should be struck out, and *two hundred* inserted.

Mr. SHERMAN objected to this motion: He said that was the constitution now to be formed, he should be for one representative to every 40,000 inhabitants, instead of 30,000, and upon that principle I was going to move, said he, that 175 be struck out, in order to insert a less number.

The representations of several of the states are too large, and have been justly complained of; the rights of the people are less secure in a large, than in a small assembly: The great object is information; and this may be acquired by a small number, and to better purpose than by a large.

It has been said that a future legislature will not encrease the number, should it be found necessary: If that supposition is true, the present house will not agree to this motion, unless we suppose that a future house will be less patriotic than the present: as to the largeness of the number being a security against corruption, I do not think it is; the British house of commons consists of upwards of 500 members, and yet money enough has always been found to corrupt a sufficient number for the minister's purpose.

Mr. MADISON observed that as the number 200 had been mentioned in the ratifications of several of the states and no substantial reason has been assigned why their expectation should not be complied with, it is reasonable to adopt this motion: Not, said he, that I would have the house give up their own judgement, when any substantial reason to the contrary is offered.

Mr. LAURANCE, Mr. GERRY, Mr. LIVERMORE, Mr. SEDGWICK, Mr. PAGE, Mr. TUCKER, and Mr. STONE, severally spoke upon this motion—which was finally carried in the affirmative—The paragraph as amended was agreed to by the committee.

The third amendment is "Art. I, Sec. 2. Par. 3—Strike out all between the words "direct" and "until such," and instead thereof, insert "*but no law varying the compensation, shall take effect, until an election of representatives shall have intervened. The members.*"

This clause was debated for a short time, and then the question being taken, it was carried.

The Congressional Register, 14 August 1789

The house then resolved itself into a committee of the whole on the amendments to the constitution.

Mr. Trumbull in the chair.

Mr. Smith wished to transpose the words of the first amendment, as they did not satisfy his mind in the manner they stood.

Mr. GERRY

Said they were not well expressed, we have it here "government being intended for the benefit of the people," this holds up an idea that all the governments of the earth are intended for the benefit of the people: Now, I am so far from being of this opinion, that I don't believe that one out of fifty is intended for any such purpose. I believe the establishment of most governments was to gratify the ambition of an individual, who by fraud, force, or accident, had made himself master of the people. If we contemplate the history of nations, ancient or modern, we shall find they originated either in fraud or force, or both; if this is demonstrable, how can we pretend to say that governments are intended for the benefit of those who are most oppressed by them. This maxim does not appear to me to be strictly true in fact, therefore I think we ought not to insert it in the constitution. I shall therefore propose to amend the clause by inserting "of right," then it will stand as it ought. I do not object to the principle, sir, it is a good one, but it does not generally hold in practice.

The question on inserting the words "of right" was put, and determined in the negative.

Mr. TUCKER.

I presume these propositions are brought forward under the idea of being amendments to the constitution; but can this be esteemed an amendment of the constitution? If I understand what is meant by the introductory paragraph, it is the preamble to the constitution; but a preamble is no part of the constitution; it is, to say the best, an useless amendment: For my part I should as soon think of amending the concluding part, consisting of general Washington's letter to the president of congress, as the preamble; but if the principle is of importance, it may be introduced into a bill of rights.

Mr. SMITH

Read the amendments on this head, proposed by the conventions of New-York, Virginia, and North-Carolina, from which it appeared that these states had expressed a desire to have an amendment of this kind.

Mr. TUCKER

Replied that the words "We the people do ordain and establish this constitution for the United States of America," was a declaration of their action; this being performed, congress have nothing to do with it: But if it was necessary to retain the principle, it might come in at some other place.

Mr. SUMTER

Thought this was not a proper place to introduce any general principle; perhaps in going through with the amendments something might be proposed subversive of what was there declared; wherefore he wished the committee would pass over the preamble until they had gone through all the amendments, and then, if alterations were necessary, they could be accommodated to what had taken place in the body of the constitution.

Mr. LIVERMORE

Was not concerned about the preamble; he did not care what kind it was agreed to form in the committee; because, when it got before the house it would be undone if one member more than one third of the whole opposed it.

Mr. PAGE

Thought the preamble no part of the constitution, but if it was, it stood in no need of amendment; the words "We the people," had a neatness and simplicity, while its expression was the most forcible of any he had ever seen prefixed to any constitution. He did not doubt the truth of the proposition brought forward by the committee, but he doubted its necessity in this place.

Mr. MADISON.

If it be a truth, and so self evident that it cannot be denied; if it be recognized, as is the fact in many of the state constitutions; and if it be desired by three important states, to be added to this, I think they must collectively offer a strong inducement to the mind desirous of promoting harmony, to acquiesce with the report; at least some strong arguments should be brought forward to shew the reason why it is improper.

My worthy colleague says the original expression is neat and simple; that loading it with more words may destroy the beauty of the sentence, and others say it is unnecessary, as the paragraph is complete without it, be it so in their opinion; yet, still it appears important in the estimation of three states, that this solemn truth should be inserted in the constitution. For my part, sir, I do not think the association of ideas any ways unnatural; it reads very well in this place, so much so that I think gentlemen who admit it should come in somewhere, will be puzzled to find a better place.

Mr. SHERMAN

Thought they ought not to come in in this place. The people of the United States have given their reasons for doing a certain act; here we propose to come in and give them a right to do what they did on motives which appeared to them sufficient to warrant their determination—to let them know that they had a right to exercise a natural and inherent privilege which they have asserted in a solemn ordination and establishment of the constitution. Now if this right is indefeasible, and the people have recognized it in practice, the truth is better asserted than it can be by any words whatever—the words "We the people" in the original constitution are copious and expressive as possible; any addition will only drag out the sentence without illuminating it; for these reasons it may be hoped the committee will reject the proposed amendment.

The question on the first paragraph of the report was put and carried in the affirmative, 27 to 23.

Second paragraph in the report was read as follows;

Art. 1. Sect. 2. Par. 3. Strike out all between the words "direct" and "and until such" and instead thereof insert "after the first enumeration, there shall be one representative for every 30,000, until the number shall amount to 100. After which the proportion shall be so regulated by congress that the number of representatives, shall never be less than one hundred, nor more than one hundred and seventy-five; but each state shall always have at least one representative."

Mr. VINING.

The duty, sir, which I owe to my constituents, and my desire to establish the constitution on a policy, dictated by justice and liberality, which will ever secure domestic tranquillity, and promote the general welfare, induces me to come forward with a motion, which I rest upon its own merits. Gentlemen who have a magnanimous policy in view, I trust will give it their support; and concede to what is proper in itself, and likely to procure a greater degree of harmony. I therefore move you, sir, to insert after the words "one hundred and seventy-five," these words, "That where the number of inhabitants of any particular state amounts to 45,000, they shall be entitled to two representatives."

This motion was negatived without a division.

Mr. AMES

Moved to strike out thirty thousand, and insert forty thousand. I am induced to this, said he, because I think my fellow citizens will be dissatisfied with too numerous a representation. The present I believe is in proportion to 1 for 40,000 the number I move to insert. I believe we have hitherto experienced no difficulty on account of the smallness of our number; if we are embarrassed, I apprehend the embarrassment will arise from our want of knowing the general interest of the nation at large; or for want of local information. If the present number is found sufficient for the purpose of legislation without any such embarrassment, it ought to be preferred, inasmuch as it is most adequate to its object.

But before we proceed in the discussion, let us consider the effect, which a representation, founded on 1 member for 30,000 citizens will produce. In the first place it will give 4 members for every 3 now intitled to seat in this house, which will be an additional burthen to the union, in point of expence in the same ratio: add to this another consideration, that probably before the first census is taken, the number of inhabitants will be considerably encreased, from what it was when the convention which formed this constitution obtained their information. This will probably encrease the expences of government to 450,000 dollars annually. Now those who have attended particularly to oeconomy; who upon the most careful calculation find that our revenue is like to fall infinitely short of our expences, will consider this saving as a considerable object, and deserving their most serious regard.

It may become dissatisfactory to the people as an intolerable burthen. Again it must be abundantly clear to every gentleman, that in proportion as you encrease the number of representatives the body degenerates, you diminish the individual usefulness, gentlemen will not make equal exertions to dispatch public business when they can lean upon others for the arrangement.

By enlarging the representation, we lessen the chance of selecting men of the greatest wisdom and abilities; because small district elections may be conducted by intrigue; but in large districts nothing but real dignity of character can secure an election. Gentlemen ought to consider how essential it is to the security and welfare of their constituents, that this branch of the government should support its independence and consequence.

Another effect of it will be an excitation, or fermentation in the representative body. Numerous assemblies are supposed to be less under the guidance of reason than smaller ones; their deliberations are confused; they will fall the prey of party spirit; they will cabal to carry measures which they would be unable to get through by fair and open argument. All these circumstances tend to retard the public business, and increase the expence; making government in the eyes of some so odious as to induce them to think it rather a curse than a blessing.

It lessens that responsibility which is annexed to the representative of a more numerous body of people. For I believe it will be found true that the representative of 40,000 citizens, will have more at risque than the man who represents a part of them; he has more dignity of character to support; and must use the most unremitting industry in their service to preserve it unsullied; he will be more sensible of the importance of his charge, and more indefatigable in his duty.

It is said that these amendments are introduced with a view to conciliate the affections of the people to the government; I am persuaded the people are not anxious to have a large representation, or a representation of one for every 30,000; they are satisfied with the representation they now enjoy. The great object which the convention of Massachusetts had in view by proposing this amendment, was to obtain a security, that congress should never reduce the representation below what they conceived to be a point of security. Their object was not an augmentation, it was certainty alone they wished for; at the next census the number of representatives will be 70 or 80, and in 20 years it will be equal to the desires of any gentleman, we shall have to guard against its growth in less than half a century. The number of proper characters to serve in the legislature of any country is small; and of those many are inclined to pursue other objects. If the representation is greatly enlarged, men of inferior abilities will undoubtedly creep in, for altho' America has as great a proportion of men of sense and judgment as any nation on earth; yet she may not have sufficient to fill a legislative body unduly enlarged. Now if it has been questioned whether this country can remain united under a government administered by men of the most consummate abilities; the sons of wisdom, and the friends of virtue. How much more doubtful will it be if the administration is thrown into different hands; and different hands must inevitably be employed if the representation is too large.

Mr. MADISON.

I cannot concur in sentiment with the gentleman last up, that 1 representative for 40,000 inhabitants will conciliate the minds of those to the government, who are desirous of amendments; because they have rather wished for an encrease, than confined themselves to a limitation.

I believe, by this motion, we shall avoid no inconvenience that can be considered of much consequence, for one member for either 30,000 or 40,000 inhabitants, will, in a few years, give the number beyond which it is proposed congress shall not go.

Now if good policy requires that we accommodate the constitution to the wishes of that part of the community who are anxious for amendments, we shall agree to something like what is proposed in the report, for the states of New-Hampshire, Massachusetts, New-York, Virginia and North-Carolina, have desired an alteration on this head; some have required an encrease as far as 200 at least: this does not look as if certainty was their sole object.

I do not consider it necessary, on this occasion, to go into a lengthy discussion of the advantages of a less or greater representation. I agree that after going beyond a certain point, the number may become inconvenient; that is proposed to be guarded against; but it is necessary to go to a certain number in order to secure the great objects of representation. Numerous bodies are undoubtedly liable to some objections, but they have their advantages also; if they are more exposed to passion and fermentation, they are less subject to venality and corruption; and in a government like this, where the house of representatives is connected with a smaller body it might be good policy to guard them in a particular manner against such abuse.

But for what shall we sacrifice the wishes of the people? Not for a momentary advantage: Yet the amendment proposed by the gentleman from Massachusetts will lose its efficacy after the second census; I think, with respect to futurity, it makes little or no difference; and as it regards the present time, 30,000 is the most proper, because it is the number agreed upon in the original constitution, and what is required by several states.

Mr. SEDGWICK

Observed, that the amendment proposed by the convention of Massachusetts was carried there, after a full discussion; since then, the whole of the amendments proposed by the convention had been recommended by the legislature of that state, to the attention of their delegates in congress. From these two circumstances he was led to believe, that his, and his colleagues' constituents, were generally in favor of the amendment as stated in the report.

He did not expect any advantage would arise from enlarging the number of representatives beyond a certain point; but he thought 175 rather too few.

Mr. GERRY.

My colleague (mr. Ames) has said that we experience no inconvenience for want of either general or local knowledge. Sir, I may dispute the fact from the difficulties we encountered in carrying through the collection bill, and on some other occasions, where we seemed much at a loss to know what were the dispositions of our constituents. But admitting this to be the fact; is information the only principle upon which we are to stand? Will that gentleman pretend to say we have as much security in a few representatives as in many? Certainly he will not. Not that I would insist upon a burthensome representation, but upon an adequate one. He supposes the expences of the government will be encreased in a very great proportion; but if he calculates with accuracy he will find the difference of the pay of the additional members not to exceed a fourth: The civil list was stated to cost 300,000 dollars, but the house of representatives does not cost more than a ninth of that sum; consequently the additional members, at the ratio of 4 for 3, could not amount to more than a thirtieth part, which would fall far short of what he seemed to apprehend. Is this such an object as to induce the people to risk every security which they ought to have in a more numerous representation?

One observation which I understood fell from him, was, that multiplying the number of representatives, diminished the dignity and importance of the individuals who compose the house. Now I wish to know whether he means that we should establish our own importance at the risk of the liberties of America, if so, it has been of little avail that we successfully opposed the lordly importance of a British parliament. We shall now, I presume, be advised to keep the representation where it is, in order to secure our dignity; but I hope it will be ineffectual, and that gentlemen will be inclined to give up some part of their consequence to secure the rights of their constituents.

My honorable colleague has said that large bodies are subject to fermentations; true, sir, but so are small ones also, when they are composed of aspiring and ambitious individuals. Large bodies in this country are likely to be composed in a great measure of gentlemen who represent the landed interest of the country; these are generally more temperate in debate than others, consequently, by encreasing the representation we shall have less of this fermentation than on the present establishment. As to the other objections, they are not of sufficient weight to induce the house to refuse adopting an amendment recommended by so large a body of our constituents.

Mr. LIVERMORE

Was against the alteration, because he was certain his constituents were opposed to it: He never heard a single person but supposed that one member was little enough to represent the interest of 30,000 inhabitants; many had thought the proportion ought to be 1 for 20 or 25,000. It would be useless to propose amendments which there was no probability of getting ratified; and he feared this would be the fate of the one under consideration, if the honorable gentleman's alteration took place.

Mr. AMES

Begged to know the reasons upon which amendments were founded: He hoped it was not purely to gratify an indigested opinion; but in every part where they retouched the edifice, it was with an intention of improving the structure; they certainly could not think of making alterations for the worse. Now, that his motion would be an improvement, was clearly demonstrable from the advantage in favor of deliberating by a less numerous body, and various other reasons already mentioned; but to those, the honorable gentleman from Virginia, (mr. Madison) replied, by saying we ought to pay attention to the amendments recommended by the states;

if this position is true, we have nothing more to do than read over their amendments, and propose them without exercising our judgment upon them. But he would undertake to say that the object of the people was rather to procure certainty, than encrease; if so, it was the duty of congress rather to carry the spirit of the amendment into operation than the letter of it.

The house of representatives will furnish a better check upon the senate, if filled with men of independent principles, integrity, and eminent abilities, than if consisting of a numerous body of inferior characters; in this opinion, said he, my colleague cannot but agree with me: Now if you diminish the consequence of the whole, you diminish the consequence of each individual, it was in this view that I contended for the importance of the members.

He said it could not be the wish of Massachusetts to have the representation numerous, because they were convinced of its impropriety in their own legislature, which might justly be supposed to require a greater number, as the objects of their deliberation extended to minute and local regulations. But that kind of information was not so much required in congress, whose power embraced national objects alone. He contended that all the local information necessary in this house, was to be found as fully among the ten members from Massachusetts, as if there had been one from every town in the state.

It is not necessary to encrease the representation, in order to guard against corruption, because no one will presume to think that a body composed like this, and encreased in a ratio of 4 to 3, will be much less exposed to sale than we are. Nor is a greater number necessary to secure the rights and liberties of the people, for the representative of a great body of people, is likely to be more watchful of its interests than the representative of a lesser body.

Mr. JACKSON.

I have always been afraid of letting this subject come before the house, for I was apprehensive that something would be offered striking at the very foundation of the constitution, by lessening it in the good opinion of the people. I conceive that the proposition for encreasing the ratio of representation will have this tendency; but I am not opposed to the motion only on the principle of expediency, but because I think it grounded on wrong principles. The honorable gentleman's arguments were as much in favor of entrusting the business of legislation to one, two, or three men as to a body of sixty or a hundred, they would dispatch business with greater facility and be an immense saving to the public; but will the people of America be gratified with giving the power of managing their concerns into the hands of one man? Can this take place upon the democratic principle of the constitution, I mean the doctrine of representation? Can one man, however consummate his abilities, however unimpeachable his integrity, and however superior his wisdom, be supposed capable of understanding, combining and managing interests so diversified as those of the people of America. It has been complained of that the representation is too small at one for 30,000, we ought not therefore attempt to reduce it.

In a republic, the laws should be founded upon the sense of the community; if every man's opinion could be obtained it would be the better; it is only in aristocracies, where the few are supposed to understand the general interests of the community more than the many: I hope I shall never live to see that doctrine established in this country.

Mr. STONE

Supposed the United States to contain 3,000,000 of people; these, at one representative for every 30,000 would give a hundred members, of which fifty-one were a quorum to do business; twenty-six men would be the majority, and give law to the United States, together with seven in the senate: If this was not a number sufficiently small to administer the government, he did not know what was; he was satisfied that gentlemen, upon mature reflection, would deem it inexpedient to reduce that number one-fourth.

Mr. SENEY

Said it had been observed by the gentleman from Massachusetts, that it would tend to diminish the expence, but he considered this object as very inconsiderable when compared with that of having a fair and full representation of the people of the United States.

Mr. Ames's motion was now put, and lost by a large majority.

Mr. SEDGWICK.

When he reflected on the country, and the increase of population which was likely to take place, he was led to believe that one hundred and seventy-five members would be a body rather too small to represent such extensive concerns—for this reason he would move to strike out a hundred and seventy-five and insert two hundred.

Mr. SHERMAN

Said if they were now forming a constitution, he should be in favor of one representative for 40,000 rather than 30,000; the proportion by which the several states are now represented in this house, was founded on the former calculation; in the convention that framed the constitution, there was a majority in favor of 40,000, and though there were some in favour of 30,000 yet that proposition did not obtain until after the constitution was agreed to, when the president had expressed a wish that 30,000 should be inserted, as more favorable to the public interest;[20] during the contest between 30 and 40,000, he believed there were not more than nine states who voted in favour of the former.

The objects of the federal government were fewer than those of the state governments; they did not require an equal degree of local knowledge; the only case, perhaps, where local knowledge would be advantageous, was in laying direct taxes; but here they were freed from an embarrassment, because the arrangements of the several states might serve as a pretty good rule on which to found their measures.

So far was he from thinking a hundred and seventy-five insufficient, that he was about to move for a reduction, because he always considered that a small body deliberated to better purpose than a greater one.

Mr. MADISON

Hoped gentlemen would not be influenced by what had been related to have passed in the convention; he expected the committee would determine upon their own sense of propriety; though as several states had proposed the number of two hundred, he thought some substantial reason should be offered to induce the house to reject it.

Mr. LIVERMORE

Said that he did not like the amendment as it was reported; he approved of the ratio being one for 30,000, but he wished the number of representatives might be increased in proportion as the population of the country increased, until the number of representatives amounted to two hundred.

Mr. TUCKER

Said the honorable gentleman who spoke last had anticipated what he was going to remark. It appeared to him that the committee had looked but a very little way forward when they agreed to fix the representation at one hundred members, on a ratio of one to every 30,000 upon the first enumeration; he apprehended the United States would be found to comprehend near 3,000,000 of people, consequently they would give a hundred members, now, by the amendment, it will lay in the power of congress to prevent any addition to that number; if it should be a prevalent opinion among the members of this house that a small body was better calculated to perform the public business than a larger one, they will never suffer their members to increase to a hundred and seventy-five, the number to which the amendment extended.

[20] On 17 September 1787, when he rose to call the question in the Federal Convention, Washington broke his rule of silence and spoke in favor of the lower figure.

Mr. GERRY

Expressed himself in favour of extending the number to two hundred, and wished that the amendment might be so modified as to insure an increase in proportion to the increase of population.

Mr. SHERMAN

Was against any increase; he thought that if a future house should be convinced of the impropriety of increasing this number to above one hundred, they ought to have it at their discretion to prevent it, and if that was likely to be the case, it was an argument why the present house should not decide. He did not consider that all that had been said with respect to the advantages of a large representation was founded upon experience; it had been intimated that a large body was more incorruptible than a smaller one; this doctrine was not authenticated by any proof, he could invalidate it by an example notorious to every gentleman in this house; he alluded to the British house of commons, which altho' it consisted of upwards of 500 members, the minister always contrived to procure votes enough to answer his purpose.

Mr. LAURANCE

Said that it was a matter of opinion upon which gentlemen held different sentiments whether a greater or less number than a certain point, was best for a deliberative body; but he apprehended that whatever number was now fixed, would be continued by a future congress, if it was left to their discretion; he formed this opinion from the influence of the senate, in which the small states were represented in an equal proportion with the larger ones: He supposed that the senators from New-Hampshire, Rhode-Island, Connecticut, Jersey, and Delaware would ever oppose an augmentation of the number of representatives; because their influence in the house would be proportionably abated. These states were incapable of extending their population beyond a certain point, inasmuch as they were confined with respect to territory; if therefore they could never have more than one representative, they would hardly consent to double that of others, by which their own importance would be diminished. If such a measure was carried by the large states through this house, it might be successfully opposed in the senate; he would therefore be in favor of encreasing the number to 200, and making its increase gradual till it arrived at that height.

Mr. GERRY.

The presumption is, that if provision is not made for the increase of the house of representatives, by the present congress, the increase never will be made. Gentlemen ought to consider the difference between the government in its infancy and when well established. The people suppose their liberties somewhat endangered; they have expressed their wishes to have them secured, and instructed their representatives to endeavour to obtain for them certain amendments, which they imagine will be adequate to the object they have in view; besides this, there are two states not in the union, but which we hope to annex to it by the amendments now under deliberation; these are inducements for us to proceed and adopt this amendment, independent of the propriety of the amendment itself, and such inducements as no future congress will have, the principle of self interest and self importance will always operate on them to prevent any addition to the number of representatives. Cannot gentlemen contemplate a difference in situation between this and a future congress on other accounts. We have neither money nor force to administer the constitution, but this will not be the case hereafter. In the progress of this government its revenues will increase, and an army will be established; a future legislature will find other means to influence the people than now exists.

This circumstance proves that we ought to leave as little as possible to the discretion of the future government; but it by no means proves that the present congress ought not to adopt the amendment moved by my colleague, Mr. Sedgwick.

Mr. AMES.

It has been observed that there will be an indisposition in future legislatures to increase the number of representatives. I am by no means satisfied that this observation is true: I think there are motives which will influence legislatures of the best kind to increase the number of its members; there is a constant tendency in a republican government to multiply what it thought to be the popular branch: If we consider that men are often more attached to their places than they are to their principles, we shall not be surprised to see men of the most refined judgment advocating a measure which will increase their chance of continuing in office.

My honorable colleague has intimated that a future legislature will be against extending the number of this branch, and that if the people are displeased, they will have it in their power, by force, to compel their acquiescence. I do not see, sir, how the legislature is strengthened by an increase of an army: I have generally understood that it gave power to the executive arm, but not to the deliberative head; the example of every nation is against him: Nor can I conceive upon what foundation he rests his reasoning; If there is a natural inclination in the government to increase the number of administrators, it will be prudent in us to endeavour to counteract its baneful influence.

Mr. LIVERMORE now proposed to strike out the words "one hundred" and insert "two hundred."

Mr. SEDGWICK suspended his motion until this question was determined, whereupon it was put and lost, there being 22 in favor of, and 27 against it.

Mr. SEDGWICK's motion was then put and carried in the affirmative

Mr. LIVERMORE

Wished to amend the clause of the report in such a manner as to prevent the power of congress from deciding the rate of increase; he thought the constitution had better fix it, and let it be gradual until it arrived at 200; after which, if that was the sense of the committee, it might be stationary, and liable to no other variation but that of being apportioned among the members of the union.

Mr. AMES

Suggested to the consideration of gentlemen, whether it would not be better to arrange the subject in such a way as to let the representation be proportioned to a ratio of 1 for 30,000 at the first census, and 1 for 40,000 at the second, so as to prevent a too rapid increase of the number of members; he did not make a motion of this nature, because he conceived it to be out of order, after the late decision of the committee, but it might be brought forward in the house, and he hoped would accommodate both sides.

Mr. GERRY

Wished that the gentleman last up, would pen down the idea he had just thrown out, he thought it very proper for the consideration of the house.

The question on the second proposition of the report as amended, was now put and carried, being 27 for, and 22 against it.

The next proposition in the report was as follows;

Art. I. Sect. 6. Between the words "United States" and "shall in all cases" strike out "they" and insert "but no law varying the compensation shall take effect, until an election of representatives shall have intervened. The members."

Mr. SEDGWICK

Thought much inconvenience, and but very little good would result from this amendment, it might serve as a tool for designing men, they might reduce the wages very low, much lower than it was possible for any gentleman to serve without injury to his private affairs, in order to procure popularity at home, provided a diminution of pay was looked upon as a desirable thing; it might also be done in order to prevent men of shining and disinterested abilities, but of indigent circumstances, from rendering their fellow citizens those services they are well able to perform, and render a seat in this house less eligible than it ought to be.

Mr. VINING

Thought every future legislature would feel a degree of gratitude to the preceeding one, which had performed so disagreeable a task for them. The committee who had made this a part of their report, had been guided by a single reason, but which appeared to them a sufficient one, there was, to say the least of it, a disagreeable sensation, occasioned by leaving it in the breast of any man to set a value upon his own work; it is true it was unavoidable in the present house, but it might, and ought to be avoided in future; he therefore hoped it would obtain without any difficulty.

Mr. GERRY

Would be in favor of this clause, if they could find means to secure an adequate representation, but he apprehended that would be considerably endangered, he should therefore be against it.

Mr. MADISON

Thought the representation would be as well secured under this clause as it would be if it was omitted; and as it was desired by a great number of the people of America, he should consent to it, though he was not convinced it was absolutely necessary.

Mr. SEDGWICK

Remarked once more, that the proposition had two aspects which made it disagreeable to him, the one was to render a man popular to his constituents, the other to render the place ineligible to his competitor.

He thought there was very little danger of an abuse of the power of laying their own wages, gentlemen were generally more inclined to make them moderate than excessive.

The question being put on the proposition, it was carried in the affirmative, 27 for, and 20 against it.

15 AUGUST 1789

The Daily Advertiser, 17 August 1789

The House went into a committee on the amendments to the Constitution.

Mr. BOUDINOT in the chair.

The committee took up the fourth amendment—Art. 1. Sec. 9. Between par. 2 and 3 insert, "no religion shall be established by law, nor shall the equal rights of conscience be infringed."

Mr. LIVERMORE moved to strike out this clause and to substitute one to the following effect—"The Congress shall make no laws touching religion or the rights of conscience." He observed that tho' the sense of both provisions was the same, yet the former might seem to wear an ill face and was subject to misconstruction.

The question on this motion was carried.

Fifth amendment—"The freedom of speech, and of the press, and of the right of the people peaceably to assemble and consult for their common good, and to apply to the government for redress of grievances, shall not be infringed."

Mr. TUCKER moved to insert between the words "common good," "and to" in this paragraph, these words "to instruct their representatives."

On this motion a long debate ensued.

Mr. HARTLEY said it was a problematical subject. The practice on this principle might be attended with danger. There were periods when from various causes the popular mind was in a state of fermentation and incapable of acting wisely—This had frequently been experienced in the mother country, and once in a sister State.[21] In such cases it was a happiness to obtain representatives who might be free to exert their abilities against the popular errors and passions. The power of instructing might be liable to great abuses; it would generally be exercised in times of public disturbance, and would express rather the prejudices of faction, than the voice of policy; thus it would convey improper influences into the government. He said he had seen so many unhappy examples of the influence of the popular humours in public bodies, that he hoped they would be provided against in this government.

Mr. PAGE was in favor of the motion.

Mr. CLYMER remarked that the principle of the motion was a dangerous one. It would take away all the freedom and independence of the representatives, it would destroy the very spirit of representation itself, by rendering Congress a passive machine instead of a deliberative body.

Mr. SHERMAN insisted that instructions were not a proper rule for the representative, since they were not adequate to the purposes for which he was delegated. He was to consult the common good of the whole, and was the servant of the people at large. If they should coincide with his ideas of the common good, they would be unnecessary; if they contradicted them, he would be bound by every principle of justice to disregard them.

Mr. JACKSON also opposed the motion.

Mr. GERRY advocated the proposition—he said the power of instructing was essential in order to check an administration which should be

[21] The right of county conventions to instruct members of the legislature had been an issue in the early stages of Shays's Rebellion in Massachusetts.

guilty of abuses. Such things would probably happen. He hoped gentlemen would not arrogate to themselves more perfection, than any other government had been found to possess, or more at all times than the body of the people. It had he said been always contended by the friends of this government that the sovereignty resided in the people. That principle seemed inconsistent with what gentlemen now asserted; if the people were the sovereign he could not conceive why they had not the right to instruct and direct their agents at their pleasure.

Mr. MADISON observed that the existence of this right of instructing was at least a doubtful right. He wished that the amendments which were to go to the people should consist of an enumeration of simple and acknowledged principles. Such rights only ought to be expressly secured as were certain and fixed. The insertion of propositions that were of a doubtful nature, would have a tendency to prejudice the whole system of amendments, and render their adoption difficult. The right suggested was doubtful, and would be so considered by many of the states. In some degree the declaration of this right might be true; in other respects false. If by instructions were meant a given advice, or expressing the wishes of the people, the proposition was true, but still was unnecessary, since that right was provided for already. The amendments already passed had declared that the press should be free, and that the people should have the freedom of speech and petitioning: therefore the people might speak to their representatives, might address them through the medium of the press, or by petition to the whole body. They might freely express their wills by these several modes. But if it was meant that they had any obligatory force, the principle was certainly false. Suppose the representatives were instructed to do any act incompatible with the constitution, would he be bound to obey those instructions? Suppose he was directed to do what he knew was contrary to the public good, would [*he*] be bound to sacrifice his own opinion? Would not the vote of a representative contrary to his instructions be as binding on the people as a different one? If these things then be true, where is the right of the constituent? or where is the advantage to result from. It must either supercede all the other obligations, the most sacred, or it could be of no benefit to the people. The gentleman says, the people are the sovereign—True. But who are the people? Is every small district, the PEOPLE? and do the inhabitants of this district express the voice of the people, when they may not be a thousandth part, and although their instructions may contradict the sense of the whole people besides? Have the people in detached assemblies a right to violate the constitution or controul the actions of the whole sovereign power? This would be setting up a hundred sovereignties to the place of one.

Mr. SMITH (S.C.) was opposed to the motion—He said the doctrine of Instructions in practice would operate partially. The States who were near the seat of government would have an advantage over those more distant. Particular instructions might be necessary for a particular measure; such could not be obtained by the members of the distant states. He said there was no need of a large representation, if in all important matters they were to be guided by express instructions—One member from each state would serve every purpose. It was inconsistent with the principle of the amendment which had been adopted the preceding day.

Mr. STONE. differed with Mr. Madison, that the members would not be bound by instruction—He said when this principle was inserted in the constitution, it would render instructions sacred and obligatory in all cases, but he looked on this as one of the greatest of evils. He believed this would change the nature of the constitution—Instead of being a representative government, it would be a singular kind of democracy, and whenever a question arose what was the law, it would not properly be decided by recurring to the codes and institutions of Congress, but by collecting and examining the various instructions of different parts of the Union.

Several of the members spoke, and the debate was continued in a desultory manner—and at last the motion was negatived by a great majority—The question on the amendment was then put, and carried in the affirmative.

Gazette of the United States, 19 August 1789

In committee of the whole, on amendments to the constitution—the fourth amendment under consideration; viz. Art. 1. Sec. 9, between Par. 2 and 3 insert "*no religion shall be established by law, nor shall the equal rights of conscience be infringed.*"

Mr. SILVESTER said he doubted the propriety of the mode of expression used in this paragraph; he thought it was liable to a construction different from what was intended by the committee.

Mr. SHERMAN. It appears to me best that this article should be omitted intirely: Congress has no power to make any religious establishments, it is therefore unnecessary.

Mr. CARROLL, Mr. HUNTINGTON, Mr. MADISON, and Mr. LIVERMORE made some observations: The last proposed that the words should be struck out to substitute these words, "Congress shall make no laws touching religion or the rights of conscience."

The question on this motion was carried.

Fifth amendment. *The freedom of speech, and of the press, and of the rights of the people peaceably to assemble and consult for their common good, and to apply to government for the redress of grievances shall not be infringed.*

Mr. SEDGWICK moved to strike out the words "assemble and." This is a self evident unalienable right of the people, said he, and it does appear to me below the dignity of this house, to insert such things in the constitution. The right will be as fully recognized if the words are struck out, as if they were retained: For if the people may converse, they must meet *for* the purpose.

This motion was opposed by Mr. GERRY, Mr. PAGE, Mr. VINING and Mr. HARTLEY; and the question being taken it was negatived.

Mr. TUCKER moved to insert these words, *to instruct their representatives*. This produced a long debate.

Mr. HARTLEY. I could wish, Mr. chairman, that these words had not been proposed. Representatives ought to possess the confidence of their constituents; they ought to rely on their honour and integrity. The practice of instructing representatives may be attended with danger; we have seen it attended with bad consequences; it is commonly resorted to for party purposes, and when the passions are up. It is a right, which even in England is considered a problematical. The right of instructing is liable to great abuses; it will generally be exercised in times of popular commotion; and these instructions will rather express the prejudices of party, than the dictates of reason and policy. I have known, Sir, so many evils arise from adopting the popular opinion of the moment, that I hope this government will be guarded against such an influence; and wish the words may not be inserted.

Mr. PAGE was in favour of the motion. He said, that the right may well be doubted in a monarchy; but in a government instituted for the sole purpose of guarding the rights of the people, it appears to me to be proper.

Mr. CLYMER: I hope, Sir, the clause will not be adopted, for if it is, we must go further, and say, that the representatives are *bound* by the instructions, which is a most dangerous principle, and is destructive of all ideas of an independent and deliberative body.

Mr. SHERMAN said, these words had a tendency to mislead the people, by conveying an idea that they had a right to controul the debates of the federal legislature. Instructions cannot be considered as a proper rule for a representative to form his conduct by; they cannot be adequate to the purpose for which he is delegated. He is to consult the good of the whole: Should instructions therefore coincide with his ideas of the common good, they would be unnecessary: If they were contrary, he would be bound by every principle of justice to disregard them.

Mr. JACKSON opposed the motion: He said this was a dangerous article, as its natural tendency is to divide the house into factions: He then adverted to the absurdities and inconsistencies which would be involved in adopting the measure.

Mr. GERRY supported the motion: He observed, that to suppose we cannot be instructed, is to suppose that we are perfect: The power of instruction is in my opinion essential to check an administration which should be guilty of abuses: No one will deny that these may not happen: To deny the people this right is to arrogate to ourselves more wisdom than the whole body of the people possess. I contend, Sir, that our constituents have not only a right to instruct, but to *bind* this legislature—It has been contended by the friends to the constitution, that the people are sovereign: if so it involves an absurdity to suppose that they cannot, not only instruct, but controul the house: Debates may create factions, as well as instructions: We cannot be too well informed; this is the best method of obtaining information, and I hope we shall never shut our ears against that information which is to be derived from the voice of the people.

Mr. MADISON observed, that the existence of this right is at least doubtful. I wish that the amendments may consist of an enumeration of simple and acknowledged principles: The insertion of propositions that are of a doubtful nature, will have a tendency to prejudice the whole system of amendments: The right now suggested is doubtful, and will be so considered by many of the States: In some respects the declaration of this right may be true, in others it is false: If we mean nothing more by it than this, that the people have a right to give advice or express their sentiments and wishes it is true; but still unnecessary, as such a right is already recognized: The press shall be free, and the people shall have the same freedom of speech and petitioning: but if it is meant that the representatives are to be bound by these instructions, the principle is false: Suppose a representative is instructed to do what is contrary to the public good? Would he be bound to sacrifice his own opinion? Or will not the vote of a representative contrary to his instruction be as binding on the people as a different one? If these things are true, where is the right of the constituent to instruct? or where is the advantage to result from it? It must either supercede all other obligations, the most sacred; or it can be of no benefit to the people. The gentleman says, the people are the sovereign; but who are the people? Is every small district the PEOPLE? And can the inhabitants of this district express the voice of the people, when they may not be a thousandth part, and all their instructions may contradict the sense of the whole people besides? Have the people in detached assemblies a right to violate the constitution or controul the whole sovereign power? This would be setting up an hundred sovereignties in the place of one.

Mr. SMITH (S.C.) was opposed to the motion: The doctrine of instructions would, in practice, operate partially: The States near the seat of government will have an obvious advantage over those remote from it: There is no necessity for so large a representation as has been determined on, if the members are to be guided in all their deliberations by positive instructions; one member from a State will serve every purpose; but then the nature of the assembly will be changed from a legislative to a diplomatic body: It would in fact be turning all our representatives into ambassadors.

Mr. STONE observed that to adopt this motion would change the nature of the constitution; instead of being a representative government, it would be a singular kind of democracy; in which, whenever a question arises, what is the law? It will not be determined by recurring to the codes and institutions of Congress, but by collecting the various instructions from different parts of the Union.

Mr. GERRY observed that several of the States had proposed this amendment, which rendered it proper to be attended to: In answer to Mr. Madison's query he said, he meant that instructions should be consistent with the laws and the constitution.

Mr. LIVERMORE said that though no particular districts could instruct, yet the Legislatures of the States most undoubtedly possessed this right.

This assertion of Mr. LIVERMORE was controverted by several gentlemen—by Mr. SEDGWICK, Mr. SMITH, Mr. AMES, and Mr. WADSWORTH: The last, speaking on the subject of instructions in general, said, I never knew merely political instructions to be observed; and I never knew a representative brought to an account for it: But I have known representatives follow instructions, contrary to their private sentiments, and they have ever been despised for it. Others have disregarded their instructions, and have been re-elected, and caressed. Now if the *people* considered it as an inherent right in *them* to instruct their representatives, they would undoubtedly have punished the violation of such instructions; but this I believe has never been the case. I consider the measure as having a mischievous tendency.

The debate was continued much longer, but in a desultory way, as the speakers appeared to take it for granted, that they might touch upon collateral circumstances. The question on the motion being at length taken, it was negatived by a large majority; and then the committee agreed to the amendment in its original form.

The Congressional Register, 15 August 1789

The house resolved itself into a committee of the whole, and resumed the consideration of the report of the committee on the subject of amendments.

Mr. BOUDINOT in the chair.

The fourth proposition under consideration being as follows:

Article 1. Sect. 9. Between paragraph 2 and 3 insert "no religion shall be established by law, nor shall the equal rights of conscience be infringed."

Mr. SILVESTER

Had some doubts of the propriety of the mode of expression used in this paragraph; he apprehended that it was liable to a construction different from what had been made by the committee, he feared it might be thought to have a tendency to abolish religion altogether.

Mr. VINING

Suggested the propriety of transposing the two members of the sentence.

Mr. GERRY

Said it would read better if it was, that no religious doctrine shall be established by law.

Mr. SHERMAN

Thought the amendment altogether unnecessary, inasmuch as congress had no authority whatever delegated to them by the constitution, to make religious establishments, he would therefore move to have it struck out.

Mr. CARROLL.

As the rights of conscience are in their nature of peculiar delicacy, and will little bear the gentlest touch of the governmental hand; and as many sects have concurred in opinion that they are not well secured under the present constitution, he said he was much in favor of adopting the words; he thought it would tend more toward conciliating the minds of the people to the government than almost any other amendment he had heard proposed. He would not contend with gentlemen about the phraseology, his object was to secure the substance in such a manner as to satisfy the wishes of the honest part of the community.

Mr. MADISON

Said he apprehended the meaning of the words to be, that congress should not establish a religion, and enforce the legal observation of it by law, nor compel men to worship God in any manner contrary to their conscience; whether the words were necessary or not he did not mean to say, but they had been required by some of the state conventions, who seemed to entertain an opinion that under the clause of the constitution, which gave power to congress to make all laws necessary and proper to carry into execution the constitution, and the laws made under it, enabled them to make laws of such a nature as might infringe the rights of conscience, or establish a national religion, to prevent these effects he presumed the amendment was intended, and he thought it as well expressed as the nature of the language would admit.

Mr. HUNTINGTON

Said that he feared with the gentleman first up on this subject, that the words might be taken in such a latitude as to be extremely hurtful to the cause of religion: He understood the amendment to mean what had been expressed by the gentleman from Virginia, but others might find it convenient to put another construction upon it. The ministers of their congregations to the eastward,[22] were maintained by the contributions of those who belonged to their society; the expence of building meeting-houses was contributed in the same manner, these things were regulated by bye laws: If an action was brought before a federal court on any of these cases, the person who had neglected to perform his engagements could not be compelled to do it; for a support of ministers, or building of places of worship might be construed into a religious establishment.

By the charter of Rhode-Island, no religion could be established by law, he could give a history of the effects of such a regulation; indeed the people were now enjoying the blessed fruits of it: He hoped therefore the amendment would be made in such a way as to secure the rights of conscience, and a free exercise of the rights of religion, but not to patronize those who professed no religion at all.

Mr. MADISON

Thought, if the word national was inserted before religion, it would satisfy the minds of honorable gentlemen. He believed that the people feared one sect might obtain a pre-eminence, or two combine together and establish a religion to which they would compel others to conform; he thought if the word national was introduced, it would point the amendment directly to the object it was intended to prevent.

Mr. LIVERMORE

Was not satisfied with that amendment, but he did not wish them to dwell long on the subject; he thought it would be better if it was altered, and made to read in this manner, that congress shall make no laws touching religion, or infringing the rights of conscience.

Mr. GERRY

Did not like the term national, proposed by the gentleman from Virginia, and he hoped it would not be adopted by the house. It brought to

[22] New England.

his mind some observations that had taken place in the conventions at the time they were considering the present constitution; it had been insisted upon by those who were called antifederalists; that this form of government consolidated the union; the honorable gentleman's motion shews, that he considers it in the same light; those who were called antifederalists at that time complained that they had injustice done them by the title, because they were in favor of a federal government, and the others were in favor of a national one; the federalists were for ratifying the constitution as it stood, and the others not until amendments were made. Their names then ought not to have been distinguished by federalists and antifederalists, but rats and antirats.

Mr. Madison

Withdrew his motion, but observed that the words "no national religion shall be established by law," did not imply that the government was a national one; the question was then taken on mr. Livermore's motion, and passed in the affirmative, 31 for, 20 against.

The next clause of the 4th proposition was taken into consideration, and was as follows: "The freedom of speech and of the press, and the right of the people peaceably to assemble and consult for their common good, and to apply to the government for redress of grievances shall not be infringed."

Mr. Sedgwick

Submitted to those gentlemen who had contemplated the subject, what effect such an amendment as this would have; he feared it would tend to make them appear trifling in the eyes of their constituents; what, said he, shall we secure the freedom of speech, and think it necessary at the same time to allow the right of assembling? If people freely converse together, they must assemble for that purpose; it is a self-evident unalienable right which the people possess; it is certainly a thing that never would be called in question; it is derogatory to the dignity of the house to descend to such minutiae—he therefore moved to strike out "assemble and."

Mr. Benson.

The committee who framed this report, proceeded on the principle that these rights belonged to the people; they conceived them to be inherent, and all that they meant to provide against, was their being infringed by the government.

Mr. Sedgwick

Replied, that if the committee were governed by that general principle, they might have gone into a very lengthy enumeration of rights; they might have declared that a man should have a right to wear his hat if he pleased, that he might get up when he pleased, and go to bed when he thought proper; but he would ask the gentleman whether he thought it necessary to enter these trifles in a declaration of rights, under a government where none of them were intended to be infringed.

Mr. TUCKER

Hoped the words would not be struck out, for he considered them of importance; beside, they were recommended by the states of Virginia and North-Carolina, though he noticed that the most material part proposed by those states was omitted, which was, a declaration that the people should have a right to instruct their representatives; he would move to have those words inserted as soon as the motion for striking out was decided.

Mr. GERRY

Was also against the words being struck out, because he conceived it to be an essential right; it was inserted in the constitutions of several states, and though it had been abused in the year 1786 in Massachusetts,[23] yet that abuse ought not to operate as an argument against the use of it; the people ought to be secure in the peaceable enjoyment of this privilege, and that can only be done by making a declaration to that effect in the constitution.

Mr. PAGE.

The gentleman from Massachusetts, (mr. Sedgwick) who has made this motion, objects to the clause; because the right is of so trivial a nature; he supposes it no more essential than whether a man has a right to wear his hat or not, but let me observe to him that such rights have been opposed, and a man has been obliged to pull off his hat when he appeared before the face of authority; people have also been prevented from assembling together on their lawful occasions, therefore it is well to guard against such stretches of authority, by inserting the privilege in the declaration of rights; if the people could be deprived of the power of assembling under any pretext whatsoever, they might be deprived of every other privilege contained in the clause.

Mr. VINING

Said if the thing was harmless, and it would tend to gratify the states that had proposed amendments, he should agree to it.

Mr. HARTLEY

Observed that it had been asserted in the convention of Pennsylvania, by the friends of the constitution, that all the rights and powers that were

---

[23]Late in the summer of 1786, farmers in central and western Massachusetts, burdened by taxes and debts, formed armed groups known as "regulators" and closed the courts of five counties. The state used the militia to crush the rebellion in January 1787, but the public rejected harsh treatment for the insurgents and a new state government pardoned those who had been condemned to death. Daniel Shays (ca. 1747–1825) was one of several leaders.

not given to the government, were retained by the states and the people thereof; this was also his own opinion, but as four or five states had required to be secured in those rights by an express declaration in the constitution, he was disposed to gratify them; he thought every thing that was not incompatible with the general good ought to be granted, if it would tend to obtain the confidence of the people in the government, and upon the whole, he thought these words were as necessary to be inserted in the declaration of rights as most in the clause.

Mr. GERRY

Said that his colleague contended for nothing, if he supposed that the people had a right to consult for the common good, because they could not consult unless they met for the purpose.

Mr. SEDGWICK

Replied that if they were understood or implied in the word consult, they were utterly unnecessary, and upon that ground he moved to have them struck out.

The question was now put upon mr. Sedgwick's motion, and lost by a considerable majority.

Mr. TUCKER then moved to insert these words, "to instruct their representatives."

Mr. HARTLEY

Wished the motion had not been made, for gentlemen acquainted with the circumstances of this country, and the history of the country from which we separated, differed exceedingly on this point; the members of the house of representatives, said he, are chosen for two years, the members of the senate for six.

According to the principles laid down in the constitution, it is presumable that the persons elected know the interests and the circumstances of their constituents, and being checked in their determinations by a division of the legislative power into two branches, there is little danger of error, at least it ought to be supposed that they have the confidence of the people during the period for which they are elected; and if, by misconduct, they forfeit it, their constituents have the power of leaving them out at the expiration of that time; thus they are answerable for the part they have taken in measures that may be contrary to the general wish.

Representation is the principle of our government; the people ought to have confidence in the honor and integrity of those they send forward to transact their business; their right to instruct them is a problematical subject. We have seen it attended with bad consequences, both in England and America. When the passions of the people were excited, instructions have been resorted to and obtained, to answer party purposes; and although the public opinion is generally respectable, yet at such moments it has been known to be often wrong; and happy is that government composed of men of firmness and wisdom to discover and resist the popular error.

If, in a small community, where the interests, habits, and manners are neither so numerous or diversified, instructions bind not: What shall we say of instructions to this body; can it be supposed that the inhabitants of a single district in a state, are better informed with respect to the general interests of the union than a select body assembled from every part? Can it be supposed that a part will be more desirous of promoting the good of the whole than the whole will of the part? I apprehend, sir, that congress will be judges of proper measures, and that instructions will never be resorted to but for party purposes, when they will generally contain the prejudices and acrimony of the party rather than the dictates of honest reason and sound policy.

In England this question has been considerably agitated, the representatives of some towns in parliament, have acknowledged, and submitted to the binding force of instructions, while the majority have thrown off the shackles with disdain. I would not have this precedent influence our decision; but let the doctrine be tried upon its own merits, and stand or fall as it shall be found to deserve.

It appears to my mind, that the principle of representation is distinct from an agency, which may require written instructions. The great end of meeting is to consult for the common good; but can the common good be discerned without the object is reflected and shewn in every light. A local or partial view does not necessarily enable any man to comprehend it clearly; this can only result from an inspection into the aggregate. Instructions viewed in this light, will be found to embarrass the best and wisest men. And were all the members to take their seats in order to obey instructions, and those instructions were as various as it is probable they would be, what possibility would there exist of so accommodating each to the other, as to produce any act whatever? Perhaps a majority of the whole might not be instructed to agree to any one point; and is it thus the people of the United States propose to form a more perfect union, provide for the common defence, and promote the general welfare?

Sir, I have known within my own time so many inconveniencies and real evils arise from adopting the popular opinions of the moment, that although I respect them as much as any man, I hope this government will particularly guard against them, at least that they will not bind themselves by a constitutional act, and by oath to submit to their influence, if they do, the great object which this government has been established to attain, will inevitably elude our grasp on the uncertain and veering winds of popular commotion.

Mr. PAGE.

The gentleman from Pennsylvania tells you, that in England this principle is doubted; how far this is consonant with the nature of the government I will not pretend to say, but I am not astonished to find that the administrators of a monarchical government are unassailable by the weak voice of the people, but under a democracy whose great end is, to form a code of laws congenial with the public sentiment, the popular opinion ought to be collected and attended to. Our present object is I presume, to secure to our constituents and to posterity these inestimable rights. Our government is derived from the people, of consequence the people have a right to consult for the common good; but to what end will this be done, if they have not the power of instructing their representatives? Instruction and representation in a republic, appear to me to be inseparably connected; but was I the subject of a monarch, I should doubt whether the public good did not depend more upon the prince's will than the will of the people. I should dread a popular assembly consulting for the public good, because under its influence, commotions and tumults might arise that would shake the foundation of the monarch's throne, and make the empire tremble in expectation. The people of England have submitted the crown to the Hanover family, and have rejected the Stuarts,[24] if instructions upon such a revolution were considered as binding, it is difficult to know what would have been the effects, it might be well therefore to have the doctrine exploded from that kingdom; but it will not be advanced as a substantial reason in favor of our treading in the same steps.

The honorable gentleman has said, that when once the people have chosen a representative, they must rely on his integrity and judgment during the period for which he is elected. I think, sir, that to doubt the authority of the people to instruct their representatives, will give them just cause to be alarmed for their fate: I look upon it as a dangerous doctrine, subversive of the great end for which the United States have confederated. Every friend of mankind, every well-wisher of his country will be desirous of obtaining the sense of the people on every occasion of magnitude; but how can this be so well expressed as in instructions to their representatives; I hope, therefore, that gentlemen will not oppose the insertion of it in this part of the report.

Mr. CLYMER.

I hope the amendment will not be adopted, but if our constituents chuse to instruct us, that they may be left at liberty to do so; do gentle-

---

[24] In the Glorious Revolution of 1689.

men foresee the extent of these words? If they have a constitutional right to instruct us, it infers that we are bound by those instructions, and as we ought not to decide constitutional questions by implication, I presume we shall be called upon to go further, and expressly declare the members of the legislature bound by the instruction of their constituents; this is a most dangerous principle, utterly destructive of all ideas of an independent and deliberative body, which are essential requisites in the legislatures of free governments, they prevent men of abilities and experience from rendering those services to the community that are in their power, destroying the object contemplated by establishing an efficient general government, and rendering congress a mere passive machine.

Mr. SHERMAN.

It appears to me, that the words are calculated to mislead the people by conveying an idea, that they have a right to control the debates of the legislature; this cannot be admitted to be just, because it would destroy the object of their meeting. I think, when the people have chosen a representative, it is his duty to meet others from the different parts of the union, and consult, and agree with them to such acts as are for the general benefit of the whole community; if they were to be guided by instructions, there would be no use in deliberation, all that a man would have to do, would be to produce his instructions and lay them on the table, and let them speak for him, from hence I think it may be fairly inferred, that the right of the people to consult for the common good can go no further than to petition the legislature or apply for a redress of grievances. It is the duty of a good representative to enquire what measures are most likely to promote the general welfare, and after he has discovered them to give them his support; should his instructions therefore coincide with his ideas on any measure, they would be unnecessary; if they were contrary to the conviction of his own mind, he must be bound by every principle of justice to disregard them.

Mr. JACKSON

Was in favor of the right of the people, to assemble and consult for the common good, it had been used in this country as one of the best checks on the British legislature in their unjustifiable attempts to tax the colonies without their consent. America had no representatives in the British parliament, therefore they could instruct none, yet they exercised the power of consultation to a good effect. He begged gentlemen to consider the dangerous tendency of establishing such a doctrine, it would necessarily drive the house into a number of factions, there might be different instructions from every state, and the representation from each state would be a faction to support its own measures.

If we establish this as a right, we shall be bound by those instructions;

now, I am willing to leave both the people and the representatives to their own discretion on this subject, let the people consult and give their opinion, let the representative judge of it, and if it is just, let him govern himself by it as a good member ought to do, but if it is otherwise, let him have it in his power to reject their advice.

What may be the consequence of binding a man to vote in all cases according to the will of others? He is to decide upon a constitutional point, and on this question his conscience is bound by the obligation of a solemn oath; you now involve him in a serious dilemma, if he votes according to his conscience, he decides against his instructions, but in deciding against his instructions he commits a breach of the constitution, by infringing the prerogative of the people secured to them by this declaration. In short, it will give rise to such a variety of absurdities and inconsistencies as no prudent legislature would wish to involve themselves in.

Mr. GERRY.

By the checks provided in the constitution, we have good grounds to believe that the very framers of it conceived that the government would be liable to mal-administration, and I presume that the gentlemen of this house do not mean to arrogate to themselves more perfection than human nature has as yet been found to be capable of; if they do not, they will admit an additional check against abuses which this, like every other government, is subject to. Instructions from the people will furnish this in a considerable degree.

It has been said that the amendment proposed by the honorable gentleman from South-Carolina, (mr. Tucker) determines this point, "that the people can bind their representatives to follow their instructions;" I do not conceive that this necessarily follows: I think the representative, notwithstanding the insertion of these words, would be at liberty to act as he pleased; if he declined to pursue such measures as he was directed to attain, the people would have a right to refuse him their suffrages at a future election.

Now, though I do not believe the amendment would bind the representatives to obey the instructions, yet I think the people have a right both to instruct and bind them. Do gentlemen conceive that on any occasion instructions would be so general as to proceed from all our constituents? If they do it is the sovereign will, for gentlemen will not contend that the sovereign will, presides in the legislature; the friends and patrons of this constitution have always declared that the sovereignty resides in the people, and that they do not part with it on any occasion; to say the sovereignty vests in the people, and that they have not a right to instruct and control their representatives, is absurd to the last degree; they must either give up their principle, or grant that the people have a right to exercise their sovereignty to control the whole government, as well as this branch of it; but the amendment does not carry the principle to such an extent, it only declares the right of the people to send instructions; the representative will, if he thinks proper, communicate his instructions to the house, but how far they shall operate on his conduct, he will judge for himself.

The honorable gentleman from Georgia (mr. Jackson) supposes that instructions will tend to generate factions in this house, but he did not see how it could have that effect, any more than the freedom of debate had. If the representative entertains the same opinion with his constituents, he will decide with them in favor of the measure; if other gentlemen, who are not instructed on the point, are convinced by argument that the measure is proper, they will also vote with them, consequently the influence of debate and of instruction is the same.

The gentleman says further, that the people have the right of instructing their representatives; if so, why not declare it? Does he mean that it shall lay dormant and never be exercised? If so, it will be a right of no utility. But much good may result from a declaration in the constitution that they possess this privilege; the people will be encouraged to come forward with their instructions, which will form a fund of useful information for the legislature; we cannot, I apprehend, be too well informed of the true state, condition, and sentiment of our constituents, and perhaps this is the best mode in our power of obtaining information. I hope we shall never shut our ears against that information which is to be derived from the petitions and instructions of our constituents. I hope we shall never presume to think that all the wisdom of this country is concentred within the walls of this house. Men, unambitious of distinctions from their fellow citizens, remain within their own domestic walk, unheard of and unseen, possessing all the advantages resulting from a watchful observance of public men and public measures, whose voice, if we would descend to listen to it, would give us knowledge superior to what could be acquired amidst the cares and bustles of a public life; let us then adopt the amendment, and encourage the dissident to enrich our stock of knowledge with the treasure of their remarks and observations.

Mr. MADISON.

I think the committee acted prudently in omitting to insert these words in the report they have brought forward; if unfortunately the attempt of proposing amendments should prove abortive, it will not arise from the want of a disposition in the friends of the constitution to do what is right with respect to securing the rights and privileges of the people of America; but from the difficulties arising from discussing and proposing abstract propositions, of which the judgment may not be convinced. I venture to say that if we confine ourselves to an enumeration of simple acknowledged principles, the ratification will meet with but little difficulty. Amendments of a doubtful nature will have a tendency to prejudice the whole system; the proposition now suggested, partakes highly of this nature; it is doubted by many gentlemen here; it has been objected to in intelligent publications throughout the union; it is doubted by many members of the state legislatures: In one sense this declaration is true, in many others it is certainly not true; in the sense in which it is true, we have asserted the right sufficiently in what we have done; if we mean nothing more than this, that the people have a right to express and communicate their sentiments and wishes, we have provided for it already. The right of freedom of speech is secured; the liberty of the press is expressly declared to be beyond the reach of this government; the people may therefore publicly address their representatives; may privately advise them, or declare their sentiments by petition to the whole body; in all these ways they may communicate their will. If gentlemen mean to go further, and to say that the people have a right to instruct their representatives in such a sense as that the delegates were obliged to conform to those instructions, the declaration is not true. Suppose they instruct a representative by his vote to violate the constitution, is he at liberty to obey such instructions? Suppose he is instructed to patronize certain measures, and from circumstances known to him, but not to his constituents, he is convinced that they will endanger the public good, is he obliged to sacrifice his own judgement to them? Is he absolutely bound to perform what he is instructed to do? Suppose he refuses, will his vote be the less valid, or the community be disengaged from that obedience which is due from the laws of the union? If his vote must inevitably have the same effect, what sort of a right is this in the constitution to instruct a representative who has a right to disregard the order, if he pleases? In this sense the right does not exist, in the other sense it does exist, and is provided largely for.

The honorable gentleman from Massachusetts, asks if the sovereignty is not with the people at large; does he infer that the people can, in detached bodies, contravene an act established by the whole people? My idea of the sovereignty of the people is, that the people can change the constitution if they please, but while the constitution exists, they must conform themselves to its dictates: But I do not believe that the inhabitants of any district can speak the voice of the people, so far from it, their ideas may contradict the sense of the whole people; hence the consequence that instructions are binding on the representative is of a doubtful, if not of a dangerous nature. I do not conceive, therefore, that it is necessary to agree to the proposition now made; so far as any real good is to arise from it, so far that real good is provided for; so far as it is of a doubtful nature, so far it obliges us to run the risk of losing the whole system.

Mr. SMITH (of S.C.)

I am opposed to this motion, because I conceive it will operate as a partial inconvenience to the more distant states; if every member is to be bound by instructions how to vote, what are gentlemen from the extremities of the continent to do?

Members from the neighbouring states can obtain their instructions earlier than those from the southern ones, and I presume that particular instructions will be necessary for particular measures, of consequence we vote perhaps against instructions on their way to us, or we must decline voting at all; but what is the necessity of having a numerous representation; one member from a state can receive the instructions, and by his vote answer all the purposes of many, provided his vote is allowed to count for the proportion the state ought to send; in this way the business might be done at a less expence than having one or two hundred members in the house, which had been strongly contended for yesterday.

Mr. STONE.

I think the clause would change the government entirely, instead of being a government founded upon representation, it would be a democracy of singular properties.

I differ from the gentleman from Virginia (mr. Madison) if he thinks this clause would not bind the representative; in my opinion it would bind him effectually, and I venture to assert, without diffidence, that any law passed by the legislature, would be of no force, if a majority of the members of this house were instructed to the contrary, provided the amendment become part of the constitution. What would follow from this? Instead of looking in the code of laws passed by congress, your judiciary would have to collect and examine the instructions from the various parts of the union. It follows very clearly from hence, that the government would be altered from a representative one to a democracy, wherein all laws are made immediately by the voice of the people.

This is a power not to be found in any part of the earth except among the Swiss Cantons; there the body of the people vote upon the laws, and give instructions to their delegates. But here we have a different form of government, the people at large are not authorised under it to vote upon the law, nor did I ever hear that any man required it. Why then are we called upon to propose amendments subversive of the principles of the constitution which were never desired.

Several members now called for the question, and the chairman being about to put the same.

Mr. GERRY.

Gentlemen seem in a great hurry to get this business through, I think, mr. chairman, it requires a further discussion; for my part I had rather do less business and do it well, than precipitate measures before they are fully understood.

The honorable gentleman from Virginia (mr. Madison) stated, that if the proposed amendments are defeated, it will be by the delay attending the discussion of doubtful propositions; and he declares this to partake of that quality. It is natural, sir, for us to be fond of our own work, we do not like to see it disfigured by other hands. That honorable gentleman brought forward a string of propositions; among them was the clause now proposed to be amended, he is no doubt ready for the question and determined not to admit what we think an improvement. The gentlemen who were on the committee, and brought in the report, have considered the subject, and are also ripe for a decision. But other gentlemen may crave a like indulgence, is not the report before us for deliberation and discussion and to obtain the sense of the house upon it, and will not gentlemen allow us a day or two for these purposes, after they have forced us to proceed upon them at this time? I appeal to their candor and good sense on the occasion, and am sure not to be refused; and I must inform them now, that they may not be surprized hereafter, that I wish all the amendments, proposed by the respective states to be considered. Gentlemen say it is necessary to finish the subject, in order to reconcile a number of our fellow citizens to the government. If this is their principle, they ought to consider the wishes and intentions which the conventions have expressed for them; if they do this, they will find that they expect and wish for the declaration proposed by the honorable gentleman over the way (mr. Tucker) and of consequence they ought to agree to it, and why it, with others recommended in the same way, were not reported, I cannot pretend to say; the committee know this best themselves.

The honorable gentleman near me (mr. Stone) says, that the laws passed contrary to instruction will be nugatory. And other gentlemen ask, if their constituents instruct them to violate the constitution, whether they must do it? Sir, does not the constitution declare that all laws passed by congress are paramount to the laws and constitutions of the several states; if our decrees are of such force as to set aside the state laws and constitutions, certainly they may be repugnant to any instructions whatever without being injured thereby. But can we conceive that our constituents would be so absurd as to instruct us to violate our oath, and act directly contrary to the principles of a government ordained by themselves. We must look upon them to be absolutely abandoned and false to their own interests to suppose them capable of giving such instructions.

If this amendment is introduced into the constitution, I do not think we shall be much troubled with instructions; a knowledge of the right will operate to check a spirit that would render instruction necessary.

The honorable gentleman from Virginia asked, will not the affirmative of a member who votes repugnant to his instructions, bind the community as much as the votes of those who conform? There is no doubt, sir, but it will; but does this tend to shew that the constituent has no right to instruct? Surely not. I admit, sir, that instructions contrary to the constitution, ought not to bind, though the sovereignty resides in the people. The honorable gentleman acknowledges that the sovereignty vests there, if so, it may exercise its will in any case not inconsistent with a previous contract. The same honorable gentleman asks if we are to give the power to the people in detached bodies to contravene the government while it exists? Certainly not, nor does the proposed proposition extend to that point, it is only intended to open for them a convenient mode in which they may convey their sense to their agents. The gentleman therefore takes for granted what is inadmissable, that congress will always be doing illegal things, and make it necessary for the sovereign to declare its pleasure.

He says the people have a right to alter the constitution, but they have no right to oppose the government. If, while the government exists, they have no right to control it, it appears they have divested themselves of the sovereignty over the constitution. Therefore, our language, with our principles, must change, and we ought to say that the sovereignty existed in the people previous to the establishment of this government. This will be ground for alarm indeed if it is true, but I trust, sir, too much to the good sense of my fellow citizens ever to believe, that the doctrine will generally obtain in this country of freedom.

Mr. Vining.

If, mr. chairman, there appears on one side too great an urgency to dispatch this business, there appears on the other an unnecessary delay and procrastination equally improper and unpardonable. I think this business has been already well considered by the house, and every gentleman in it; however, I am not for an unseemly expedition.

The gentleman last up, has insinuated a reflection upon the committee for not reporting all the amendments proposed by some of the state conventions. I can assign him a reason for this, the committee conceived some of them superfluous or dangerous, and found many of them so contradictory that it was impossible to make any thing of them, and this is a circumstance the gentleman cannot pretend ignorance of.

Is it not inconsistent in that honorable member to complain of hurry, when he comes day after day reiterating the same train of arguments, and demanding the attention of this body by rising six or seven times on a question. I wish, sir, this subject discussed coolly and dispassionately, but I hope we shall have no more reiterations or tedious discussions; let gentlemen try to expedite public business, and their arguments will be conducted in a laconic and consistent manner. As to the business of instruction, I look upon it inconsistent with the general good. Suppose our constituents were to instruct us to make paper money, no gentleman pretends to say it would be unconstitutional, yet every honest mind must shudder at the thought. How can we then assert that instructions ought to bind us in all cases not contrary to the constitution?

Mr. LIVERMORE

Was not very anxious whether the words were inserted or not, but he had a great deal of doubt about the meaning of this whole amendment, it provides that the people may meet and consult for the common good; does this mean a part of the people in a township or district, or does it mean the representatives in the state legislatures? If it means the latter, there is no occasion for a provision that the legislature may instruct the members of this body.

In some states the representatives were chosen by districts, in this case, perhaps, the instructions may be considered as coming from the districts, but in other states, each representative was chosen by the whole people; in New-Hampshire it was the case there, the instructions of any particular place would have but little weight, but a legislative instruction would have considerable influence upon each representative. If, therefore, the words mean that the legislature may instruct, he presumed it would have considerable effect, though he did not believe it binding. Indeed he was inclined to pay a deference to any information, he might receive from any number of gentlemen, even by a private letter, but as for full binding force, no instructions contained that quality. They could not, nor ought not to have it, because different parties pursue different measures, and it might be expedient, nay absolutely necessary, to sacrifice them in mutual concessions.

The doctrine of instructions would hold better in England than here, because the boroughs and corporations might have an interest to pursue, totally immaterial to the rest of the kingdom, in this case it would be prudent to instruct their members in parliament.

Mr. GERRY

Wished the constitution amended without his having any hand in it, but if he must interfere he would do his duty. The honorable gentleman from Delaware, had given him an example of moderation and laconic and consistent debate that he meant to follow, and would just observe to the worthy gentleman last up, that several states had proposed the amendment, and among the rest New-Hampshire.

There was one remark which escaped him, when he was up before, the gentleman from Maryland (mr. Stone) had said that the amendment would change the nature of the government and make it a democracy; now he had always heard that it was a democracy, but perhaps he was mislead, and the honorable gentleman was right in distinguishing it by some other appellation, perhaps an aristocracy was a term better adapted to it.

Mr. SEDGWICK

Opposed the idea of the gentleman from New-Hampshire, that the state legislatures had the power of instructing the members of this house; he looked upon it as a subornation of the rights of the people to admit such an authority. We stand not here, said he, the representatives of the state legislatures as under the former congress,[25] but as the representatives of the great body of the people. The sovereignty, the independence, and the rights of the states, are intended to be guarded by the senate; if we are to be viewed in any other light, the greatest security the people have for their rights and privileges is destroyed.

But with respect to instructions, it is well worthy of consideration how they are to be procured, it is not the opinion of an individual that is to control my conduct; I consider myself a representative of the whole union. An individual may give me information, but his sentiments may be in opposition to the sense of the majority of the people: If instructions are to be of any efficacy, they must speak the sense of the majority of the people, at least of a state. In a state so large as Massachusetts it will behoove gentlemen to consider how the sense of the majority of the freemen is to be obtained and communicated. Let us take care to avoid the insertion of crude and indigested propositions, more likely to produce acrimony, than that spirit of harmony which we ought to cultivate.

Mr. LIVERMORE

Said that he did not understand the honorable gentleman, or was not understood by him; he did not presume peremptorily to say what degree of influence the legislative instructions would have on a representative, he knew it was not the thing in contemplation here, and what he had said respected only the influence it would have on his private judgments.

Mr. AMES

Said there would be a very great inconvenience attending the establishment of the doctrine contended for by his colleague, those states who had selected their members by districts would have no right to give them instructions, consequently the members ought to withdraw, in which case

[25] Members of the Continental and Confederation Congresses, 1774–89, were chosen by the state legislatures, with the exception of the delegations from Rhode Island after 1777 and Connecticut after 1779, which were popularly elected.

the house might be reduced below a majority, and not be able, according to the constitution, to do any business at all.

According to the doctrine of the gentleman from New-Hampshire, one part of the government would be annihilated, for of what avail is it that the people have the appointment of a representative, if he is to pay obedience to the dictates of another body.

Several members now rose and called for the question.

Mr. Page

Was sorry to see gentlemen so impatient, the more so as he saw there was very little attention paid to any thing that was said, but he would express his sentiments if he was only heard by the chair; he discovered clearly, notwithstanding what had been observed by the most ingenious supporters of the opposition, that there was an absolute necessity for adopting the amendment, it was strictly compatible with the spirit and the nature of the government, all power vests in the people of the United States, it is therefore a government of the people, a democracy; if it was consistent with the peace and tranquillity of the inhabitants, every freeman would have a right to come and give his vote upon the law, but inasmuch as this cannot be done, by reason of the extent of territory, and some other causes, the people have agreed that their representatives shall exercise a part of their authority; to pretend to refuse them the power of instructing their agents, appears to me to deny them a right. One gentleman asks how the instructions are to be collected. Many parts of this country have been in the practice of instructing their representatives; they found no difficulty in communicating their sense: Another gentleman asks if they were to instruct us to make paper money, what we would do? I would tell them, said he, it was unconstitutional, alter that, and we will consider on the point; unless laws are made satisfactory to the people, they will lose their support, they will be abused or done away; this tends to destroy the efficiency of the government.

It is the sense of several of the conventions that this amendment should take place; I think it my duty to support it, and fear it will spread an alarm among our constituents if we decline to do it.

Mr. Wadsworth.

Instructions have frequently been given to the representatives throughout the United States, but the people did not claim as a right that they should have any obligation upon the representative; it is not right that they should: In troublesome times designing men have drawn the people to instruct the representatives to their harm; the representatives have, on such occasions, refused to comply with their instructions. I have known, myself, that they have been disobeyed, and yet the representative was not brought to account for it, on the contrary, he was carressed and re-elected, while those who have obeyed them, contrary to their private sentiments, have ever after been despised for it: Now, if the people considered it an inherent right in them to instruct their representatives, they would have undoubtedly punished the violation of them. I have no idea of instructions, unless they are obeyed; a discretionary power is incompatible with them.

The honorable gentleman who was up last says, if he was instructed to make paper money, he would tell his constituents it was unconstitutional; I believe that is not the case, for this body would have a right to make paper money, but if my constituents were to instruct me to vote for such a measure, I would disobey them let the consequence be what it would.

Mr. SUMTER.

The honorable gentlemen who are opposed to the motion of my colleague, do not treat it fairly; they suppose that it is meant to bind the representative to conform to his instructions, the mover of this question, I presume to say, has no such thing in idea; that they shall notice them and obey them as far as is consistent and proper, may be very just; perhaps they ought to produce them to the house, and let them have as much influence as they deserve; but nothing further, I believe, is contended for.

I rose on this occasion, not so much to make any observations upon the point immediately under consideration, as to beg the committee to consider the consequences that may result from an undue precipitancy and hurry; nothing can distress me more than to be obliged to notice what I conceive to be somewhat improper in the conduct of so respectable a body. Gentlemen will reflect how difficult it is to remove error when once the passions are engaged in the discussion, temper and coolness are necessary to complete what must be the work of time; it cannot be denied but what the present constitution is imperfect, we must therefore take time to improve it. If gentlemen are pressed for want of time, and are disposed to adjourn the sessions of congress at a very early period, we had better drop the subject of amendments, and leave it until we have more leisure to consider and do the business effectually; for my part I would rather sit till this day twelve month, than have this all-important subject inconsiderately passed over; the people have already complained that the adoption of the constitution was done in too hasty a manner, what will they say of us if we press the amendments with so much haste.

Mr. BURKE.

It has been asserted, mr. chairman, that the people of America do not require this right; I beg leave to ask the gentleman from Massachusetts, whether the constitution of that state does not recognize that right, and the gentlemen from Maryland, whether their declaration of rights does not expressly secure it to the inhabitants of that state? These circumstances, added to what has been proposed by the state conventions as amendments to this constitution, pretty plainly declares the sense of the people to be in favor of securing to themselves and to their posterity, a right of this nature.

Mr. SENEY

Said that the declaration of rights prefixed to the constitution of Maryland, secured to every man a right of petitioning the legislature for a redress of grievances, in a peaceable and orderly manner.

Mr. BURKE.

I am not positive with respect to the particular expression in the declaration of rights of the people of Maryland, but the constitutions of Massachusetts, Pennsylvania and North-Carolina, all of them recognize, in express terms, the right of the people to give instruction to their representatives. I do not mean to insist particularly upon this amendment, but I am very well satisfied that those that are reported and likely to be adopted by this house, are very far from giving satisfaction to our constituents; they are not those solid and substantial amendments which the people expect; they are little better than whip-syllabub, frothy and full of wind, formed only to please the palate, or they are like a tub thrown out to a whale, to secure the freight of the ship and its peaceable voyage;[26] in my judgment they will not be gratified by the mode we have pursued in bringing them forward; there was a committee of eleven appointed, and out of them I think there were five who were members of the convention that formed the constitution, such gentlemen having already given their opinion with respect to the perfection of the work, may be thought improper agents to bring forward amendments; upon the whole, I think it will be found that we have done nothing but lose our time, and that it will be better to drop the subject now, and proceed to the organization of the government.

Mr. SINNICKSON

Enquired of mr. chairman, what was the question before the committee, for really debate had become so desultory, as to induce him to think it was lost sight of altogether.

Mr. LAURANCE

Was averse to entering on the business at first, but since they had proceeded so far, he hoped they would finish it; he said, if gentlemen would confine themselves to the question, when they were speaking, that the business might be done in a more agreeable manner; he said he was against the amendment proposed by the gentleman from S. Carolina (mr.

[26] "Seamen have a custom, when they meet a whale, to fling him out an empty tub by way of amusement, to divert him from laying violent hands upon the ship" (Jonathan Swift, *Tale of a Tub* [1704]. The phrase, "a tub to the whale," became a metaphor for a diversionary tactic.

Tucker,) because every member on this floor ought to consider himself the representative of the whole union, and not of the particular district which had chosen him, as their decisions were to bind every individual of the confederated states, it was wrong to be guided by the voice of a single district, whose interests might happen to clash with that of the general good, and unless instructions were to be considered as binding, they were altogether superfluous.

Mr. MADISON

Was unwilling to take up any more of the time of the committee, but on the other hand, he was not willing to be silent after the charges that had been brought against the committee, and the gentleman who introduced the amendments, by the honorable members on each side of him, (mr. Sumter and mr. Burke.) Those gentlemen say that we are precipitating the business, and insinuate that we are not acting with candor; I appeal to the gentlemen who have heard the voice of their country, to those who have attended the debates of the state conventions, whether the amendments now proposed, are not those most strenuously required by the opponents to the constitution? It was wished that some security should be given for those great and essential rights which they had been taught to believe were in danger. I concurred, in the convention of Virginia, with those gentlemen, so far as to agree to a declaration of those rights which corresponded with my own judgment, and the other alterations which I had the honor to bring forward before the present congress. I appeal to the gentlemen on this floor who are desirous of amending the constitution, whether these proposed are not compatible with what are required by our constituents; have not the people been told that the rights of conscience, the freedom of speech, the liberty of the press, and trial by jury, were in jeopardy; that they ought not to adopt the constitution until those important rights were secured to them.

But while I approve of these amendments, I should oppose the consideration at this time, of such as are likely to change the principles of the government, or that are of a doubtful nature; because I apprehend there is little prospect of obtaining the consent of two-thirds of both houses of congress, and three-fourths of the state legislatures, to ratify propositions of this kind; therefore, as a friend to what is attainable, I would limit it to the plain, simple, and important security that has been required. If I was inclined to make no alteration in the constitution I would bring forward such amendments as were of a dubious cast, in order to have the whole rejected.

Mr. BURKE

Never entertained an idea of charging gentlemen with the want of candor; but he would appeal to any man of sense and candor, whether the amendments contained in the report were any thing like the amendments required by the states of New-York, Virginia, New-Hampshire and Carolina, and having these amendments in his hand, he turned to them to shew the difference, concluding that all the important amendments were omitted in the report.

Mr. SMITH, (of S.C.)

Understood his colleague, who has just sat down, to have asserted that the amendment under consideration was contained in the constitution of the state of South-Carolina, this was not the fact.

Mr. BURKE

Said he mentioned the state of North-Carolina, and there it was inserted in express terms.

The question was now called for from several parts of the house, but a desultory conversation took place before the question was put; at length the call becoming very general, it was stated from the chair, and determined in the negative, 10 rising in favor of it, and 41 against it.

The question was now taken on the 2d clause of the 4th proposition as originally reported and agreed to.

Mr. AMES

Moved the committee to rise and report progress, which being agreed to;

Mr. Speaker having resumed the chair,

Mr. AMES

Moved to discharge the committee from any further proceeding, he was led to make the motion from two considerations; First, That as the committee were not restrained in their discussions, a great deal of time was consumed in unnecessary debate; And second, That as the constitution required two thirds of the house to acquiesce in amendments, the decisions of the committee, by a simple majority, might be set aside for want of the constitutional number to support them in the house. He further observed that it might have an evil influence, if alterations agreed to in committee were not adopted by the house.

Mr. Smith (of S.C.) was in favor of the motion.

Mr. GERRY

Thought that the object of the motion was to prevent such a thorough discussion of the business as the nature of it demanded. He called upon gentlemen to recollect the consistency of his honorable colleague, who had proposed to refer the subject to a select committee, lest an open and full examination should lay bare the muscles and sinews of the constitution; he had succeeded on that occasion, and the business was put into the hands of a select committee, he now proposes to curtail the debate, because gentlemen will not swallow the propositions as they stand, when their judgment and their duty requires to have them improved. Will this house, said he, agree that an important subject like this shall have less consideration than the most trifling business yet come before us? I hope they will not; if they are tired of it, let it be postponed until another session, when it can be attended with leisure and good temper. Gentlemen now feel the weather warm, and the subject is warm, no wonder it produces some degree of heat; perhaps as our next will be a winter session, we may go thro' more coolly and dispassionately.

Mr. SEDGWICK

Seconded Mr. Ames's motion, thinking there was little probability of getting through with the business, if gentlemen were disposed to offer motions, and dwell long upon them in committee, when there was no likelihood they would meet the approbation of two-thirds of both houses, and three-fourths of the state legislatures.

Mr. Gerry moved to call the yeas and noes on the motion.

Mr. PAGE

Begged gentlemen to consider, that the motion tended to deprive the members of that freedom of debate which they had heretofore been indulged in, and prevented the speaker from giving his sentiments; he was sorry to see this hurry, and hoped the subject would be fairly treated, otherwise the people might think they were unjustly dealt by. They would have a right to suppose with the honorable gentleman from Carolina (mr. Burke) that we meant nothing more than to throw out a tub to the whale.

Mr. BURKE

Would oppose the motion, and join in calling the yeas and nays, because its object must be to preclude debate. He was certain the subject was so variegated, and at the same time so important, that it could not be thoroughly discussed in any other manner than in a committee of the whole; and unless it was discussed in a satisfactory manner he apprehended it would occasion a great deal of mischief. He said the people knew, and were sensible that in ratifying the present constitution, they parted with their liberties, but it was under a hope that they would get them back again: Whether this was to be the case or not, he left it to time to discover, but the spirit which seemed now to prevail in the house was no favorable omen. He begged gentlemen to treat the subject with fairness and candor, and not depart from their usual mode of doing business.

Mr. SMITH (of S.C.)

Had said he would support the motion under an impression, that it was useless to carry a measure through the committee by a small majority, which was unlikely to meet the approbation of two-thirds of the house;

but as gentlemen appeared so desirous of pursuing the common routine of doing business, he would withdraw his support.

Mr. TUCKER

Was in hopes the honorable mover would have seen the impropriety of his motion, and have withdrawn it, but as he had not, he would presume to ask him upon what principle it was founded. Is it to precipitate the business, and prevent an investigation; or is it because the committee have spent some time on it, and made no progress? He thought the latter was not the case, because the committee had proceeded as far in it as could reasonably be expected for the time. The gentleman, says he, is apprehensive it may do harm to have propositions agreed to in committee, and rejected by the house; certainly there is no foundation for this apprehension, or the clause in the constitution, requiring the consent of two thirds of the legislature to amendments, is formed on wrong principles. If the propositions are reasonable in themselves, they ought to be admitted, but if they are improper, they ought to be rejected; we would not presume to prevent our constituents from contemplating the subject in their own mind.

Is this haste produced by a desire to adjourn? He was as desirous of adjourning as any member; but he would not sacrifice the duty he owed the public to his own private convenience.

Mr. LIVERMORE

Hoped the gentleman would withdraw his motion, because it would have a disagreeable aspect to leave the business in the unfinished state it now stood; he thought it had better been altogether let alone.

Mr. AMES

Withdrew his motion, and laid another on the table requiring two thirds of the committee to carry a question, and after some desultory conversation the house adjourned.

17 AUGUST 1789

Gazette of the United States, 22 August 1789

In Committee of the whole House.

7th Amendment. "No soldier shall in time of peace be quartered in any house without the consent of the owner, nor in time of war, but in a manner to be prescribed by law."

Mr. SUMTER moved to strike out the words "in time of peace" and also the last words of the paragraph from the word "owner."

Mr. SHERMAN said he thought this was going too far; occasion might arise in which it would be extremely injurious to put it in the power of any man to obstruct the public service: He adverted to the British regulations in this case, of quartering soldiers in public houses. This motion was negatived.

Mr. GERRY said, that he conceived the article might be so altered as to relieve the minds of the citizens of the United States. It is said, government will take care of the rights of the people; but these amendments are designed to prevent the arbitrary exercise of power. He then moved to insert between the words "but" and "in a manner," the words *by a civil magistrate*. Negatived.

The amendment was agreed to.

8th Amendment. "No person shall be subject, except in case of impeachment, to more than one trial for the same offence, nor shall be compelled to be a witness against himself, nor be deprived of life, liberty or property, without due process of law, nor shall private property be taken for public use without just compensation."

Mr. BENSON observed, that it was certainly a fact, that a person might be tried more than once for the same offence: Instances of this kind frequently occured. He therefore moved to strike out the words "one trial or." This was negatived.

Mr. SHERMAN was in favor of the motion.

Mr. LIVERMORE was opposed to it: He said: The clause appears to me essential; if it is struck out, it will hold up the idea that a person may be tried more than once for the same offence. Some instances of this kind have taken place; but they have caused great uneasiness: It is contrary to the usages of law and practice among us; and so it is to those of that country from which we have adopted our laws. I hope the clause will not be struck out.

Mr. PARTRIDGE moved to insert after the words "same offence," the words *by any law of the United States*. Negatived.

Mr. LAURANCE moved to insert after the words "nor shall" these words *in any criminal case*. This amendment was agreed to.

9th Amendment. "Excessive bail shall not be required, nor excessive fines imposed, nor cruel and unusual punishments inflicted."

Mr. LIVERMORE said, the clause appears to express much humanity, as such, he liked it; but as it appeared to have no meaning, he did not like it: As to bail, the term is indefinite, and must be so from the nature of things: and so with respect to fines; and as to punishments, taking away life is sometimes necessary, but because it may be thought cruel, will you therefore never hang any body—the truth is, matters of this kind must be left to the discretion of those who have the administration of the laws.

This amendment was adopted.

10th Amendment. "The rights of the people to be secure in their persons, houses, papers and effects, shall not be violated without probable cause, supported by oath or affirmation, and not particularly describing the places to be searched, and the persons or things to be seized."

Mr. BENSON moved to insert after the words "and effects," these words *against unreasonable seizures, and searches.*

This was carried.

Mr. GERRY objected to the words, "by warrants issuing"—He said the provision was good, as far as it went; but he thought it was not sufficient: He moved that it be altered to *and no warrant shall issue.* This was negatived.

The question was then put on the amendment and carried.

12th Amendment. Art. I, Sec. 10, between the 1st and 2d par. insert, "No state shall infringe the equal rights of conscience, nor freedom of speech, or of the press, nor of the right of trial by jury in criminal cases."

Mr. TUCKER moved to strike out these words altogether, as they were an interference with the Constitutions: The Constitution of the United States, he said, interfered too much already.

Mr. MADISON said he hoped the clause would be retained. I think, said he, these abuses are most likely to take place under the State governments; and if they are to be restrained in any thing, this appears to me the most necessary: We shall do what will be grateful to the people by retaining the clause.

Mr. TUCKER's motion was negatived.

The words on motion of Mr. LIVERMORE were then transposed, and the amendment agreed to.

13th Amendment. Art. 3. Sec. 2, add to the 2d par. "But no appeal to such court shall be allowed, where the value in controversy shall not amount to one thousand dollars; nor shall any fact triable by jury, according to the course of common law, be otherwise re-examinable than according to the rules of common law."

Mr. BENSON moved to strike out the first part of the paragraph respecting the limitation of appeals.

Mr. MADISON observed, that except some adequate substitute was proposed, he thought it would be necessary to retain the clause: There is, said he, perhaps no danger of any court in the United States, granting an appeal where the value in dispute does not amount to 1,000 dollars; still the possibility of such an event has excited the greatest apprehensions in the minds of many citizens of the United States: The idea that opulent persons might carry a cause from one end of the continent to another has caused serious fears in the minds of the people: I think it best to retain the clause.

The motion was negatived.

Mr. SEDGWICK, to strengthen the clause, moved to strike out 1,000 dollars, and to insert 3,000. This motion was seconded and supported by Mr. Livermore, but was negatived, and the amendment accepted.

The Congressional Register, 17 August 1789

The house went into a committee of the whole, on the subject of amendments. The 3d clause of the 4th proposition in the report was taken into consideration, being as follows; "A well regulated militia, composed of the body of the people, being the best security of a free state; the right of the people to keep and bear arms shall not be infringed, but no person, religiously scrupulous, shall be compelled to bear arms."

Mr. GERRY.

This declaration of rights, I take it, is intended to secure the people against the mal-administration of the government; if we could suppose that in all cases the rights of the people would be attended to, the occasion for guards of this kind would be removed. Now I am apprehensive, sir, that this clause would give an opportunity to the people in power to destroy the constitution itself. They can declare who are those religiously scrupulous, and prevent them from bearing arms.

What, sir, is the use of a militia? It is to prevent the establishment of a standing army, the bane of liberty. Now it must be evident, that under this provision, together with their other powers, congress could take such measures with respect to a militia, as make a standing army necessary. Whenever government mean to invade the rights and liberties of the people, they always attempt to destroy the militia, in order to raise an army upon their ruins. This was actually done by Great Britain at the commencement of the late revolution. They used every means in their power to prevent the establishment of an effective militia to the eastward. The assembly of Massachusetts, seeing the rapid progress that administration were making, to divest them of their inherent privileges, endeavored to counteract them by the organization of the militia, but they were always defeated by the influence of the crown.

Mr. SENEY

Wished to know what question there was before the committee, in order to ascertain the point upon which the gentleman was speaking?

Mr. GERRY

Replied, that he meant to make a motion, as he disapproved of the words as they stood. He then proceeded, No attempts that they made, were successful, until they engaged in the struggle which emancipated them at once from their thralldom. Now, if we give a discretionary power to exclude those from militia duty who have religious scruples, we may as well make no provision on this head; for this reason he wished the words to be altered so as to be confined to persons belonging to a religious sect, scrupulous of bearing arms.

Mr. JACKSON

Did not expect that all the people of the United States would turn Quakers or Moravians, consequently one part would have to defend the other, in case of invasion; now this, in his opinion, was unjust, unless the constitution secured an equivalent, for this reason he moved to amend the clause, by inserting at the end of it "upon paying an equivalent to be established by law."

Mr. SMITH, (of S.C.)

Enquired what were the words used by the conventions respecting this amendment; if the gentleman would conform to what was proposed by Virginia and Carolina, he would second him: He thought they were to be excused provided they found a substitute.

Mr. JACKSON

Was willing to accommodate; he thought the expression was, "No one, religiously scrupulous of bearing arms, shall be compelled to render military service in person, upon paying an equivalent."

Mr. SHERMAN

Conceived it difficult to modify the clause and make it better. It is well-known that those who are religiously scrupulous of bearing arms, are equally scrupulous of getting substitutes or paying an equivalent; many of them would rather die than do either one or the other—but he did not see an absolute necessity for a clause of this kind. We do not live under an arbitrary government, said he, and the states respectively will have the government of the militia, unless when called into actual service; beside, it would not do to alter it so as to exclude the whole of any sect, because there are men amongst the quakers who will turn out, notwithstanding the religious principles of the society, and defend the cause of their country. Certainly it will be improper to prevent the exercise of such favorable dispositions, at least whilst it is the practice of nations to determine their contests by the slaughter of their citizens and subjects.

Mr. VINING

Hoped the clause would be suffered to remain as it stood, because he saw no use in it if it was amended so as to compel a man to find a substitute, which, with respect to the government, was the same as if the person himself turned out to fight.

Mr. STONE

Enquired what the words "Religiously scrupulous" had reference to, was it of bearing arms? If it was, it ought so to be expressed.

Mr. BENSON,

Moved to have the words "But no person religiously scrupulous shall be compelled to bear arms" struck out. He would always leave it to the benevolence of the legislature—for, modify it, said he, as you please, it will be impossible to express it in such a manner as to clear it from ambiguity. No man can claim this indulgence of right. It may be a religious persuasion, but it is no natural right, and therefore ought to be left to the discretion of the government. If this stands part of the constitution, it will be a question before the judiciary, on every regulation you make with respect to the organization of the militia, whether it comports with this declaration or not? It is extremely injudicious to intermix matters of doubt with fundamentals.

I have no reason to believe but the legislature will always possess humanity enough to indulge this class of citizens in a matter they are so desirous of, but they ought to be left to their discretion.

The motion for striking out the whole clause being seconded, was put, and decided in the negative, 22 members voting for it, and 24 against it.

Mr. GERRY

Objected to the first part of the clause, on account of the uncertainty with which it is expressed: A well-regulated militia being the best security of a free state, admitted an idea that a standing army was a secondary one. It ought to read "a well regulated militia, trained to arms," in which case it would become the duty of the government to provide this security, and furnish a greater certainty of its being done.

Mr. GERRY's motion not being seconded, the question was put on the clause as reported, which being adopted,

Mr. BURKE

Proposed to add to the clause just agreed to, an amendment to the following effect: "A standing army of regular troops in time of peace, is dangerous to public liberty, and such shall not be raised or kept up in time of peace but from necessity, and for the security of the people, nor then without the consent of two-thirds of the members present of both houses, and in all cases the military shall be subordinate to the civil authority." This being seconded,

Mr. VINING

Asked whether this was to be considered as an addition to the last clause, or an amendment by itself? If the former, he would remind the gentleman the clause was decided; if the latter, it was improper to introduce new matter, as the house had referred the report specially to the committee of the whole.

Mr. BURKE

Feared that what with being trammelled in rules, and the apparent disposition of the committee, he should not be able to get them to consider any amendment; he submitted to such proceeding because he could not help himself.

Mr. HARTLEY

Thought the amendment in order, and was ready to give his opinion of it. He hoped the people of America would always be satisfied with having a majority to govern. He never wished to see two-thirds or three-fourths required, because it might put it in the power of a small minority to govern the whole union.

The question on mr. Burke's motion was put, and lost by a majority of 13.

The 4th clause of the 4th proposition was taken up as follows: "No soldier shall in time of peace, be quartered in any house, without the consent of the owner, nor in time of war but in a manner to be prescribed by law."

Mr. SUMTER

Hoped soldiers would never be quartered on the inhabitants, either in time of peace or war, without the consent of the owner: It was a burthen, and very oppressive, even in cases where the owner gave his consent; but where this was wanting, it would be a hardship indeed: Their property would lie at the mercy of men irritated by a refusal, and well disposed to destroy the peace of the family.

He moved to strike out all the words from the clause but "No soldier shall be quartered in any house without the consent of the owner."

Mr. SHERMAN

Observed that it was absolutely necessary that marching troops should have quarters, whether in time of peace or war, and that it ought not to be put in the power of an individual to obstruct the public service; if quarters were not to be obtained in public barracks, they must be procured elsewhere. In England, where they paid considerable attention to private rights, they billetted the troops upon the keepers of public houses, and upon private houses also, with the consent of the magistracy.

Mr. SUMTER's motion being put was lost by a majority of 16.

Mr. GERRY

Moved to insert between "but" and "in a manner" the words "by a civil magistrate" observing that there was no part of the union but what they could have access to such authority.

Mr. HARTLEY

Said those things ought to be entrusted to the legislature; that cases might arise where the public safety would be endangered by putting it in the power of one person to keep a division of troops standing in the inclemency of the weather for many hours, therefore he was against inserting the words.

Mr. GERRY said either his amendment was essential, or the whole clause was unnecessary.

On putting the question 13 rose in favor of the motion, 35 against it, and then the clause was carried as reported.

The 5th clause of the 4th proposition was taken up, viz. "no person shall be subject, in case of impeachment, to more than one trial or one punishment for the same offence, nor shall be compelled to be a witness against himself, nor be deprived of life, liberty or property, without due process of law, nor shall private property be taken for public use without just compensation."

Mr. BENSON

Thought the committee could not agree to the amendment in the manner it stood, because its meaning, appeared rather doubtful, it says that no person shall be tried more than once for the same offence, this is contrary to the right heretofore established, he presumed it was intended to express what was secured by our former constitution, that no man's life should be more than once put in jeopardy for the same offence, yet it was well known, that they were intitled to more than one trial; the humane intention of the clause was to prevent more than one punishment, for which reason he would move to amend it by striking out the words "one trial or."

Mr. SHERMAN

Approved of the motion, he said, that as the clause now stood, a person found guilty could not arrest the judgment, and obtain a second trial in his own favor, he thought that the courts of justice would never think of trying and punishing twice for the same offence, if the person was acquitted on the first trial, he ought not to be tried a second time, but if he was convicted on the first, and any thing should appear to set the judgment aside, he was intitled to a second, which was certainly favorable to him. Now the clause as it stands would deprive him of this advantage.

Mr. LIVERMORE

Thought the clause very essential, it was declaratory of the law as it now stood, striking out the words, would seem as if they meant to change the law by implication, and expose a man to the danger of more than one trial; many persons may be brought to trial for crimes they are guilty of, but for want of evidence may be acquitted; in such cases it is the universal practice in Great-Britain, and in this country, that persons shall not be brought to a second trial for the same offence, therefore the clause is proper as it stands.

Mr. SEDGWICK thought, instead of securing the liberty of the subject, it would be abridging the privileges of those who were prosecuted.

The question on Mr. Benson's motion being put, was lost by a considerable majority.

Mr. PARTRIDGE moved to insert after "same offence," the words, "by any law of the United States;" this amendment was lost also.

Mr. LAURANCE

Said this clause contained a general declaration, in some degree contrary to laws passed, he alluded to that part where a person shall not be compelled to give evidence against himself; he thought it ought to be confined to criminal cases, and moved an amendment for that purpose, which amendment being adopted, the clause as amended was unanimously agreed to by the committee, who then proceeded to the 6th clause of the 4th proposition in these words, "excessive bail shall not be required, nor excessive fines imposed, nor cruel and unusual punishments inflicted."

Mr. SMITH (of S.C.) objected to the words "nor cruel and unusual punishments," the import of them being too indefinite.

Mr. LIVERMORE.

The clause seems to express a great deal of humanity, on which account I have no objection to it; but as it seems to have no meaning in it, I do not think it necessary. What is meant by the terms excessive bail? Who are to be the judges? What is understood by excessive fines? It lays with the court to determine. No cruel and unusual punishment is to be inflicted; it is sometimes necessary to hang a man, villains often deserve whipping, and perhaps having their ears cut off; but are we in future to be prevented from inflicting these punishments because they are cruel? If a more lenient mode of correcting vice and deterring others from the commission of it could be invented, it would be very prudent in the legislature to adopt it, but until we have some security that this will be done, we ought not to be restrained from making necesary laws by any declaration of this kind.

The question was put on the clause, and it was agreed to by a considerable majority.

The committee went on to the consideration of the 7th clause of the 4th proposition, being as follows; "the right of the people to be secured in their persons, houses, papers and effects, shall not be violated by warrants issuing without probable cause, supported by oath or affirmation, and not particularly describing the place to be searched, and the persons or things to be seized."

Mr. Gerry

Said he presumed there was a mistake in the wording of this clause, it ought to be "the right of the people to be secure in their persons, houses, papers and effects, against unreasonable seizures and searches," and therefore moved that amendment.

This was adopted by the committee.

Mr. Benson

Objected to the words "by warrants issuing," this declaratory provision was good as far as it went, but he thought it was not sufficient, he therefore proposed to alter it so as to read "and no warrant shall issue."

The question was put on this motion, and lost by a considerable majority.

Mr. Livermore objected to the words "and not" between "affirmative and particularly." He moved to strike them out, in order to make it an affirmative proposition.

But the motion passed in the negative.

The clause as amended being now agreed to,

The 8th clause of the 4th proposition was taken up, which was "The enumeration in this constitution of certain rights shall not be construed to deny or disparage others retained by the people."

Mr. Gerry said it ought to be "deny or impair," for the word "disparage" was not of plain import; he therefore moved to make that alteration, but not being seconded, the question was taken on the clause, and it passed in the affirmative.

The committee then proceeded to the 5th proposition.

Art. 1. sect. 10. between the 1st and 2d paragraph insert "no state shall infringe the equal rights of conscience, nor the freedom of speech, or of the press, nor of the right of trial by jury in criminal cases."

Mr. Tucker.

This is offered, I presume, as an amendment to the constitution of the United States, but it goes only to the alteration of the constitutions of particular states; it will be much better, I apprehend, to leave the state governments to themselves, and not to interfere with them more than we already do, and that is thought by many to be rather too much; I therefore move, sir, to strike out these words.

Mr. Madison

Conceived this to be the most valuable amendment on the whole list; if there was any reason to restrain the government of the United States from infringing upon these essential rights, it was equally necessary that they should be secured against the state governments; he thought that if they provided against the one, it was as necessary to provide against the other, and was satisfied that it would be equally grateful to the people.

Mr. LIVERMORE had no great objection to the sentiment, but he thought it not well expressed. He wished to make it an affirmative proposition; "the equal rights of conscience, the freedom of speech, or of the press, and the right of trial by jury in criminal cases shall not be infringed by any state."

This transposition being agreed to, and mr. Tucker's motion being rejected, the clause was adopted.

The 6th proposition, art. 3. sect. 2. add to the 2d paragraph "But no appeal to such court shall be allowed, where the value in controversy shall not amount to one thousand dollars; nor shall any fact, triable by jury according to the course of the common law, be otherwise re-examinable than according to the rules of common law."

Mr. BENSON

Moved to strike out the first part of the paragraph respecting the limitation of appeals, because the question in controversy might be an important one, though the action was not to the amount of a thousand dollars.

Mr. MADISON.

If the gentleman will propose any restriction to answer his purpose, and for avoiding the inconvenience he apprehends, I am willing to agree to it, but it will be improper to strike out the clause without a substitute.

There is little danger that any court in the United States will admit an appeal where the matter in dispute does not amount to a thousand dollars, but as the possibility of such an event has excited in the minds of many citizens, the greatest apprehension that persons of opulence would carry a cause from the extremities of the union to the supreme court, and therefore prevent the due administration of justice, it ought to be guarded against.

Mr. LIVERMORE thought the clause was objectionable, because it comprehended nothing more than the value.

Mr. SEDGWICK

Moved to insert 3,000 dollars, in lieu of 1,000, but on the question, this motion was rejected, and the proposition accepted in its original form.

The committee then proceeded to consider the 7th proposition in the words following;

Art. 3, Sect. 2. Strike out the whole of the 3d paragraph, and insert, "In all criminal prosecutions, the accused, shall enjoy the right to a speedy and public trial, to be informed of the nature and cause of the accusation, to be confronted with the witnesses against him, to have compulsory process for obtaining witnesses in his favor, and to have the assistance of counsel for his defence."

Mr. BURKE

Moved to amend this proposition in such a manner, as to leave it in the power of the accused to put off their trial to the next session, provided he made appear to the court, that the evidence of the witnesses, for whom process was granted, but not served, was material to his defence.

Mr. HARTLEY

Said that in securing him the right of compulsory process, the government did all it could, the remainder must lay in the discretion of the court.

Mr. SMITH (of S.C.) thought the regulation would come properly in, as part of the judicial system.

The question on mr. Burke's motion was taken, and lost. Affirmative 9, negative 41.

Mr. LIVERMORE moved to alter the clause, so as to secure to the criminal the right of being tried in the state where the offence was committed.

Mr. STONE observed, that full provision was made on the subject in the subsequent clause.

On the question, Mr. Livermore's motion was adopted.

Mr. BURKE

Said he was not so much discouraged by the fate of his former motions, but what he would venture upon another, he therefore proposed to add to the clause, that no criminal prosecution should be had by way of information.

Mr. HARTLEY only requested the gentleman to look to the clause, and he would see the impropriety of inserting it in this place.

A desultory conversation rose, respecting the foregoing motion, and after some time mr. Burke withdrew it for the present.

18 AUGUST 1789

The Daily Advertiser, 19 August 1789

Mr. GERRY moved for the following order, that such of the amendments proposed by the several states, as are not in substance comprised in the report of the select committee appointed to consider amendments, be referred to a committee of the whole house, and that all the amendments which shall be agreed to by the committee last mentioned, be included in one report.

To this motion it was objected, that, as the amendments proposed by the different states had been referred to a committee of eleven, and their report was now referred to a committee of the whole; the amendments of the states were of course before the committee of the whole, as necessarily accompanying the report of the special committee, being part of the subject referred to them, and the documents on which their report was founded: It was therefore contended that it was out of order to make such a commitment. Mr. GERRY still persisting in his motion, the previous question was moved by Mr. VINING.

The previous question was then put, viz. "shall the main question be now put?" and the yeas and nays being called, it passed in the negative.

The Daily Advertiser, 20 August 1789

In publishing the proceedings of the house of Tuesday, we inserted a motion made by Mr. Gerry for referring to a committee of the whole house, such of the amendments proposed by the several states, as are not in substance comprised in the report of the select committee appointed to consider amendments and we observed that to this motion it was objected, that the amendments proposed by the different states were before the committee of the whole, and that the motion was therefore out of order—We should have observed that these objections were over ruled by the Speaker, who declared that the motion of Mr. Gerry was in order, it appearing by the Journals of the house that no reference had been made to the committee of the whole house of the amendments proposed by the states—the proceedings of the house were therefore on a regular motion of Mr. Gerry's: and as from our statement of it, a different impression may be made on the minds of the public, we hope this paragraph will be inserted by the printers who may have inserted the proceedings aforesaid.

Gazette of the United States, 19 August 1789

Mr. GERRY introduced a motion upon the subject of amendments, to this purport, That such amendments to the Constitution of the United States as have been proposed by the different States, which are not in the report of the select committee, be referred to a committee of the whole house—and that those, with the amendments proposed by that committee, be included in one report. This motion was introduced by a lengthy speech upon the subject of amendments at large and was seconded by Mr. Sumter—This brought on a warm debate, which continued till near one o'clock—when the question being called for from various parts of the house, the AYES and NOES were required by Mr. GERRY. Upon which Mr. VINING called for the previous question, and the Ayes and Noes were then required upon that also—this occasioned a further debate—at length the Speaker directed the Clerk to call the Ayes and Noes on *Shall the main question be put?*

Gazette of the United States, 22 August 1789

Committee of the whole on the subject of amendments.

Mr. Boudinot in the chair.

The committee took up the fifteenth amendment, which is

"The trial of all crimes (except in cases of impeachment, and in cases arising in the land or naval forces, or in the militia, when in actual service in time of war or public danger) shall be by an impartial jury of freeholders of the vicinage, with the requisite of unanimity for conviction, the right of challenge, and other accustomed requisites; and no person shall be held to answer for a capital, or otherwise infamous crime, unless on a presentment or indictment by a grand jury; but if a crime be committed in a place in the possession of an enemy, or in which an insurrection may prevail, the indictment and trial may by law be authorized in some other place within the same state; and if it be committed in a place not within a state, the indictment and trial may be at such place or places as the law may have directed."

Mr. BURKE moved to strike out "vicinage," and to insert "*county or district in which the offence has been committed.*" The gentleman enforced this motion by a variety of observations; and among others said that it was agreeable to the practice of the state he represented, and would give the constitution a more easy operation; that it was a matter of serious alarm to the good citizens of many of the States, the idea that they might be dragged from one part of the State perhaps 2 or 300 miles to the other for trial.

Mr. GERRY objected to the word "district" as too indefinite.

Mr. SEDGWICK said, that he conceived that the proposed amendment is not so adequate to the gentleman's object as the word "vicinage"—the latter part of the clause is sufficient for the gentleman's purpose.

The motion was negatived.

Mr. BURKE then proposed to add a clause to prevent prosecutions upon informations: This was objected to, as the object of the clause was to provide that high crimes, &c. should be by presentment of a grand jury; but that other things should take the course heretofore practised. This motion was lost.

And then the paragraph was adopted.

17th amendment: Immediately after art. 6, the following to be inserted as art. 7. "The powers delegated by this Constitution to the government of the United States shall be exercised as therein appropriated, so that the Legislative shall never exercise the powers vested in the Executive or the Judicial; nor the Executive the powers vested in the Legislative or Judicial; nor the Judicial the powers vested in the Legislative or Executive."

Mr. SHERMAN objected to this: He said it is unnecessary.

Mr. MADISON observed, that its adoption will satisfy the people: This separation of the powers is expected: It will serve to explain many cases that may arise under the Constitution, and can do no harm.

Mr. LIVERMORE said, that he objected to the clause altogether as in its operation it is subversive of the Constitution.

Mr. SEDGWICK, Mr. BENSON, and Mr. GERRY were in favor of this amendment, which was finally carried.

18th Amendment: "The powers not delegated by this Constitution, nor prohibited by it to the States, are reserved to the States respectively."

Mr. TUCKER proposed an introductory clause to this amendment, viz. *all power being derived from the people.*

Mr. MADISON objected to this, as confining the government within such limits as to admit of no implied powers, and I believe, said he, that no government ever existed which was not necessarily obliged to exercise powers by implication. This question was agitated in the Convention of Virginia; it was brought forward by those who were opposed to the Constitution, and was finally given up by them.[27]

Mr. SHERMAN observed, that all corporations are supposed to possess all the powers incidental to their corporate capacity: It is not in human wisdom to provide for every possible contingency.

This motion was negatived.

Mr. GERRY then proposed to add, after the word "States," *and people thereof.*

Mr. CARROLL objected to the addition, as it tended to create a distinction between the people and their legislatures.

The motion was negatived, and the amendment agreed to.

The Congressional Register, 18 August 1789

Mr. GERRY

Moved, "That such of the amendments to the constitution proposed by the several states, as are not in substance comprised in the report of the select committee, appointed to consider amendments, be referred to a

[27]The *GUS*, 26 Aug., reported that these observations were made after Gerry moved to insert the word "expressly" between "not" and "delegated" in the resolution. The insertion of that word was the question Madison said was agitated in the Convention of Virginia.

committee of the whole house; and that all amendments which shall be agreed to by the committee last mentioned, be included in one report."

Mr. TUCKER

Remarked, that many citizens expected that the amendments proposed by the conventions, would be attended to by the house, and that several members conceived it to be their duty to bring them forward; if the house should decline taking them into consideration, it might tend to destroy that harmony which had hitherto subsisted, and which did great honor to their proceedings, it might effect all their future measures, and promote such feuds as might embarrass the government exceedingly. The states who had proposed these amendments would feel some degree of chagrin at having misplaced their confidence in the general government; five important states have pretty plainly expressed their apprehensions of the danger to which the rights of their citizens are exposed; finding these cannot be secured in the mode they had wished, they will naturally occur to the alternative, and endeavor to obtain a federal convention, the consequence of this may be disagreeable to the union; party spirit may be revived, and animosities rekindled obstructive of tranquillity. States that exert themselves to obtain a federal convention; and those that oppose the measure, may feel so strongly the spirit of discord as to sever the union asunder.

If in this conflict the advocates for a federal convention should prove successful, the consequences may be alarming, we may lose many of the valuable principles now established in the present constitution; if on the other hand a convention should not be obtained, the consequences resulting are equally to be dreaded, it would render the administration of this system of government weak, if not impracticable; for no government can be administered with energy, however energetic its system, unless it obtains the confidence and support of the people, which of the two evils is the greatest would be difficult to ascertain.

It is essential to our deliberations that the harmony of the house be preserved, by it alone we shall be enabled to perfect the organization of the government; a government but in embryo, or at best but in its infancy.

My idea, relative to this constitution whilst it was dependant upon the assent of the several states was, that it required amendment, and that the proper time for amendment was previous to the ratification; my reasons were, that I conceived it difficult, if not impossible to obtain essential amendments by the way pointed out in the constitution; nor have I been mistaken in this suspicion, it will be found, I fear, still more difficult than I apprehended, for perhaps these amendments, should they be agreed to, by two-thirds of both houses of congress, will be submitted for ratification to the legislatures of the several states, instead of state conventions, in which case the chance is still worse. The legislatures of almost all the states consist of two independent distinct bodies, the amendments must be adopted by three-fourths of such legislatures, that is to say, it must meet the approbation of the majority of each of eighteen deliberative assemblies. But notwithstanding all these objections to obtaining amendments after the ratification of the constitution, it will tend to give a great degree of satisfaction to those who are desirous of them, if this house shall take them up and consider them with that degree of candor and attention they have hitherto displayed on the subjects that have come before them; consider the amendments separately, and after fair deliberation, either approve or disapprove of them; by such conduct, we answer in some degree the expectations of those citizens in the several states who have shewn so great a tenacity to the preservation of those rights and liberties they secured to themselves by an arduous persevering, and successful conflict.

I have hopes that the states will be reconciled to this disappointment, in consequence of such procedure.

A great variety of arguments might be urged in favor of the motion; but I shall rest it here, and not trespass any further upon the patience of the house.

Mr. MADISON

Was just going to move to refer these amendments, in order that they might be considered in the fullest manner; but it would be very inconvenient to have them made up into one report, or all of them discussed at the present time.

Mr. VINING

Had no objection to the bringing them forward in the fullest point of view; but his objection arose from the informality attending the introduction of the business.

The order of the house, was to refer the report of the committee of eleven to a committee of the whole, and therefore it was improper to propose any thing additional. A desultory conversation arose on this motion, when mr. Vining moved the previous question, in which being supported by five members, it was put, and the question was, shall the main question, to agree to the motion, be now put, the ayes and noes being demanded by one fifth of the members present, on this last motion they were taken.

So the motion was lost.

The house now resolved itself into a committee of the whole on the subject of amendments, and took into consideration the 2d clause of the 7th proposition, in the words following, "The trial of all crimes (except in cases of impeachment, and in cases arising in the land or naval forces, or in the militia when in actual service in time of war, or public danger) shall be by an impartial jury of freeholders of the vicinage, with the requisite of unanimity for conviction, the right of challenge, and other accustomed requisites; and no person shall be held to answer for a capital, or otherwise infamous crime, unless on a presentment, or indictment, by a grand jury; but if a crime be committed in a place in the possession of an enemy, or in which an insurrection may prevail, the indictment and trial may by law be authorised in some other place within the same state; and if it be committed in a place not within a state, the indictment and trial may be at such place or places as the law may have directed."

Mr. BURKE

Moved to change the word "vicinage" into "district or county in which the offence has been committed," he said this was conformable to the practice of the state of South Carolina, and he believed to most of the states in the union, it would have a tendency also to quiet the alarm entertained by the good citizens of many of the states for their personal security, they would no longer fear being dragged from one extremity of the state to the other for trial, at the distance of 3 or 400 miles.

Mr. LEE

Thought the word "vicinage" was more applicable than that of "district, or county," it being a term well understood by every gentleman of legal knowledge.

The question on mr. Burke's motion being put was negatived.

Mr. BURKE then revived his motion for preventing prosecutions upon information, but on the question this was also lost.

The clause was now adopted without amendment.

The 3d clause of the 7th proposition as follows, "In suits at common law, the right of trial by jury shall be preserved," was considered and adopted.

The 8th proposition in the words following, was considered, "Immediately after art. 6, the following to be inserted as art. 7."

"The powers delegated by this constitution to the government of the United States, shall be exercised as therein appropriated, so that the legislative shall not exercise the powers vested in the executive or the judicial; nor the executive the power vested in the legislative or judicial; nor the judicial the powers vested in the legislative or executive."

Mr. SHERMAN conceived this amendment to be altogether unnecessary, inasmuch as the constitution assigned the business of each branch of the government to a separate department.

Mr. MADISON

Supposed the people would be gratified with the amendment, as it was admitted, that the powers ought to be separate and distinct, it might also tend to an explanation of some doubts that might arise respecting the construction of the constitution.

Mr. LIVERMORE, thinking the clause subversive of the constitution, was opposed to it, and hoped it might be disagreed to.

On the motion being put, the proposition was carried.

The 9th proposition in the words following was considered, "The powers not delegated by the constitution, nor prohibited by it to the states, are reserved to the states respectively."

Mr. TUCKER

Proposed to amend the proposition by prefixing to it, "all powers being derived from the people," thought this a better place to make this assertion than the introductory clause of the constitution, where a similar sentiment was proposed by the committee. He extended his motion also, to add the word "expressly" so as to read "The powers not expressly delegated by this constitution."

Mr. MADISON

Objected to this amendment, because it was impossible to confine a government to the exercise of express powers, there must necessarily be admitted powers by implication, unless the constitution descended to recount every minutiae. He remembered the word "expressly" had been moved in the convention of Virginia, by the opponents to the ratification, and after full and fair discussion was given up by them, and the system allowed to retain its present form.

Mr. SHERMAN

Coincided with mr. Madison in opinion, observing that corporate bodies are supposed to possess all powers incident to a corporate capacity, without being absolutely expressed.

Mr. TUCKER

Did not view the word "expressly" in the same light with the gentleman who opposed him; he thought every power to be expressly given that could be clearly comprehended within any accurate definition of the general power.

Mr. TUCKER's motion being negatived,

The committee then rose and reported the amendments as amended by the committee.

19 AUGUST 1789

The Congressional Register, 19 August 1789

The house then took into consideration the amendments to the constitution, as reported by the committee of the whole.

Mr. SHERMAN renewed his motion for adding the amendments to the constitution by way of supplement.

Hereupon ensued a debate similar to what took place in the committee of the whole [*on 13 August*] but on the question, mr. Sherman's motion was carried by two-thirds of the house, of consequence it was agreed to.[28]

The first proposition of amendment was rejected because two-thirds of the members present did not support it.

Mr. AMES

Then brought forward his motion respecting the representation; suggested, [*on 14 August*]. A desultory conversation took place, and several amendments of the motion were attempted, but the house adjourned without coming to any determination.

20 AUGUST 1789

Gazette of the United States, 22 August 1789

The subject of amendments resumed.

Mr. AMES's proposition was taken up. Five or six other gentlemen brought in propositions on the same point; and the whole by mutual consent, were laid on the table.

Mr. SCOTT objected to the clause in the sixth amendment, "No person religiously scrupulous shall be compelled to bear arms." He said, if this becomes part of the constitution, we can neither call upon such persons for services nor an equivalent; it is attended with still further difficulties, for you can never depend upon your militia. This will lead to the violation of another article in the constitution, which secures to the people the right of keeping arms, as in this case you must have recourse to a standing army. I conceive it is a matter of legislative right altogether. I know there are many sects religiously scrupulous in this respect: I am not for abridging them of any indulgence by law; my design is to guard against those who are of no religion. It is said that religion is on the decline; if this is the case, it is an argument in my favour; for when the time comes that there is no religion, persons will more generally have recourse to these pretexts to get excused.

Mr. BOUDINOT said that the provision in the clause or something like it appeared to be necessary. What dependence can be placed in men who are conscientious in this respect? Or what justice can there be in compelling them to bear arms, when, if they are honest men they would rather

[28]The *GUS*, 22 Aug., stated that Sherman's motion received the votes of "more than three fourths of the members present."

die than use them. He then adverted to several instances of oppression in the case which occurred during the [*revolutionary*] war. In forming a militia we ought to calculate for an effectual defence, and not compel characters of this description to bear arms. I wish that in establishing this government we may be careful to let every person know that we will not interfere with any person's particular religious profession. If we strike out this clause, we shall lead such persons to conclude that we mean to compel them to bear arms.

Mr. VINING and Mr. JACKSON spake upon the question. The words *in person* were added after the word "arms," and the amendment was adopted.

21 AUGUST 1789

The Congressional Register, 21 August 1789

The house proceeded in the consideration of the amendments to the constitution reported by the committee of the whole, and took up the 2d clause of the 7th proposition.

Mr. GERRY

Then proposed to amend it by striking out these words, "public danger" and to insert foreign invasion; this being negatived, it was then moved to strike out the last clause, "and if it be committed, &c." to the end. This motion was carried, and the amendment was adopted.

The house then took into consideration the 3d clause of the 7th proposition, which was adopted without debate.

The 8th proposition was agreed to in the same manner.

The 9th proposition, mr. Gerry proposed to amend by inserting the word "expressly" so as to read the powers not expressly delegated by the constitution, nor prohibited to the states, are reserved to the states respectively or to the people; as he thought this an amendment of great importance, he requested the ayes and noes might be taken. He was supported in this by one fifth of the members present, whereupon they were taken.

Mr. SHERMAN

Moved to alter the last clause so as to make it read, the powers not delegated to the United States, by the constitution, nor prohibited by it to the states, are reserved to the states respectively, or to the people.

This motion was adopted without debate.

Mr. BURKE.

The majority of this house may be inclined to think all our propositions unimportant, as they seemed to consider that upon which the ayes and noes were just now called. However, to the minority they are important; and it will be happy for the government, if the majority of our citizens are not of their opinion; but be this as it may, I move you, sir, to add to the articles of amendment, the following, "Congress shall not alter, modify, or interfere in the times, places, or manner of holding elections of senators, or representatives, except when any state shall refuse or neglect, or be unable, by invasion or rebellion, to make such election."

Mr. AMES

Thought this one of the most justifiable of all the powers of congress, it was essential to a body representing the whole community, that they should have power to regulate their own elections, in order to secure a representation from every part, and prevent any improper regulations, calculated to answer party purposes only. It is a solecism in politics, to let others judge for them, and is a departure from the principles upon which the constitution was founded.

Mr. LIVERMORE

Said, this was an important amendment, and one that had caused more debate in the convention of New-Hampshire than any other whatever. The gentleman just up, said it was a solecism in politics, but he could cite an instance in which it had taken place. He only called upon gentlemen to recollect the circumstance of mr. Smith's (of South-Carolina) election, and answer him was not that decided by the state laws? Was not his qualification as a member of the federal legislature, determined upon the laws of South-Carolina? It was not supposed by the people of South-Carolina, that the house would question a right derived by their representative from their authority.[29]

Mr. MADISON.

If this amendment had been proposed at any time either in the committee of the whole or separately in the house, I should not have objected to the discussion of it. But I cannot agree to delay the amendments now agreed upon, by entering into the consideration of propositions not likely to obtain the consent of either two-thirds of this house or three-fourths of the state legislatures. I have considered this subject with some degree of attention, and upon the whole, am inclined to think the constitution stands very well as it is.

---

[29] David Ramsay, one of the candidates for election to the U.S. House of Representatives from Charleston, S.C., and its environs, protested to the House that the winner, William Smith, did not meet the seven-year citizenship requirement of Article I of the U.S. Constitution. On 22 May 1789 the House resolved that Smith satisfied the requirement.

Mr. GERRY

Was sorry that gentlemen objected to the time and manner of introducing this amendment, because it was too important in its nature to be defeated by want of form. He hoped, and he understood it to be the sense of the house that each amendment should stand upon its own ground; if this was, therefore, examined on its own merits, it might stand or fall as it deserved, and there would be no cause for complaint on the score of inattention.

His colleague, (mr. Ames,) objected to the amendment, because he thought no legislature was without the power of determining the mode of its own appointment, but he would find, if he turned to the constitution of the state he was a representative of, that the times, places and manner of chusing members of their senate and council were prescribed therein.

Why, said he, are gentlemen desirous of retaining this power? Is it because it gives energy to the government? It certainly has no such tendency; then why retain a clause so obnoxious to almost every state? But this provision may be necessary in order to establish a government of an arbitrary kind, to which the present system is pointed in no very indirect manner: In this way, indeed, it may be useful. If the United States are desirous of controlling the elections of the people, they will in the first place, by virtue of the powers given them by the 4th sect. of the 1st art. abolish the mode of balloting,[30] then every person must publicly announce his vote, and it would then frequently happen that he would be obliged to vote for a man or the friend of a man to whom he was under obligations. If the government grows desirous of being arbitrary, elections will be ordered at remote places, where their friends alone will attend. Gentlemen will tell me that these things are not to be apprehended; but if they say that the government has the power of doing them, they have no right to say the government will never exercise such powers, because it is presumable that they will administer the constitution at one time or another with all its powers, and whenever that time arises, farewell to the rights of the people, even to elect their own representatives.

Mr. STONE

Called upon gentlemen to shew what confederated government had the power of determining on the mode of their own election. He apprehended

[30] Article I, Section 4 of the Constitution provides that "Congress may at any time by Law make or alter such [*election*] Regulations, except as to the Places of chusing Senators."

there were none; for the representatives of states were chosen by the states in the manner they pleased. He was not afraid that the general government would abuse this power, and as little afraid that the states would; but he thought it was in the order of things that the power should vest in the states respectively, because they can vary their regulations to accommodate the people in a more convenient manner than can be done in any general law whatever. He thought the amendment was generally expected, and therefore on the principles of the majority ought to be adopted.

Mr. SMITH (of S.C.)

Said he hoped it would be agreed to, that eight states had expressed their desires on this head, and all of them wished the general government to relinquish their control over the elections. The eight states he alluded to were New-Hampshire, Massachusetts, New-York, Pennsylvania, Maryland, Virginia, North-Carolina, and South-Carolina.

Mr. CARROLL denied that Maryland had expressed the desire attributed to her.

Mr. FITZSIMONS. The remark was not just as it respected Pennsylvania.

Mr. SMITH (of S.C.) said the convention of Maryland, appointed a committee to recommend amendments, and among them was the one now under consideration.

Mr. STONE replied there was nothing of the kind noticed on the journals of that body.

Mr. SMITH (of S.C.)

Did not know how they came into the world, but he had certainly seen them. As to Pennsylvania there was a very considerable minority, he understood one third, who had recommended the amendment. Now, taking all circumstances into consideration, it might be fairly inferred that a majority of the United States was in favor of this amendment. He had studied to make himself acquainted with this particular subject, and all that he had ever heard in defence of the power being exercised by the general government was, that it was necessary, in case any state neglected or refused to make provision for the election. Now these cases were particularly excepted by the clause proposed by his honorable colleague; and therefore he presumed there was no good argument against it.

Mr. SEDGWICK

Moved to amend the motion by giving the power to congress to alter the times, manner and places of holding elections, provided the states made improper ones; for as much injury might result to the union from improper regulations, as from a neglect or refusal to make any; it is as much to be apprehended that the states may abuse their powers, as that the United States may make an improper use of theirs.

Mr. AMES

Said, that inadequate regulations were equally injurious, as having none; and that such an amendment as was now proposed, would alter the constitution; it would vest the supreme authority in places where it was never contemplated.

Mr. SHERMAN

Observed, that the convention were very unanimous in passing this clause, that it was an important provision, and if it was resigned it would tend to subvert the government.

Mr. MADISON

Was willing to make every amendment that was required by the states, which did not tend to destroy the principles, and the efficacy of the constitution; he conceived that the proposed amendment would have that tendency, he was therefore opposed to it.

Mr. SMITH, (of S.C.)

Observed, that the states had the sole regulation of elections, so far as it respected the president. Now he saw no good reason why they should be indulged in this, and prohibited from the other, but the amendment did not go so far; it admitted that the general government might interfere whenever the state legislature refused or neglected; and it might happen that the business would be neglected without any design to injure the administration of the general government; it might be that the two branches of the legislature could not agree, as happened he believed in the legislature of New-York, with respect to their choice of senators at their late session.

Mr. TUCKER.

Objected to mr. Sedgwick's motion of amendment, because it had a tendency to defeat the object of the proposition brought forward by his colleague, (mr. Burke.) The general government would be the judge of inadequate or improper regulations, of consequence they might interfere in any or every law which the states might pass on that subject.

He wished that the state legislatures might be left to themselves to perform every thing they were competent to, without the guidance of congress, he believed there was no great danger, but they knew they would pursue their own good, as well when left to their discretion, as they would under the direction of a superior. It seemed to him as if there was a strong propensity in this government to take upon themselves the guidance of the state government, which to his mind implied a doubt of their capacity, to govern themselves, now his judgment was convinced that the particular state governments could take care of themselves, and deserved more to be trusted than this did, because the right of the citizens were more secure under it.

It had been supposed by some states, that electing by districts was the most convenient mode of chusing members to this house; others have thought that the whole state ought to vote for the whole number of members to be elected for that state. Congress might, under like impressions, set their regulations aside. He had heard that many citizens of Virginia (which state was divided into eleven districts) supposed themselves abridged of nine-tenths of their privilege by being restrained to the choice of one man instead of ten, the number that state sends to this house.

With respect to the election of senators, the mode is fixed, every state but New-York, has established a precedent, there is therefore but little danger of any difficulty on this account. As to New-York, she suffers by her want of decision, it is her own loss, but probably they may soon decide the point, and then no difficulty can possibly arise hereafter;[31] from all these considerations he was induced to hope mr. Sedgwick's motion would be negatived, and his colleague's agreed to.

Mr. GOODHUE

Hoped the amendment never would obtain. Gentlemen should recollect there appeared a large majority against amendments, when the subject was first introduced, and he had no doubt but that majority still existed. Now, rather than this amendment should take effect, he would vote against all that had been agreed to. His greatest apprehensions were, that the state governments would oppose and thwart the general one to such a degree as finally to overturn it: Now, to guard against this evil, he wished the federal government to possess every power necessary to its existence.

Mr. BURKE

Was convinced there was a majority against him, but nevertheless he would do his duty, and propose such amendments as he conceived essential to secure the rights and liberties of his constituents. He begged permission to make an observation or two, not strictly in order; the first was on an assertion that had been repeated more than once in this house, "That this revolution or adoption of the new constitution was agreeable to the public mind, and that those who opposed it at first are now satisfied with it." I believe, sir, said he, that many of those gentlemen who agreed to the ratification without amendments, did it from principles of patri-

[31] In New York a dispute between the Antifederalist assembly and the Federalist senate prevented the state from electing U.S. senators. Federalists won control of both houses in the election of 1789 and Gov. George Clinton called the legislature into special session on 6 July. The senators were elected on 16 July and took their seats at the end of the month.

otism, but they knew at the same time, that they parted with their liberties, yet they had such reliance on the virtue of a future congress, that they did not hesitate, expecting that they would be restored to them unimpaired as soon as the government commenced its operations, conformably to what was mutually understood at the sealing and delivering up those instruments.

It has been supposed that there is no danger to be apprehended from the general government of an invasion of the rights of election. I will remind gentlemen of an instance in the government of Holland. The patriots in that country, fought no less strenuously for that prize than the people of America; yet, by giving to the states general powers not unlike those in this constitution, their right of representation was abolished. That they once possessed it is certain, and that they made as much talk about its importance as we do; but now the right has ceased, all vacancies are filled by the men in power. It is our duty, therefore, to prevent our liberties from being foolled away in a similar manner; consequently we ought to adopt the clause, which secures to the general government every thing that ought to be required.

Mr. MADISON

Observed, that it was the state governments in the Seven United Provinces which had assumed to themselves the power of filling vacancies, and not the general government, therefore the gentleman's application did not hold.

The question on mr. Sedgwick's motion for amending mr. Burke's proposition was put and lost.

The question was then put on mr. Burke's motion, and the ayes and noes being demanded by the constitutional number; they were taken.

So it was determined in the negative.

The house then resumed the consideration of the proposition respecting the apportioning of the representation to a certain ratio, proposed by mr. Ames.

When, after some desultory conversation, it was agreed to as follows; "After the first enumeration, required by the first article of the constitution, there shall be one representative for every 30,000, until the number shall amount to one hundred. After which, the proportion shall be so regulated by congress, that there shall be not less than one hundred representatives, nor less than one representative for every 40,000 persons, until the number of the representatives shall amount to two hundred; after which the proportion shall be so regulated by congress, that there shall not be less than two-hundred representatives, nor less than one representative for 50,000 persons."

22 August 1789

Gazette of the United States, 26 August 1789

The amendments to the Constitution as altered and agreed to by the House, were read.

Mr. TUCKER then proposed the following amendment in substance: That Congress shall not exercise the power of levying direct taxes, except in cases where any of the States shall refuse, or neglect to comply with their requisitions.

Mr. PAGE said, although I wish the way may be always open for every member of this house to propose amendments to the Constitution—yet as the business is so far completed with respect to the report of the committee, I think it will be best to proceed and finish this report, and in the mean time refer this to the select committee of eleven.

Mr. TUCKER: I hope, Sir, the proposition will be attended to at the present time—as the house is upon the subject, and considerable progress is made, this amendment may be added with ease, if it should be agreed to—I think it best to finish the whole business now Congress has it before them.

Mr. JACKSON opposed the proposition: I hope, Sir, that the experience we have had will be sufficient to prevent Congress ever divesting themselves of this power—This experience forcibly points out the impropriety of adopting this amendment—requisitions upon several States it is well known, tho made several years since, remain uncomplied with to this day; and no inducements in future can ever be supposed to be sufficiently operative, to induce so universal a compliance with requisitions, as to secure the public good, if a sense of common danger, war, and the facility of payment in a paper medium were not sufficient to do it: But this plan of requisitions is pregnant with difficulties of various kinds—it will excite jealousies—insurrections—and civil war, dissolve the Union, and expose us to the contempt and invasion of foreign powers: For if this power is taken from Congress, you divest the United States of the means of protecting the Union, or providing for the existence and continuation of the government.

Mr. LIVERMORE supported the motion: He said, it is more important than all that has been agreed to: This is an amendment to some purpose, and which a number of the States have particularly called for: Without some to more purpose is held out to the people, that I have the honor to represent, they will consider these as a mere musketo bite—they will not give a pinch of snuff for them all.

Mr. PAGE observed, that this proposition is one about which the warmest friends to amendments have differed in opinion: Some of them have entirely ceased urging it, and others have become the most strenuous advocates for the reverse; and now say that the government ought never to give up this power: For my part, experience has fully evinced that no dependence can be placed upon requisitions: If in a time of war, and when we made paper money by hogsheads full, they were disregarded, I have no expectation that any dependence in future can be placed in them—I shall therefore be against the proposition.

Mr. GERRY moved, that it be referred to a select committee.

Mr. TUCKER objected to this motion, he said the subject of amendments is still open—as the report of the committee is not yet completed.

Mr. GERRY advocated the object of the motion; but he did not think that object fully comprehended in the motion now before the house: He then entered into a general discussion of the question, and pointed out the consequences of the exercise of this power by the general government, as involving the annihilation of the State governments.

Mr. TUCKER: I do not see the arguments in favour of giving Congress this power in so strong a light as some gentlemen do: It will be to erect an *imperium in imperio*;[32] which is always considered as subversive of all government. Whenever Congress shall exercise this power, it will raise commotions in the states; whereas the mode of requisitions will operate in such an easy way, by being consonant to the habits of the people, that the supplies will be sooner realized into the public treasury in this, than by the other mode. Much time must be spent in forming a uniform system of taxation, which shall operate equally and justly through all the States, if it is possible to form such a system. It is said that requisitions have not been complied with in former times; but it is to be expected that there will not be so much difficulty in future. The requisitions will be greatly diminished by reason of the supplies from the impost; besides, should any of the States not comply, they will in that case be liable to the exercise of the power of Congress in the very heart of such States as are delinquent; this power would be so disagreeable, that the dread of it would serve to stimulate the States to an immediate and prompt compliance with the requisitions. This amendment is proposed by several of the States, and some of the most important; and for this, and other reasons which have been offered, I hope the amendment will be adopted.

Several methods of disposing of this question for the present were proposed, but the motion for its lying on the table being put and negatived, Mr. PARTRIDGE, referring to his instructions, was solicitous that this

[32] A state within a state.

amendment should not be too suddenly decided upon, moved the previous question, which was negatived.

Mr. SEDGWICK observed, that he believed he felt the force of the instructions from his constituents which they ought to have upon his mind, and to as great a degree as other gentlemen; but Sir, said he, a government entrusted with the freedom, and the very existence of the people, ought surely to possess, in the most ample manner, the means of supporting its own existence; and as we do not know what circumstances we *may* be in, nor how necessary it may be for Congress to exercise this power, I should think it a violation of the oath I have taken to support this constitution, were I now to vote for this amendment.

Mr. SHERMAN observed that if congress should exercise this power, the taxes would be laid by the immediate representatives of the people; nor would there be any necessity for adopting one uniform method of collecting direct taxes: The several states may be accommodated by a reference to their respective modes of taxation.

The question upon the paragraph being called for from all parts of the house, the ayes and noes stand thus:[33]

The Congressional Register, 22 August 1789

The house resumed the consideration of the amendments to the constitution. When

Mr. TUCKER

Moved the following as a proposition to be added to the same. "The congress shall never impose direct taxes but where the monies arising from the duties, imposts and excise are insufficient for the public exigencies, nor then until congress shall have made a requisition upon the states to assess, levy, and pay their respective proportions of such requisitions. And in case any state shall neglect, or refuse to pay its proportion, pursuant to such requisition, then congress may assess, and levy such states proportioned, together with the interest thereon at the rate of 6 per cent. per annum, from the time of payment prescribed by such requisition."

Mr. PAGE

Said that he hoped every amendment to the constitution would be considered separately in the manner this was proposed, but he wished them considered fully; it ought to have been referred to the committee of eleven, reported upon, and then to the committee of the whole. This was

[33] The *NYDA*, 24 Aug., stated that Livermore called for the yeas and nays.

the manner in which the house had decided upon on all those already agreed to, and this ought to be the manner in which this should be decided, he should be sorry to delay what was so nearly completed on any account; the house has but little time to sit, and the subject has to go before the senate, therefore it requires of us, all the expedition we can possibly give it. I would prefer putting a finishing hand to what has been already agreed to, and refer this to the committee of eleven, for their consideration.

Mr. TUCKER.

This proposition was referred to the committee, along with many others in the gross; but the committee of eleven declined reporting upon it. I understood it to be in any gentleman's power to bring it forward when he thought proper, and it was under this influence that I proposed it, nor do I conceive it to be an improper time. The house is engaged in the discussion of amendments; they have made some progress; and I wish them to go on to complete what they have begun. This may be added without inconvenience if it meets the sense of the house; but if it does not, I wish my constituents to be acquainted with our decision on the whole subject, and therefore hope it may be decided upon at this time.

Mr. JACKSON.

The gentleman has an undoubted right to bring forward the proposition; but I differ greatly with respect to its propriety. I hope, sir, the experience we have had, will be sufficient to prevent us from ever agreeing to a relinquishment of such an essential power. The requisitions of the former congress were ineffectual to obtain supplies; they remain to this day neglected by several states. If a sense of common danger, if war, and that a war of the noblest kind, a contest for liberty, were not sufficient to stimulate the states to a prompt compliance, when the means was abundant, by reason of the immense quantities of paper medium, can we ever expect an acquiescence to a requisition in future, when the only stimulus is honesty, to enable the confederation to discharge the debts incurred by the late war?

But suppose requisitions were likely to be, in some degree, complied with, (which by the by I never can admit) in every case where a state had neglected or refused to furnish its quota, congress must come in, assess and collect it. Now in every such case, I venture to affirm, that jealousies would be excited, discontent would prevail, and civil wars break out. What less can gentlemen picture to themselves, when a government has refused to perform its obligations, but that it will support its measures by the point of the bayonet.

Without the power of raising money to defray the expences of government, how are we to be secure against foreign invasion? What, can a government exert itself, with its sinews torn from it? We can expect neither strength nor exertion; and without these are acquired and preserved, our union will not be lasting; we shall be rent assunder by intestine commotion, or exterior assault, and when that period arrives, we may bid adieu to all the blessings we have purchased at the price of our fortunes, and the blood of our worthiest heroes.

Mr. LIVERMORE

Thought this an amendment of more importance than any yet obtained; that it was recommended by five or six states, and therefore ought to engage their most serious consideration. It had been supposed that the United States will not attempt to levy direct taxes, but this is certainly a mistake; he believed nothing but the difficulty of managing the subject would deter them: The mode of levying and collecting taxes pursued by the several states are so various, that it is an insuperable obstacle to an attempt by the general government.

He was sensible the requisitions of the former congress had not been fully complied with, and the defect of the confederation was, that the government had no powers to enforce a compliance. The proposition now under consideration obviated that difficulty. Suppose one or two states refused to comply, certainly the force of the others could compel them, and that is all that ought to be required; because it is not to be supposed that a majority of the states will refuse, as such an opposition must destroy the union. He hoped the states would be left to furnish their quotas in a manner the most easy to themselves, as was requested by more than the half of the present union.

Unless something more effectual was done to improve the constitution, he knew his constituents would be dissatisfied. As to the amendments already agreed to, they would not value them more than a pinch of snuff, they went to secure rights never in danger.

Mr. PAGE

Wished the proposition might be recommitted, for he was certain there was neither time nor inclination to add it to those already agreed upon.

He observed that the warmest friends to amendments differed in opinion on this subject; many of them have ceased urging it, while others have become strenuous advocates for the reverse: The most judicious and discerning men now declare that the government ought never to part with this power. For his part, experience had convinced him that no reliance was to be had on requisitions, when the states had treated them with contempt in the hour of danger, and had abundant means of compliance. The public credit stood at this moment in the utmost need of support, and he could not consent to throw down one of its strongest props. He thought there was no danger of an abuse of this power, for the government would not have recourse to it while the treasury could be supplied from any other source, and when they did, they would be studious of adapting their law to the convenience of the states. He hoped when the gentleman returned home to New-Hampshire, his constituents would give him credit for his exertions, and be better satisfied with the amendments than he now supposed them to be.

Mr. SUMTER

Felt himself so sensibly impressed with the importance of the subject, that if he apprehended the proposition would not have a fair discussion at this time, he would second the motion of commitment, and had not a doubt but the house would acquiesce in it.

Gentlemen had said that the states had this business much at heart. Yes, he would venture to say more, that if the power was not relinquished by the general government, the state governments would be annihilated. If every resource is taken from them, what remains in the power of the states for their support, or the extinguishment of their domestic debt.

Mr. GERRY

Thought if the proposition was referred, that it ought to go to a committee of the whole, for he wished it to have a full and candid discussion. He would have something left in the power of every state to support itself independent of the United States, and therefore was not satisfied with the amendment proposed. The constitution in its original state gives to congress the power of levying and collecting taxes, duties, imposts and excise, the fault here is, that every thing is relinquished to the general government. Now the amendments give the same power with qualification, that there shall have been a previous requisition. This by no means came up to his idea; he thought that some particular revenue ought to be secured to the states so as to enable them to support themselves.

He apprehended when this clause in the constitution was under the consideration of the several state conventions, they would not so readily have ratified it, if they had considered it more fully in the point of view, he had now placed it, but if they had ratified it, it would have been under a conviction that congress would admit such amendments as were necessary to the existence of the state governments. At present the states are divested of every means to support themselves; if they discover a new source of revenue, after congress shall have diverted all the old ones into their treasury, the rapacity of the general government can take that from them also. The states can have recourse to no tax, duty, impost or excise but what may be taken from them whenever the congress shall be so disposed, and yet gentlemen will say that the annihilation of the state governments must be followed by the ruin of this.

Now what is the consequence of the amendment? Either the states will or will not comply with the requisitions; if they comply, they voluntarily surrender their means of support; if they refuse the arms of congress are raised to compel them, which in all probability may lay the foundation for civil war. What umbrage must it give every individual to have two setts of collectors and tax-gathers surrounding their doors, the people then sowered, and a direct refusal by the legislature will be the occasion of perpetual discord. He wished to alter this proposition in such a manner as to secure the support of the federal government, and the state governments likewise, and therefore wished the amendment referred to a committee of the whole house.

Mr. TUCKER.

I do not see the arguments in favor of giving congress this power in so forcible a light as some gentlemen do: It will be to erect an *imperium in imperio*,[34] which is generally considered to be subversive of all government. At any time that congress shall exercise this power, it will raise commotions in the states; whereas the mode of requisitions will operate in so easy a way, by being consonant to the habits of the people, that the supplies will be sooner realized in the treasury by this means than by any other. It will require a length of time to form an uniform system of taxation, that shall operate equally and justly through all the states; though I doubt the possibility of forming such a system. It has been said that requisitions have not been complied with in former times, but it is to be hoped that there will not be so much difficulty in future. The supplies from the impost will greatly diminish the requisitions; besides, should any of the states refuse to comply, they will be liable to the exercise of the power of congress in the very heart of their country. This power will be so disagreeable, that the very dread of it will stimulate the states to an immediate and prompt compliance with the requisitions. This amendment has been proposed by several of the states, and by some of the most important ones; for this and other reasons that have been offered on the subject, I hope the amendment will be adopted.

Several methods were proposed for disposing of this question for the present, but the motion for its lying on the table being put and negatived, mr. Partridge, referring to his instructions, was solicitous that this amendment should not be too precipitately decided upon, moved the previous question, which was negatived.

Mr. SEDGWICK

Said that he believed his mind was as strongly impressed with the force of the instructions he had received from his constituents, as that of other gentlemen. But, sir, said he, a government entrusted with the freedom, and the very existence of the people, ought surely to possess in the most

[34] A state within a state.

ample manner, the means of supporting its own existence; and as we do not know what circumstances we may be in, nor how necessary it may be for congress to exercise this power, I should deem it a violation of the oath I have taken to support the constitution, were I now to vote for this amendment.

Mr. SHERMAN

Remarked that if congress should exercise this power, the taxes would be laid by the immediate representatives of the people; neither would it be necessary to adopt one uniform method of collecting direct taxes. The several states might be accommodated by a reference to their respective modes of taxation.

The question upon the paragraph being called for from every part of the house, the ayes and noes were taken.

PART III

Letters and Other Documents

Most of this section is made up of excerpts from letters to or from members of the First Federal Congress that relate to amending the Constitution. Portions of several letters by other persons in a position to influence the process are also printed. A paragraph from George Washington's Inaugural Address, the resolutions of the states of Virginia and New York calling for a second constitutional convention, and newspaper pieces by Roger Sherman ("A Citizen of New Haven") and Noah Webster ("Pacificus" to James Madison, Jr.) complete the documentary record.

The documents were selected after a reading of all manuscripts in the files of the First Federal Congress Project for the period 1 March through 30 September 1789. Letters that were repetitive of others or simply supplied information available in the legislative history of the amendments were omitted, as were letters between persons who were not members of Congress and had no first hand information about events on the floor.

Documents that discuss amendments to the Constitution and were written between the passage of the Constitution and March 1789 have been or will be printed in the *DHROC*. Documents relating to the Amendments and their ratification dated after October 1789 will appear in either the *DHFFC* or the *DHROC*.

The documents are sparsely annotated. Identification of all authors and recipients appears in a biographical gazetteer following this section.

March 1789

Abraham Baldwin to Joel Barlow
1 March 1789

The advocates for amendments will be but few, perhaps two from Massachusetts, four from New York, four from Virginia, and three from South Carolina in the house of representatives, and the Senators of Virginia, and of this state [*New York*] if they ever agree to appoint any; I should rather say antifeds, for perhaps the feds. may agree—to propose some amendments after they have got through the business of their first session.

Abraham Baldwin Papers, CtY.

Miles King to James Madison
3 March 1789

I hope Congress will take up the Amendments proposd. by the States and do What is Necessary without there being a New Convention, I think Many of the Amendments are good & Necessary, but the great point of Direct Taxation will be of the Most Importance, When your Body Meets together and they should think it best for Congress to Retain that, I am perfectly Satisfyd. they Should Retain it I am very Willing to trust them, but Many of the Opposers to the Goverment will not agree Congress should have that power.

James Madison Papers, DLC.

Tench Coxe to George Thatcher
12 March 1789

If due attention be paid to removing the jealousies & fears of the honest part of the Opposition we may gain strength & respectability without impairing one essential power of the constitution. Some declarations concerning the liberty of the press, of conscience &ca. ought perhaps to be frankly made parts of the constitution.

Independence National Historical Park, Philadelphia.

Thomas Jefferson to James Madison
15 March 1789

your thoughts on the subject of the Declaration of rights in the letter of Oct. 17. I have weighed with great satisfaction. some of them had not occurred to me before but were acknoleged just in the moment they were presented to my mind. in the arguments in favor of a declaration of rights you omit one which has a great weight with me, the legal check which it puts into the hands of the judiciary. this is a body, which if rendered independent, & kept strictly to their own department merits great confidence for their learning & integrity. in fact what degree of confidence would be too much for a body composed of such men as Wythe Blair & Pendleton?[1] on characters like these the "civium ardor prava jubentium"[2] would make no impression. I am happy to find that on the whole you are a friend to this amendment. the Declaration of rights is like all other human blessings alloyed with some inconveniences: and not accomplishing fully it's object. but the good in this instance vastly overweighs the evil. I cannot refrain from making short answers to the objections which your letter states to have been missed. 1. that the rights in question are reserved by the manner in which the federal powers are granted. answer. a constitutive act may certainly be so formed as to need no declaration of rights. the act itself has the force of a declaration as far as it goes: and if it goes to all material points nothing more is wanting. in the draught of a constitution which I had once a thought of proposing in Virginia & printed afterwards I endeavored to reach all the great objects of public

---

[1]These three jurists were considered elder statesmen of Virginia. George Wythe (1726–1806), signer of the Declaration of Independence and member of the Federal Convention, moved the resolution to ratify at the Virginia convention. John Blair (1732–1800), chief justice of Virginia, signer of the Constitution, and member of the Virginia ratification convention, served in 1776 on the committee that drafted the Virginia Constitution and Declaration of Rights. For Pendleton, see the Biographical Gazetteer.

[2]From Horace, *Odes*, bk. III, ode III: "the frenzy of his fellow citizens bidding what is wrong."

liberty, and did not mean to add a declaration of rights. probably the object was imperfectly executed: but the deficiencies would have been supplied by others in the course of discussion. but in a constitutive act which leaves some precious article unnoticed, and raises implications against others, a declaration of rights becomes necessary by way of supplement. this is the case of our new federal constitution. this instrument forms us into one state as to certain objects, and gives us a legislative & executive body for these objects. it should therefore guard us against their abuses of power within the feild submitted to them. 2. a positive declaration of some essential rights could not be obtained in the requisite latitude. answer. half a loaf is better than no bread. if we cannot secure all our rights, let us secure what we can. 3. the limited powers of the federal government & jealousy of the subordinate governments afford a security which exists in no other instance. answer. the first member of this seems resolvable into the 1st. objection before stated. the jealousy of the subordinate governments is a precious reliance. but observe that those governments are only agents. they must have principles furnished them whereon to found their opposition. the declaration of rights will be the text whereby they will try all the acts of the federal government. in this view it is necessary to the federal government also: as by the same text they may try the opposition of the subordinate governments. 4. experience proves the inefficacy of a bill of rights. true. but tho it is not absolutely efficacious under all circumstances, it is of great potency always, and rarely inefficacious. a brace the more will often keep up the building which would have fallen with that brace the less. There is a remarkeable difference between the characters of the Inconveniencies which attend a Declaration of rights, & those which attend the want of it. the inconveniences of the Declaration are that it may cramp government in it's useful exertions. but the evil of this is shortlived, moderate, & reparable. the inconveniencies of the want of a Declaration are permanent, afflicting & irreparable: they are in constant progression from bad to worse. the executive in our governments is not the sole, it is scarcely the principal object of my jealousy. the tyranny of the legislatures is the most formidable dread at present, and will be for long years. that of the executive will come in it's turn, but it will be at a remote period. I know there are some among us who would now establish a monarchy. but they are inconsiderable in number and weight of character. the rising race are all republicans. we were educated in royalism: no wonder if some of us retain that idolatry still. our young people are educated in republicanism. an apostacy from that to royalism is unprecedented & impossible. I am much pleased with the prospect that a declaration of rights will be added: and hope it will be done in that way which will not endanger the whole frame of the government, or any essential part of it.

James Madison Papers, DLC. This is the climax of Jefferson's and Madison's correspondence on the bill of rights. Jefferson raised the issue of its absence when he first commented on the Constitution to his friend in December 1787.

Tench Coxe to James Madison
18 March 1789

I have reflected since I had the pleasure of seeing you on the form of a declaration to be introduced into the constitution in favor of religious liberty, and I think the Idea of extending the powers of the union to an interposition between the state legislatures & their respective constituents might be accomplished to universal satisfaction, by something like the 4th. Sec. of the 4th. Article relating to a republican form of Government—It would give great eclat to the constitution in Europe, and would give it an honest Triumph over the disingenuousness of those, who have opposed it on that score against their better knowlege.

James Madison Papers, DLC.

A Citizen of New Haven [*Roger Sherman*]
24 March 1789

ALL the difficulties proposed to be remedied by amendments, that have come within my notice, may be provided for by law, without altering the Constitution, except the following, on which I would make a few observations, and submit to the public, whether it is proper or necessary to make those alterations.

1. It has been proposed that the consent of two thirds, or three fourths of the members in each branch of Congress should be made requisite for passing certain acts.

But why should a majority in Congress, joined with the concurrent voice of the President, be controuled by a minority? If the President dissents, the Constitution requires the consent of two thirds of the members in each branch to pass any act. It is a general maxim in popular government, that the majority should govern.

2. It is objected that the Senate is not the proper tribunal for the trial of impeachments.

But what good reason can be assigned for this objection? The members being elegible by the Legislatures of the several States, they will doubtless be persons of wisdom and probity, and proper guardians of the rights of the community, who can have no motive from the nature of their office to partiality in judgment.

3. It is objected, that the President ought not to have power to grant pardons in cases of high treason.

But what great mischief can arise from the exercise of this power by the President? He cannot pardon in cases of impeachment, so that offenders may be excluded from office notwithstanding his pardon.

4. It is proposed to make the President and Senators inelegible after certain periods.

But this would abridge the liberty of the people, and remove one great motive to fidelity in office. The danger of having the same persons continued long in office is intirely removed, if they are dependent on the people for their continuance by re-election; and by long experience they will be better qualified for usefulness, and nothing renders government more unstable than a frequent change of the persons that administer it.

5. It has been proposed that members of Congress be rendered inelegible to any other office, during the time for which they are elected members of that body.

This is an objection that will admit of something plausible to be said on both sides. The mischief intended to be avoided is, their instituting offices with large salaries, with a view of filling them themselves; but that difficulty is obviated by the provision in the Constitution, that they shall not be elegible to any office that shall have been instituted or the emoluments encreased while they were members. On the other hand a person may be best qualified for some office by means of the knowledge of public affairs acquired by being a member of Congress; and it seems reasonable that the public should be at liberty to employ any of the citizens in offices wherein they can be most useful.

6. It has been proposed that no treaty of commerce should be made without the consent of two thirds of the Senators, nor any cession of territory or right of navigation or fishery without the consent of three fourths of the members present in each branch of Congress.

It is provided that the President with the concurrence of two thirds of the Senators present may make treaties, and as each State has an equal representation and suffrage in the Senate, their rights in this respect will be as secure under the new Constitution as under the old; and it is not probable that they would ever make a cession of any important national right, without the consent of Congress. The King of Great-Britain has power by the Constitution of that nation to make treaties, yet in matters of great importance he consults the Parliament.

7. The amendment proposed by the Convention of South-Carolina, respecting religious tests, is an ingenious one, but not very important, because the Constitution as it now stands, will have the same effect, as it would have with that amendment.

On the whole, will it not be best to make a fair trial of the Constitution, before any attempts are made to alter it? It is now become the only frame of government for the United States, and must be supported and conformed to, or they will have no government at all as confederated States. Experience will best shew whether it is deficient or not; on trial it may appear that the alterations proposed are not necessary, or that others not yet thought of may be necessary. Every thing that tends to disunion, ought to be carefully avoided. Instability in government and laws, tends to weaken a State, and render the rights of the people precarious. The Constitution which is the foundation of law and government ought not to be changed without the most pressing necessity. When experience has convinced, the people in general that alterations are necessary, they may be easily made, but attempting it at present may be detrimental, if not fatal to the union of the States, and to their credit with foreign nations.

The New-York Packet, 24 March 1789.

John Avery to George Thatcher
25 March 1789

The District of Hampshire and Berkshire seem to struggle hard in their choice, but am in hopes the next tryal will produce a Member, indeed I sincerely wish it, as it will save me great trouble:[1] by the Way, why can't there be an Alteration in this mode when you come upon the subject of Amendments, that when there is no choice by the People, for the several Legislatures to determine the Matter as in the case of Senators &c. &c.

Chamberlain Collection, MB.

[1]At this time Theodore Sedgwick was a candidate for election to the House of Representatives from western Massachusetts. He won a plurality of the votes in the elections held on 18 December 1788 and 30 March 1789, but not those held on 29 January and 2 March 1789. He was finally elected by a majority of the votes on 11 May 1789. Avery, as Massachusetts secretary of state, was responsible for the paperwork on elections.

Paine Wingate to Timothy Pickering
25 March 1789

Nobody thinks that a general convention will be called. Possibly in a convenient time Congress make [*may*] take up the consideration of amendments or alterations, and may recommend some that may quiet the fears & jealousies of the well designing & not affect the essentials of the present-system: I am rather inclined to suppose that this cannot be attended to immediately, but must be postponed for other more important matters.

Pickering Papers, MHi.

Edmund Randolph to James Madison
27 March 1789

There is a general calm of politicks. The discontented themselves seem willing to wait with temper, until congress shall open their views. It gave me much pleasure to read your letter to Colo. T. M. Randolph;[1] as it shews a consciousness of amendments being necessary, and a disposition to procure them. Altho' I am convinced, that nothing will soften the rancour of some men, I believe that a moderate and conciliating conduct in our foederal rulers will detach from their virulence those, who have been opposed from principle. A very injudicious, and ill written publication, which you have seen under the signature of Decius,[2] may impede perhaps this salutary effect; by keeping in a state of irritation those minds, which are well affected to the object of his bitterness. His facts are of a trivial cast, and his assertions are not always correct; and he thus becomes vulnerable in almost every part. The liberty of the press is indeed a bless-

---

[1]On 13 January 1789, in the middle of his hotly contested election campaign against Antifederalist James Monroe, Madison wrote the Antifederal leader Thomas Mann Randolph, Sr., to express his support for amendments to the Constitution. The letter appeared in the Antifederal Richmond *Virginia Independent Chronicle* on 28 January and was widely republished throughout the United States. For the letter, see the Introduction, n. 5.

[2]The letters of Decius appeared in the *Virginia Independent Chronicle* between January and July 1789. They were a scathing attack on Virginia Antifederalists, particularly Patrick Henry, who was accused of enriching himself at public expense when he was governor.

ing, which ought not to be surrendered but with blood; and yet it is not an illfounded expectation in those, who deserve well of their country, that they should be assailed by an enemy in disguise, and have their characters deeply wounded, before they can prepare for defence. I apply not this to any particular person.

James Madison Papers, DLC.

Samuel A. Otis to Nathan Dane
28 March 1789

I should suppose however there was no great prospect of a Convention, and when such men as father Sherman[1] says "try it first" do I much expect an early attempt at amendments.

Nathan Dane Papers, DLC.

[1] Roger Sherman's "Citizen of New Haven," from *The New-York Packet* of 24 March, is printed above.

Charles Pinckney to James Madison
28 March 1789

Are you not, to use a full expression, abundantly convinced that the theoretical nonsense of an election of the members of Congress by the people in the first instance, is clearly and practically wrong. that it will in the end be the means of bringing our councils into contempt & that the legislature are the only proper judges of who ought to be elected?

Are you not fully convinced that the Senate ought at least to be double their number to make them of consequence & to prevent their falling into the same comparative state of insignificance that the State Senates have, merely from their smallness?

Do you not suppose that giving to the federal Judicial *retrospective jurisdiction in any case whatsoever*—from the difficulty of determining to what periods to look back from it's being an ex post facto provision, & from the confusion & opposition it will give rise to, will be the surest & speediest mode to subvert our present system & give it's adversaries the majority?

Do not suffer these and other queries I may hereafter put to you to startle your opinion with respect to my principles. I am more than ever a friend to the federal constitution, not I trust from that fondness which men sometimes feel for a performance in which they have been concerned but from a conviction of it's intrinsic worth. from a conviction that on it's efficacy our political welfare depends. my wish is to see it divested of those improprieties which I am sure will sooner or later subvert or what is worse bring it into contempt.

James Madison Papers, DLC.

Richard Bland Lee to Leven Powell 29 March 1789

There will be little doubt that all the amendments tending to the greater security of civil Liberty will be obtained. The Voice of Congress is almost unanimous against a second convention, as leading directly to anarchy & the most fatal discord. From the moderation and wisdom which center in this body from every part of America, I have no doubt that the most proper, and happy measures will be pursued, as well to conciliate the affections, as to promote the peace and prosperity of the People of U. States. All reasonable & proper amendments will be obtained, those tending to sap the foundations of United government will be discarded.

Leven Powell Papers, DLC.

James Madison to Thomas Jefferson 29 March 1789

With regard to the Constitution, it is pretty well decided that the disaffected party in the Senate amounts to two or three members only; and that in the other House it does not exceed a very small minority, some of which will also be restrained by the federalism of the States from which they come. Notwithstanding this character of the Body, I hope and expect that some conciliatory sacrifices will be made, in order to extinguish opposition to the system, or at least break the force of it, by detaching the deluded opponents from their designing leaders.

PJM 12:38.

Thomas Hartley to Stephen Chambers
30 March 1789

Amendments will be spoke of by some Gentlemen—but there will be so much good Temper respecting this Business that there is a probability that all will end well.

Stauffer Collection, PHi.

Patrick Henry to William Grayson
31 March 1789

Federal and anti seem now scarcely to exist; for our highest toned Feds say we must have the amendments. But the Enumeration stops at direct Taxation Treatys Trade &c. &c., so that I perceive it will be a Question of prudence. How far the Temper of the Times will carry the condiscention of party or whether apprehensions will extort concession to any salutary purpose I from my secluded situation cannot guess—You perhaps can tell me how far the appearances tend that way. I hear nothing worth telling you.

Virginia Magazine of History and Biography 14(1906–1907):202–4.

April 1789

Ralph Izard to Thomas Jefferson
3 April 1789

Every Man of common Sense, & common affection for America must be strongly affected by the consideration of the humiliating State into which we are plunged. The evil has arisen principally from the want of an efficient, & energetic Government, pervading every part of the United States. By whatever appellation therefore Gentlemen may choose to be distinguished; whether by federal, or antifederal, I hope we shall not be wasting time with Idle discussions about amendments of the Constitution; but that we shall go to work immediately about the Finances, & endeavour to extricate ourselves from our present embarrassed, & disgraceful situation.

Ralph Izard Papers, ScU.

Ezra Stiles to William S. Johnson
3 April 1789

Give me Leave to ask whether the Senators are not equally Representatives with the house of Representatives? Why had it not been better to have said, Congress shall consist of Representatives in two Branches; the one of the States as States, & the other of the People at large? to be denominated the upper & lower House of Congress or some new Name not founded upon Antiquity but on our own Circumstances. By callg. the lower House the House of Representatives we seem to exclude the Senate from being considered as a Representation. Both are Representatives of different Descriptions. Congress has always been the Represente. of the United States, standg. on Election; not a patrician Body as the Roman Senate, or that of Venice hereditary & perpetual. In the new federal Cong.

all are representatives, altho' not *Pares*; for the *Legati*[1] of the States *as States*, are certainly of a distinct, & I think in their own nature an Order of higher Dignity than that now called the House of Representatives. But this cannot be now altered, if indeed it would be best to alter. I could wish to have somethg. clearly intelligible. The Senatus Romanus we know consisted of Patricians Originally of one Order only. Perhaps we are not so well acquainted with the true Formation of the Senate of Carthage. But since the roman ages we have Senates innumerable, & of so different natures & Powers, that the Name no longer indicates the Powers. . . .

Had our federal Constn. directed that the President & Vice Prest. shd. have been voted for separately, the Contingence wh. was aimed at by the Antifederalists had been avoided; and Dr. Adams might have come in as unanimously as Genl. Washington.

We shall do well upon the present federal Constitution. Perhaps some Things might be amended. But if none but the Trifles I have mentioned above were found expedient to amend, I look upon them of so little Importance, that I shd. pray God they might never be amended. But there are probably others of some Moment & Magnitude & worthy to be amended hereafter. But I wish to have no Amendmts. made these 20 years; or not until by Experience & cool Judgt. we shd. be able to discern what Amendmts. are necessary. The Constitution is so good & excellent, that I do not wish to have it shaken by any speedy Alteration. However desirous a number of States may be for a speedy Convention & Revision, I wish it may be evaded & put off until we are as a public, able to judge upon Experiment.

Beinecke Library, CtY.

[1] *Pares*: equals; *legati*: ambassadors.

Theodore Sedgwick to Samuel Henshaw
6 April 1789

In your obliging letter of the 25th. ult. you are pleased to observe that many people in this district within the compass of your information have several objections to my being a representative in the national government. I thank you for that frankness and friendship which you discover in naming the objections, and for your candor & delicacy in observing on them; and I shall endeavor to give you the satisfaction required.

You observe that the primary objection is, "that I have not publickly declared my sentiments in favor of amending the national constitution of government; and that therefore the people conclude I am against any amendments at all." I am not, my dear sir, answerable for such conclusions—They may be drawn with equal propriety against the objectors themselves, and against every person in the district who has not publickly declared himself to be of different sentiments. My friends and acquaintances know, and all with whom I have had the pleasure of conversing on the subject know, that I have been and am now a zealous advocate for many amendments. Before the constitution was ratified by this state, I did every thing in my power to forward its adoption; because I then thought and do now think that the happiness, the permanent happiness of the people would be established by it. Not the happiness of any professional order of men, or of the great [*illegible*] but of the bulk of citizens—of the various artizans and innumerable yeomanry of the county. Sure I was in my mind if government could begin to operate on the leading principles of the constitution, the farmer, the manufacturer and the laboring poor would soon reap vast advantages from the efficiency of our national union. But I never once dreamed but what the constitution would be perfected agreeably to the provision in the 5th. article—And those amendments which will render it more perfect—more congenial to the sentiments and feelings of the PEOPLE who are to live under it and to support it, can never meet with successful oposition from any quarter. But, my friend we must guard against partial or local amendments—Should amendments of this kind which are proposed by some of the states be adopted, the most essential advantages of a commercial nature would be lost to this state.

Autograph Collection, MH.

James Madison to Edmund Pendleton
8 April 1789

The subject of amendments has not yet been touched. From appearances there will be no great difficulty in obtaining reasonable ones. It will depend however entirely on the temper of the federalists, who predominate as much in both branches, as could be wished. Even in this State [*New York*], notwithstanding the violence of its antifederal symtoms, three of its six representatives at least will be zealous friends to the Constitution, and it is not improbable that a fourth will be of the same description.

James Madison Papers, DLC.

James Sullivan to Richard Henry Lee
11 April 1789

but our people are disposed to live quietly, and when Congress shall pay a proper attention to the amendments proposed to the general Constitution all will be easy; unless a particular partiality is shewn by the General Government to those who have affected to be the Champions of it.

Lee Family Papers, PPAmP.

James Madison to Edmund Randolph
12 April 1789

On the subject of amendments nothing has been publickly and very little privately said. Such as I am known to have espoused, will as far as I can gather, be attainable from the federalists, who sufficiently predominate in both branches; though with some, the concurrence will proceed from a spirit of conciliation rather than conviction. Connecticut is least inclined though I presume not inflexibly opposed, to a moderate revision. A paper wch. will probably be republished in the Virga. Gazettes, under the signature of a Citizen of New Haven, unfolds *Mr. Shermans* opinions. Whatever the amendments may be it is clear that they will be attempted in no other way then thro' Congress. Many of the warmest of the opponents of the Govt. disavow the Mode contended for by Virginia.[1]

James Madison Papers, DLC.

[1] A second federal convention.

Tench Coxe to James Madison
21 April 1789

It is very certain that the attention paid by the old Government to the Overtures of Spain, and the resolutions relative to the Navigation of the Missisipi were improper, and, in principle, dangerous in a free country.[1] They were therefore unjustifiable in ours, and impolitic in the highest degree considering the lax & feeble cords by which the temper & situation

[1] On 24 August 1785 Congress instructed Secretary of Foreign Affairs John Jay to insist, in his negotiations with Spain, on "free Navigation of the Mississippi, from the source to the Ocean." A year later Congress repealed the instruction. On 16

of the Western people bind them to us. It is but reasonable that they should be alarmed—that they should doubt our justice and regard for those rights, which, whether the eastern or western people are the claimants, are not to be dispensed with, or infringed. Tis manifest that such doubts and Apprehensions have been excited by the measures of Congress, and it is very certain that the hesitation about the new Constitution in that quarter arose in a greater part from those causes, than from any faults they found in it as a System of Government. Besides the obligations of justice and liberty, which must govern the Administrators of our affairs in every place, and with every part of our Citizens there is another light in which the Western people must be viewed, which should be most seriously considered. They alone are possibly to be converted into powerful neighbouring enemies. The Northern country of G. Britain is so bound up for a great part of the Year, its soil is so bad in one part and its Government in another, that little is to be feared from that quarter. The Climate & soil of the Floridas, and the civil & religious objections to the Spanish Government with the difficult approach of the Mouth of the Missisipi and the want of enterprize & policy in that court leave little ground of Apprehension from them. But the Western Country if seperated from us, in close connexion with either, especially the latter, would expose the remainder of the Union to a very troublesome & growing Enemy.

As these considerations impress our Minds wth. the necessity of keeping them not only friendly but connected with us in Government, it seems a very important Object in our Affairs to devise the most likely Methods of allaying their fears, reviving their confidence and encreasing their Attachments to the Union; and at the same [*time*] to establish our plans in such a way that we may draw revenue from them. All these Appear to me practicable.

To allay their fears we must candidly examine the conduct that has offended them—and frankly give them efficient securities for our refraining from such Attempts in future. A part of the ideas in the 2d. division of the 7th. Amendment of Virginia[2] might perhaps be safely modified and adopted, if the subject of Amendments is touched. A Majority of every legislature in the Union would I am of Opinion ratify such an Amendment should Congress send it forward. Frankly to remove fears and do justice always revives confidence & encreases affection—and I am satisfied the measure proposed would have that effect in an eminent degree on a

September 1788 Congress resolved that free navigation of the river was "a clear and essential right of the United States" and referred the subject to the new federal government.

[2]See p. 20 above.

people governed exceedingly by their feelings, and whose situation seperates them from all the world but their relatives on the one hand, & two powers whom they either despise or dislike on the other.

James Madison Papers, DLC.

James Sullivan to Elbridge Gerry
22 April 1789

I rather incline to believe that our people in this part of the union will be very quiet without any amendments untill some measure shall be adopted by the General Government which they may deem oppressive, upon which they will grow uneasy and charge it upon the want of alterations whether it arises from that cause or not.

Elbridge Gerry Papers, MHi.

William Ellery to Benjamin Huntington
25 April 1789

I don't hear a word about amendments. Money is indeed the first and most important object. Neither civil nor military wheels can turn easily without it. But it had seemed to me that the Delegates from those States which had ordered them to move and urge amendments, would have started them as soon as a Congress was formed. I am glad that a matter of much greater consequence has been brought upon the tapis; and perhaps it would not be amiss to try whether the new government would not do without any alteration.

It is probable whenever amendments are proposed some degree of ill humour may take place of that harmony which I am told, prevails, and I hope will prevail in Congress.

Benjamin Huntington Papers, R-Ar.

Richard Henry Lee to Samuel Adams
25 April 1789

The issue of your government election gives me singular pleasure for many reasons, and especially because the hot headed *federalists* as they call themselves, placed the contest upon Mr. Hancocks proposition to your

Convention for amenments to our new Constitution.[1] This procedure argues the extremity of Art, deception, and impudence in these people—because they joined with the idea as a most happy means of procuring Union, and obtaining a ratification of the proffered plan—But now that they have gained their point, they are traducing the Men, and wish to neglect the conditions upon which probably their success was founded. Deceit, whether in public or in private life, seldom fails in the end to injure those who practice it. I observe that you mention *efficient* government—I assure you my dear friend that there lives not a Man who more cordially wishes for a Government possessed of the fullest means for procuring the happiness, prosperity, and security of our union—But for these salutary ends it is not in my judgement necessary to establish a system full of ambiguity respecting old and long esteemed Safeguards, whilst the ways, in some instances, to pernicious exertions of power are left much too open. I might object some fundamental errors, such as the idea too prevalent, of one Government, founded on the ruin of State Governments—The want of safety to Elections, and the utter want of responsibility. I hope the idea of Amendments is not lost in Massachusetts where we have been used to find the firmest defenders of Civil liberty. It is probable that this Session of Congress will pass Laws of a nature so gracious as to quiet alarms among those who reflect not, that "the safety of liberty depends not so much upon the *gracious manner*, as upon the *Limitation of Power.*"

Samuel Adams Papers, NN.

[1]One of the issues in the Massachusetts lieutenant governor's election of 1789 between Benjamin Lincoln and Samuel Adams was this proposal for amendments to the Constitution. Adams was elected.

George Washington's Inaugural Address 30 April 1789

Besides the ordinary objects submitted to your care, it will remain with your judgment to decide, how far an exercise of the occasional power delegated by the fifth article of the Constitution, is rendered expedient at the present juncture by the nature of objections which have been urged against the system, or by the degree of inquietude which has given birth to them. Instead of undertaking particular recommendations on this subject, in which I could be guided by no lights derived from official opportunities, I shall again give way to my entire confidence in your discernment and pursuit of the public good. For I assure myself that whilst you carefully avoid every alteration which might endanger the benefits of an united and effective government, or which ought to await the future lessons of experience; a reverence for the characteristic rights of freemen, and a regard for the public harmony, will sufficiently influence your deliberations on the question, how far the former can be more impregnably fortified, or the latter be safely and advantageously promoted.

HJ, p. 42.

May 1789

Arthur Campbell to [*Andrew Moore?*]
May 1789

As to the subject of Amendments it is a weighty matter, and may bid fairest for a proper decision by delaying the subject for some time; cannot we venture to bring a little experience to the aid of all the prescience of opponents in order to form a right judgement. In short we trust that such an enlightened and benificent policy will pervade all the acts of the national Legislature; that instead of the State governments awing them into improper measures, they will serve for a model to look up to (for to enable them to square their local regulations by the general ones). A government of wise laws, faithfully administered will soon reconcile every body, and restore the Commonwealth to its pristine vigour.

All this we may expect to see brought about in time, under the superintendence of our wise and good President. But still we may dread commiting an error, by having our expectations too high raised, we attempt to precipitate such matters, that require time to mature.

Arthur Campbell Papers, Filson Club, Louisville, Kentucky.

Virginia's Application for a Second Convention
5 May 1789

In General Assembly, 14 November 1788

Resolved, That an application be made in the name and on behalf of the Legislature of this Commonwealth to the Congress of the United States, in the words following, to wit:

"The good people of this Commonwealth, in Convention assembled, having ratified the Constitution submitted to their consideration, this Legislature has, in conformity to that act and the resolutions of the United States in Congress assembled to them transmitted, thought proper to make the arrangements that were necessary for carrying it into effect.

Having thus shown themselves obedient to the voice of their constituents, all America will find that so far as it depended on them, that plan of government will be carried into immediate operation.

"But the sense of the people of Virginia would be but in part complied with and but little regarded, if we went no farther. In the very moment of adoption, and coeval with the ratification of the new plan of government, the general voice of the Convention of this State pointed to objects no less interesting to the people we represent, and equally entitled to our attention. At the same time that, from motives of affection to our sister States, the Convention yielded their assent to the ratification, they gave the most unequivocal proofs, that they dreaded its operation under the present form.

"In acceding to the government under this impression, painful must have been the prospect, had they not derived consolation from a full expectation of its imperfections being speedily amended. In this resource, therefore, they placed their confidence, a confidence that will continue to support them, whilst they have reason to believe that they have not calculated upon it in vain.

"In making known to you the objections of the people of this Commonwealth to the new plan of government, we deem it unnecessary to enter into a particular detail of its defects, which they consider as involving all the great and unalienable rights of freemen. For their sense on this subject, we beg leave to refer you to the proceedings of their late Convention, and the sense of the House of Delegates as expressed in their resolutions of the thirtieth day of October, one thousand seven hundred and eighty-eight.

"We think proper, however, to declare, that, in our opinion, as those objections were not founded in speculative theory, but deduced from principles which have been established by the melancholy example of other nations in different ages; so they will never be removed, until the cause itself shall cease to exist. The sooner, therefore, the public apprehensions are quieted, and the government is possessed of the confidence of the people, the more salutary will be its operations, and the longer its duration.

"The cause of amendments we consider as a common cause, and since concessions have been made from political motives, which, we conceive, may endanger the republic, we trust, that a commendable zeal will be shown for obtaining those provisions, which, experience has taught us, are necessary to secure from danger the unalienable rights of human nature.

"The anxiety with which our countrymen press for the accomplishment of this important end, will ill admit of delay. The slow forms of congressional discussion and recommendation, if, indeed, they should ever agree to any change, would, we fear, be less certain of success. Happily for their wishes, the Constitution hath presented an alternative, by admitting the submission to a convention of the states. To this, therefore, we resort, as the source from whence they are to derive relief from their present apprehensions.

"We do, therefore, in behalf of our constituents, in the most earnest and solemn manner, make this application to Congress, that a Convention be immediately called of deputies from the several states, with full power to take into their consideration the defects of this Constitution that have been suggested by the state Conventions, and report such amendments thereto, as they shall find best suited to promote our common interests, and secure to ourselves and our latest posterity, the great and unalienable rights of mankind."

Signed JOHN JONES, Sp. Senate
THOMAS MATHEWS, Sp. H. Del.

HJ, pp. 47–48. The application was presented to the House of Representatives by Rep. Theodorick Bland on 5 May.

New York's Application for a Second Convention 6 May 1789

In ASSEMBLY, 5 February 1789

RESOLVED, If the honorable the Senate concur therein, that an application be made to the Congress of the United States of America, in the name and behalf of the Legislature of this State, in the words following, to wit:

The people of the state of New-York having ratified the Constitution agreed to on the seventeenth day of September, in the year of our Lord one thousand seven hundred and eighty-seven, by the Convention then assembled at Philadelphia, in the state of Pennsylvania, as explained by the said ratification, in the fullest confidence of obtaining a revision of the said Constitution by a general Convention; and in confidence, that certain powers in and by the said Constitution granted, would not be exercised, until a convention should have been called and convened for proposing amendments to the said Constitution. In compliance therefore, with the unanimous sense of the Convention of this State, who all united in opinion, that such a revision was necessary to recommend the said Constitution to the approbation and support of a numerous body of their constituents; and a majority of the members of which conceived several articles of the Constitution so exceptionable, that nothing but such confidence, and an invincible reluctance to separate from our sister States, could have prevailed upon a sufficient number to assent to it, without stipulating for previous amendments: And from a conviction that the apprehensions and discontents which those articles occasion, cannot be removed or allayed, unless an act to revise the said Constitution, be among the first that shall be passed by the new Congress, We, the Legislature of the state of New-York, do in behalf of our constituents, in the most earnest and solemn manner, make this application to the Congress, that a Convention of Deputies from the several States be called as early as possible, with full powers to take the said Constitution into their consideration, and to propose such amendments thereto, as they shall find best calculated to promote our common interests, and secure to ourselves and our latest posterity, the great and unalienable rights of mankind.

By order of the Assembly,
JOHN LANSING, Junior, Speaker

In SENATE, February 7, 1789
By order of the SENATE,
PIERRE VAN CORTLANDT, President

HJ, p. 50. The application was presented to the House of Representatives by Rep. John Laurance on 6 May.

Aedanus Burke to Richard Hampton
10 May 1789

Our House of Representatives here are to take up the business of Amendments on the last Tuesday in this month. but unless your Legislature interpose, we shall make no hand of it I fear—for tis necessary by the Constitution for ¾ of the States to apply for it before Amendmts. can take place. God grant you unanimity in that affair, tho' I fear he will not. Your high flying monarchical Gentry (and I am sorry to find they abound in New York, as well as in Carolina) will oppose all amendments. The wealthy powerful families in general throughout the union, ridicule the notion, and will prevent if possible [*amendments*] taking place, Rely on that.

James T. Mitchell Autograph Collection, PHi.

Richard Henry Lee to Samuel Adams
10 May 1789

I believe it is not denied by any sober person, that the Congress possesses power adequate to the great purposes of the Union, and I know of no good man who desires that they should have less. But many wise Men are of opinion that the expressions conveying power are too loose, and too much exposed to latitudinary construction. You have given Sir the truest and the best reasons why this is improper—Mr. Madison lately gave notice to the H. of Representatives that he should shortly propose to take up the consideration of that Article in the Constitution which points the way to amendments—I should hope that a very great majority will concur in proposing such as may secure Civil liberty, and such as by giving content to all reasonable Men, may procure that Union which is now wanting, and which is so necessary for the common safety. . . . I congratulate you Sir on the event of your elections. they display the wisdom of the people when some hot headed men had broached an opposition upon the principle that Mr. Hancock had been the proposer of the plan for Amendments—Although those very Men had abundant reason to think that your Convention would not have adopted the Constitution if that expedient had not been proposed.

Western Americana Collection, Beinecke Rare Book Manuscript Library, CtY.

Edward Carrington to James Madison
12 May 1789

Our Antifederal districts have become perfectly calm and generally shew a disposition to acquiesce in whatever may be the fate of the proposed alterations, relying upon their meeting with due consideration.

James Madison Papers, DLC.

Stephen Hall to George Thatcher
12 May 1789

Congress, I guess, will cut the matter of amendments pretty short in Righteousness: for I believe they will consider the federal Government, as a Government of thirteen, or at present, of Eleven great & honest, & good Personages, each too important easily to be affronted. Therefore having declared the Idea in which they adopted the federal Constitution, by the Amendments proposed, I think they are pretty safe without Congress reducing Those Amendments to a regular system; for if my memory serves me, their general tendency is to secure a good administration of the Constitution, rather than really to alter it. This you will say is very general reasoning. I mean it only as an hint; for to be particular upon the subject, when writing to a Member of Congress would rather savour of arrogance.

Chamberlain Collection, MB.

Samuel Chase to Richard Henry Lee
16 May 1789

I observed that a Day is appointed to consider Amendments to the new Constitution. I am one of the Number that expect no essential alterations. I hope I may be mistaken. I fear that no Check will be placed on the Exercise of any of the powers granted. I am satisfied that, every Amendment must flow from Grace & favor. our people will not contend for any, the most important. In this State [*Maryland*] We are prepared to submit to any government. the Hearts of our people are broke, they are bow down to the Earth with their Debts.

Lee Family Papers, ViU.

James Madison to Thomas Jefferson
27 May 1789

The subject of amendments was to have been introduced on monday last; but is postponed in order that more urgent business may not be delayed. On Monday sevennight it will certainly come forward. A Bill of rights, incorporated perhaps into the Constitution will be proposed, with a few other alterations most called for by the opponents of the Government and least objectionable to its friends.

James Madison Papers, DLC.

Richard Henry Lee to Patrick Henry
28 May 1789

So far as this has gone, I am satisfied to see a spirit prevailing that promises to send this system out free from those vexations and abuses that might have been warranted by the terms of the constitution. It must never be forgotten, however, that the liberties of the people are not so safe under the gracious manner of government, as by the limitation of power. Mr. Madison has given notice, that, on Monday s'n-night he will call for the attention of the house to the subject of amendments. I apprehend that his ideas, and those of our convention, on this subject, are not similar. We shall carefully attend to this, and when the plan comes to the senate, we shall prepare to abridge, or enlarge, so as to effect, if possible, the wishes of our legislature. I think, from what I hear and see, that many of our amendments will not succeed, but my hopes are strong that such as may effectually secure civil liberty will not be refused. As two-thirds of the legislatures have refused to apply for a general convention, the Congress, it seems, can constitutionally only submit their propositions of amendments to the legislatures, or to state conventions; but, I suppose, neither of these modes will fail, where the design is more effectually to secure civil liberty; the wish to do which, was, I assure you, the sole reason that could have influenced me to come here, ...

William Wirt Henry, *Patrick Henry: Life, Correspondence and Speeches*, 3 vols. (New York, 1891), 3:387–89.

Jeremy Belknap to Paine Wingate
29 May 1789

You will see in the speech wh. our *new* Lieut. Governor [*Samuel Adams*] made at his investiture that he has not thrown off the old idea of "*independence*" as an attribute of each individual State in the "confederated Republic"—& you will know in what light to regard his "devout & fervent wish" that "the people may enjoy well grounded confidence that their *personal & domestic* rights are *secure*." This is the same Language or nearly the same which he used in the Convention when he moved for an addition to the proposed Amendments—by inserting a clause to provide for the Liberty of the press—the right to keep arms—Protection from seizure of person & property & the *Rights of Conscience*. By which motion he gave an alarm to both sides of the house & had nearly overset the whole business which the Friends of the Constitution had been labouring for several Weeks to obtain. Should a Man tell me that he devoutly wished I might not break into his house & rob his desk—I think I should have a right to suspect that he viewed me in no better light than a Burglar. So if a Man publickly expresses a *devout* wish that the new Government may not rob him of his personal & domestic rights—I think it not uncharitable to conclude that he has a jealousy of its intentions.

The *dear* insurgents[1] must be treated with tenderness because they mean well tho' under some mistakes—but the staunch, tired defenders of American Liberty must be guarded against with a "devout wish" that they may not violate personal & domestic rights!

Chamberlain Collection, MB.

[1]Shays' Rebellion. See Part II, n. 23.

Nathan Dane to George Thatcher
31 May 1789

As to amendments—I do not think them as difficult as to the principal points it has ever appeared to me that the one party has contended but for little more than the other has admitted . . . .

Will not declaring the rights expressly and fortifying the liberties of the Country more explicitly induce confidence and there by in fact add Strength to the government, produce punctuality in the execution of the laws, and make a system good in the outlines of it, more complete.

Chamberlain Collection, MB.

George Washington to James Madison
[*31*] May 1789

As far as a momentary consideration has enable me to judge, I see nothing exceptionable in the proposed amendments. Some of them, in my opinion, are importantly necessary, others, though of themselves (in my conception) not very essential, are necessary to quiet the fears of some respectable characters and well-meaning men. Upon the whole, therefore, not foreseeing any evil consequences that can result from their adoption, they have my wishes for a favorable reception in both houses.

Lee-Kohns Collection, NN.

June 1789

Benjamin Hawkins to James Madison
1 June 1789

a circumstance trivial indeed, but from its effect here, important, deserves to be told. The opponents had predicted that Congress being once possessed with power, the friends to the new Government would never consent to make any amendments. your motion on that great and delicate subject directly contradicts it. And they swear that they will never forget Bland, Grayson and their other friends for suffering any business however important to be done in Congress prior to the subject of amendments. and moreover for suffering this important prophecy by their tardiness to be contradicted.

If you can do something by way of amendments without any material injury to the system, I shall be much pleased, and as far as I can learn it will be pleasing to my countrymen or a majority of them I mean, we certainly are more friendly than we were at the meeting of our Convention, several counties who were much opposed to it, are now decidedly very friendly and I count on its being adopted at Our next convention.

James Madison Papers, DLC.

Roger Sherman to Henry Gibbs
1 June 1789

I now enclose two News papers, of the 20th & 24th of March, containing Observations on the New Federal Constitutions, and the alterations proposed as amendments Signed *A Citizen of New Haven* for your perusal, and if you Shall think it may be useful, that they may be published in the Salem Paper, & any other Papers in your State—It will be best to put the whole into one Paper, and I wish to have one of them transmitted to me when you write again—I believe the contention about amendments of the

Constitution has pretty much Subsided every where, and I trust the people will be Still more reconciled to it, as the Laws that will from time to time be made under it Shall be published.

Gibbs Family Collection, CtY.

Richard Bland Lee to David Stuart 4 June 1789

Poor Bland has been very ill and left us early yesterday morning for home—He was much better before he went away—and expects to return to us in the course of a month. He very reluctantly left us as Monday next is the day appointed to take in consideration the fifth article of the Constitution; and amendments will be prepared and recommended without his aid or advice.

McGregor Library Manuscripts, ViU.

Christopher Gore to Rufus King 7 June 1789

Our [*state*] Senate is federal to an high degree—not more than eight bad can be counted—these can in no instance, be a majority—therefore evil may be prevented—the house has hitherto shewn no disposition to interfere with the fed. govt.—a motion was made to raise a committee for the purpose of considering the expediency of an application to Congress on the subject of amendments—I requested the mover to withdraw his motion as it was contrary to the sence of the people that a convention shou'd be called & this was the only mode in wh. the legislature cou'd interfere—and Congress had already assignd a time for the consideration of this subject—he refus'd to withdraw, as the object of his motion was only to consider the expediency of adopting some measure—on which I made some good naturd observations, & assured myself that the House had too much regard for the time & money of their constituents to spend either so wantonly, as considering such questions—the gentn. who seconded withdrew his support & no other appeard to promote the idea—& it died—this I considerd as a favorable symptom, & conclusive evidence that no plan has yet been agreed on to oppose the govt. . . . .

Rufus King Papers, NHi.

George Clymer to Richard Peters
8 June 1789

Madison this morning is to make an essay towards amendments—but whether he means merely a tub to the whale,[1] or declarations about the press liberty of conscience &c. or will suffer himself to be so far frightened with the antifederalism of his own state as to attempt to lop off essentials I do not know—I hope however we shall be strong enough to postpone. . . .
Afternoon—Madison's has proved a tub on a number of Ad. but Gerry is not content with them alone, and proposes to treat us with all the amendments of all the antifederalists in America.

Richard Peters Papers, PHi.

---

[1]See Part II, n. 26 above.

William R. Davie to James Madison
10 June 1789

You are well acquainted with the political situation of this State [*North Carolina*], its unhappy attachment to paper money, and that wild scepticism which has prevailed in it since the publication of the Constitution. It has been the uniform cant of the enemies of the Government, that Congress would exert all their influence to prevent the calling of a Convention, and would never propose an amendment themselves, or consent to an alteration that would in any manner diminish their powers. The people whose fears had been already alarmed, have received this opinion as fact, and become confirmed in their opposition; your notification however of the 4th. of May has dispersed almost universal pleasure, we hold it up as a refutation of the gloomy profecies of the leaders of the opposition, and the honest part of our antifederalists have publickly expressed great satisfaction on this event. Our Convention meet again in November, with powers to adopt the Constitution and any Amendments, that may be proposed; this renders it extremely important that the amendments, if any, should be proposed before that time. And although we may be nominally a foreign State, yet I hope the alterations will come officially addressed to the people of this Country, an attention however trifling in itself, that will be of importance in the present state of the public mind here.

That farago of Amendments borrowed from Virginia is by no means to be considered as the sense of this Country; they were proposed amidst the violence and confusion of party heat, at a critical moment in our convention, and adopted by the opposition without one moment's consideration. I have collected with some attention the objections of the honest and serious—they are but few & perhaps necesary—They require some explanations rather than alteration of power of Congress over elections—an abridgment of the Jurisdiction of the federal Court in a few instances, and some fixed regulations respecting appeals—they also insist on the trial by jury being expressly secured to them in all cases—and a constitutional guarantee for the free exercise of their religious rights and priveledges—the rule of representation is thought to be too much in the power of Congress—and the Constitution is silent with respect to the existing paper money an important and interesting property. Instead of a Bill of rights attempting to enumerate the rights of the Indivi[*du*]al or the State Governments, they seem to prefer some general negative confining Congress to the exercise of the powers particularly granted, with some express negative restriction in some important cases. I am extremely anxious to know the progress of this delicate and interesting business; and if you could find leisure from the duties of office and the obligations of Friendship to give me some information on this subject, it might perhaps be of some consequence to this Country, and would in any event be gratefully acknowledged . . . .

James Madison Papers, DLC.

Peter Muhlenberg to Benjamin Rush
10 June 1789

I do myself the Honor to enclose You The Amendments, brought before The House by Mr. Maddison on Monday last.[1] as They are not to be made Public at present, I will thank you to keep them for your own perusal, and to let me know Your sentiments, relative to the propriety &

[1]Rush's replies to this and other letters he received from members of Congress have never been found. We are printing a comment he made to John Adams on 15 June on the assumption that he made the same suggestion to one of his congressional correspondents:

> Many pious people wish the name of the Supreme Being had been introduced somewhere in the new Constitution. Perhaps an acknowledgement may be made of his goodness or of his providence in the proposed amendments. In all enterprises and parties I believe the *praying* are better allies than the *fighting* part of communities (Adams Family Manuscript Trust, MHi).

necessity of them—They were well received by the House, as it was alledged, that unless some amendments took place, some States, who were at present otherwise inclined, might be induced to Join in demanding a Convention. Mr. Gerry spoke warmly on this Subject—reprobated the idea of a Convention & concluded with saying, That if The present Government would not do, he despaird of any other; & dreaded that a Military one would follow its rejection &c. . . .P.S. This matter will not be brought forward again until the revenue System is complete. I will thank you to communicate them to Doctor Franklin.

Mr. John F. Reed, King of Prussia, Pennsylvania, 1974.

Fisher Ames to Thomas Dwight
11 June 1789

Mr. Madison has introduced his long expected Amendments. They are the fruit of much labour and research. He has hunted up all the grievances and complaints of newspapers—all the articles of Conventions—and the small talk of their debates. It contains a Bill of Rights—the right of enjoying property—of changing the govt. at pleasure—freedom of the press—of conscience—of juries—exemption from general Warrants gradual increase of representatives till the whole number at the rate of one to every 30,000 shall amount to and allowing two to every State, at least this is the substance. There is too much of it—O. I had forgot, the right of the people to bear Arms.

Risum teneatis amici[1]—

Upon the whole, it may do good towards quieting men who attend to sounds only, and may get the mover some popularity—which he wishes.

Fisher Ames Papers, Dedham Historical Society, Massachusetts.

[1] Could you forbear the laughter of a friend?

Fisher Ames to George R. Minot
12 June 1789

The civil departments will employ us next, and the judiciary the Senate. They will finish their stint, as the boys say, before the House has done. Their number is less, and they have matured the business in committee. Yet Mr. Madison has inserted, in his amendments, the increase of representatives, each State having two at least. The rights of conscience, of bearing arms, of changing the government, are declared to be inherent in the people. Freedom of the press, too. There is a prodigious great dose for a medicine. But it will stimulate the stomach as little as hasty-pudding. It is rather food than physic. An immense mass of sweet and other herbs and roots for a diet drink.

Seth Ames, ed., *The Works of Fisher Ames*, 2 vols. (Boston, 1854), 1:54.

Benjamin Contee to John Eager Howard
12 June 1789

perhaps the propositions (to be grafted on the constitution, if the intention of the motion succeeds) brought forward by Mr. Maddison may make some noise in Maryland—Mr. Duvall has a copy of them. It may be seen from thence that some of them are inapplicable in a great degree, as being needless stipulations between—not a people and a separate and independent power—but between a people and their representatives—in other between a people and—who—why themselves. For it I esteem it a real truth that the Govt. is a Govt. of the people—as much so as any ever was or can be instituted for the successful conduct of the affairs of our extensive Union—extensive I mean in its locality as well as in the importance of its various concerns—which embrace almost innumerable Objects, and many esteemed highly consequential in the Eye of the present improved and enlightened policy of nations—the enclosed paper contains some strictures which may shew the inexpediency of some of the proposed articles.

But a postponement of the business was necessarily induced by other of more importance. at least, it must be acknowledged by all to be, of more immediate importance.

Executive Papers, 1778–1865, Maryland State Archives.

William Grayson to Patrick Henry
12 June 1789

I am exceedingly sorry it is out of my power to hold out to you any flattering expectations on the score of amendments; it appears to me that both houses are almost wholly composed of foederalists: those who call themselves Antis are so extremely luke warm, as scarcely to deserve the appelation: Some gentlemen here from motives of policy have it in contemplation to effect amendments which shall affect personal liberty alone, leaving the great points of the Jud[*iciar*]y & direct taxation &c. to stand as they are; their object is in my opinion unquestionably to break the spirit of the party by divisions; after this I presume many of the most sanguine expect to go on coolly, in sapping the independence of the State legislatures: In this system however of *divide* & *impera*,[1] they are opposed by a very heavy column, from the little states, who being in possession of rights they had no pretensions to in justice, are afraid of touching a subject which may bring into investigation & controversy their fortunate situation: last munday a string of amendments were presented to the lower House; these altogether respected personal liberty; & I would now inclose you a copy did I not know that Parker had done it already: Even these amendments were opposed by Georgia New Hampshire & Connecticut: they were however submitted to a comm[*itt*]ee. of the whole on the state of the nation, & it is thought will not be taken up again for one while. I understood that the mover was so embarass'd in the course of the business that he was once or twice on the point of withdrawing the motion & it was thought by some that the commitment was more owing to personal respect than a love of the subject introduced.

In the Senate I think that prospects are even less favorable although no direct proposition has yet been brought forward; I have suggested to my colleague the propriety of bringing forward the amendments of the state before the Senate, but he thinks it will be best to wait till they come up from the representatives.

George N. Meissner Collection, Washington University Libraries.

[1]Divide and conquer.

Richard Bland Lee to Leven Powell
12 June 1789

The enclosed paper will shew you the amendments which Mr. Madison has submitted to the consideration of our house. A very desultory conversation took place on this occasion—Some objected to recommending any amendments till experience should demonstrate the necessity of them—Others considered the investigation of that Subject premature and that it ought to be delayed for some months till the weighty business before us should be dispatched. However I believe the amendments which Mr. Madison proposed will be finally recommended to the Legislatures of the respective States—provided attempts should not be made to introduce others which would destroy the efficacy of the Government—in which case the attainment of any might be risked. The further consideration of this subject will be defered till the important business which presses for immediate decision shall be determined on.

Leven Powell Papers, The College of William and Mary.

Abraham Baldwin to Joel Barlow
14 June 1789

A few days since, Madison brought before us propositions of amendment agreeably to his promise to his constituents. Such as he supposed would tranquillize the minds of honest opposers without injuring the system. viz. "That what is not given is reserved, that liberty of the press & trial by jury shall remain *inviolable*. that the representation shall never be less than one for every 30,000 &c. ordered to lie on the table. We are too busy at present in cutting away at the whole cloth, to stop to do any body's patching. There is no such thing as antifederalism heard of. R[*hode*] I[*sland*] and N[*orth*] C[*arolina*] had local reasons for their conduct, and will come right before long.

Abraham Baldwin Collection, CtY.

Thomas Fitzsimons to Benjamin Rush
15 June 1789

Last week a proposition for Amendments was brot. forward by Mr. Madison. No Opinion could at the *time* be formed how farr they were Acceptable but I have reason to think they were thot. Nugatory & premature I inclose the paper that you may make your observation. I suppose next week—they will be considered.

Gratz Collection, PHi.

James Madison to Edmund Randolph
15 June 1789

The inclosed paper contains the proposition made on monday last on the subject of amendments. It is limited to points which are important in the eyes of many and can be objectionable in those of none. The structure & stamina of the Govt. are as little touched as possible. Nothing of a controvertible nature can be expected to make its way thro' the caprice &

discord of opinions which would encounter it in Congs. when ⅔ must concur in each House, & in the State Legislatures ¾ of which will be requisite to its final success. The article which I fear most for is that which respects the representation. The small States betray already a coolness towards it. And I am not sure that another local policy may not mingle its poisin in the healing experiment.

James Madison Papers, DLC.

Samuel Nasson to George Thatcher
16 June 1789

As to the Inteligence you give me I Skipt. over the first part and come to what you Say of Amendments you think that they will be agreed two soon or Quick Demised I hope you will be Enabled to do your Duty I am more and more Convinced that they are Necessary you think that we are in no Dangour from Congress I hope in God they will be keept from doing what will finaly End in the Distruction of our Libertys.
I am Convinced that if we allways have men in the house and Senate that feel for the people then we Shall not be in any Dangour nor Should we if we had not a Constitution But Sir I would that we had Such a one that they might not have power to make laws which would affect the Libertys of the people.

George Thatcher Papers, MSaE.

George Lee Turberville to James Madison
16 June 1789

Upon the Subject of amendments, altho I shou'd be happy to know what are thought essential & what are likely to be adopted by Congress—I assure you I am totally unsollicitous for any. where there is such responsibility—where the public Voice so thoroughly pervades every department of Government—& where age is made the qualification for Office it is to me very apparent that the interest of the Ruler & the people of the Representative & Constituent are the same—And beside when it is recollected (& it can never be forgotten) that the government originated with, & was the result of the reason & deliberation of—The People—is it possible that it can ever be converted into an oppression upon those people? for the aggrandizement & benefit of a few—without such a total depravity of manners such corruption—such pusillanimity takes possession of the people as shall fit them like the ancient Cappadocians for the exercise of Despotic government alone—and at Such a period shou'd it ever arrive (which may heavan prevent) The Constitution with all its amendments will be ineffectual to protect (us or) our posterity from the Evils which will inevitably await them.

Madison Collection, NN.

George Gale to William Tilghman
17 June 1789

I send you by Mr. James Holeyday's servant the paper which Contains Mr. Madison's Amendments—I trust you will think the most of them Innocent and were it not that the Opponents to the Government might exult perhaps insultingly would have little Objection to their being Adopted.

William Tilghman Papers, PHi.

Tench Coxe to James Madison
18 June 1789

I observe you have brought forward the amendments you proposed to the federal Constitution. I have given them a very careful perusal, and have attended particularly to their reception by the public. The most decided friends of the constitution admit (generally) that they will meliorate the government by removing some points of litigation and jealousy, and by heightening and strengthening the barriers between necessary power and indispensible liberty. In short the most ardent & irritable among our friends are well pleased with them. On the part of the opposition, I do not observe any unfavorable animadversion. Those who are honest are well pleased at the footing on which the press, liberty of conscience, original right & power, trial by jury &ca. are rested. Those who are not honest have hitherto been silent, for in truth they are stript of every rational, and most of the popular arguments they have heretofore used. I will not detain you with further remarks, but feel very great satisfaction in being able to assure you generally that the proposed amendments will greatly tend to promote harmony among the late contending parties and a general confidence in the patriotism of Congress. It has appeared to me that a few well tempered observations on these propositions might have a good effect. I have therefore taken an hour from my present Engagements, which on account of my absence are greater than usual, and have thrown together a few remarks upon the first part of the Resolutions. I shall endeavour to pursue them in one or two more short papers. It may perhaps be of use in the present turn of the public opinions in New York state that they should be republished there. It is in fed. Gazette of 18th instant.[1]

James Madison Papers, DLC.

[1]Coxe's "Remarks on the . . . Amendments to the Federal Constitution" appeared in the [Philadelphia] *Federal Gazette* on 18 and 30 June over the signature of "A Pennsylvanian."

James Madison to Samuel Johnston
21 June 1789

In the inclosed paper is a copy of a late proposition in Congress on the subject of amending the Constitution. It aims at the twofold object of removing the fears of the discontented and of avoiding all such alterations as would either displease the adverse side, or endanger the success of the measure. I need not remark to you the hazard of attempting any thing of a controvertible nature which is to depend on the concurrence of ⅔ of both Houses here, and the ratification of ¾ of the State Legislatures. It will be some time before the proposed amendments will become a subject of discussion in Congress; The bills relating to revenue, and the organization of the Judiciary and Executive Departments, being likely to remain for some time on hand.

PJM 12:250.

Joseph Jones to James Madison
24 June 1789

I thank you for the copy of the amendments proposed to the constitution which you lately inclosed to me—they are calculated to secure the personal rights of the people so far as declarations on paper can effect the purpose, leaving unimpaired the great Powers of the government—they are of such a nature as to be generally acceptable and of course more likely to obtain the assent of Congress than wo'd any proposition tending to separate the powers or lessen them in either branch. The Part that speaks of facts triable by Jury not otherwise reexaminable than may consist with the principles of the common law means I suppose that the Court of app[*ea*]ls. shall not re-examine the facts but by a Jury, or what is the true meaning?

James Madison Papers, DLC.

James Madison to Tench Coxe
24 June 1789

It is much to be wished that the discon[*ten*]ted part of our fellow Citizens could be reconciled to the Government they have opposed, and by means as little as possible unacceptable to those who approve the Constitution in its present form. The amendments proposed in the H. of Reps. had this twofold object in view; besides the third one of avoiding all controvertible points which might endanger the assent of ⅔ of each branch of Congs. and ¾ of the State Legislatures. How far the experiment may succeed in any of these respects is wholly uncertain. It will however be greatly favored by explanatory strictures of a healing tendency, and is therefore already indebted to the co-operation of your pen.

James Madison Papers, DLC.

Peter Muhlenberg to Benjamin Rush
25 June 1789

I wrote You on the 4th. instant, and on the 10th. mailed you a Copy of Madisons Propositions for amending the Constitution; at that time it was not intended they should be made public, until The House should be ready to act upon them, but one of the printers having obtained a Copy, imediately gave them to the Public—I was & am still anxious to know what your sentiments are relative to these Propositions, but as I have not been Honord with a line from You during the Present Month, I am doubtfull whether my Letters are come to hand.

Feinstone Collection, David Library of the American Revolution, on deposit, PPAmP.

Edward Stevens to James Madison
25 June 1789

It affords me no small pleasure to inform you that your proposition of amendments to the Constitution, among all my acquaintances that I have had communication with; gives general Satisfaction, and I trust if adopted will shut the mouths of many.

James Madison Papers, DLC.

Oliver Wolcott, Sr., to Oliver Ellsworth
27 June 1789

With these Veiws I sincerely Wish that Congress would not relax from the Principles of the Constitution, nor attempt to effect (what some, I believe, Very erroneously call) *Amendments* thereto—To bind a government with Fetters of Iron which is founded on periodical Elections is in my Opinion, to guard against Evils of the Most Visionary Nature—The Executive will, in my Judgment, require a constant and active Support, otherwise a constitutional Defect will be found in that Branch of Government, especially after the great and confidential Character, who now possesses it, shall leave it.

Wolcott Manuscripts, Connecticut Historical Society.

George Clymer to Tench Coxe
28 June 1789

I fancy the Antifederalists with you wish to be let down easy, or they would not shew so much satisfaction at Madison's amendments—Like a sensible physician he has given his malades imaginaires[1] bread pills powder of paste & neutral mixtures to keep them in play—I am really glad of this disposition in them having greatly feared that as such amendments were not wanted by the federal party so they would not at all have come up to the hopes of the anti-federal.

Coxe Papers, PHi.

---

[1] Imaginary illnesses.

John Dawson to James Madison
28 June 1789

You have it in contemplation, I hear, to adjourn in August. Surely you will not do this without recommending those alterations which have been so ardently desird by many of the states, most of which will not materially effect the system, but will render it more secure, and more agreable in the eyes of those who were oppos'd to its establishment. I rejoice to find that you come forward at an early day with a proposition for amendments, altho I coud have wish'd they had been more extensive. Experience, as well as sound policy point out, in my humble opinion, the propriety of the amendment propos'd by this state for rendering more secure our Western territory, & for guarding against the danger of the surrender of the Mississippi—that in the commercial regulations there will be efforts in the part of the Continent to throw the weight of the duties on the other, is apprehended by many and therefore the amendment propos'd to this part of the system is thought to be of importance.[1]

James Madison Papers, DLC.

[1] See p. 20 above.

James Sullivan to Elbridge Gerry
28 June 1789

they are much displeased with and Disappointed in the great Man from Virginia they think he appears too serious in his motion for amendments but some of us think that he is going so far and laying aside the Amendments proposed by the Several states in order to prevent any thing being done on the subject, so we the people have our opinions and as yet in some instances dare to speak them. and we believe that through your Exertions and those of others we shall yet hold that priviledge.

James S. Copley Library, La Jolla, California.

Edmund Randolph to James Madison
30 June 1789

The amendments, proposed by you, are much approved by the *strong* foederalists here and at the Metropolis [*Richmond*]; being considered as an anodyne to the discontented. Some others, equally affectionate to the union, but less sanguine, expect to hear at the next session of assembly that a real melioration of the Constitution was not so much intended, as a soporific draught to the restless. I believe indeed, that nothing, nay not even the abolishment of direct taxation would satisfy those, who are most clamorous. But I confess, I am still in hopes to see reported from your mouth some review of the various amendments proposed, and reasons against the fitness of such, as appear'd improper for adoption.

James Madison Papers, DLC.

July 1789

Peter Silvester to Peter Van Schaack
1 July 1789

You have seen Madisons proposals of amendts. when that comes on I should like to say something clever in favor of it so far as it does not injure the system & I should like at some of your leisure moments you would draw up some suitable speech for me not to long nor to short when you are in a humour for it & send it to me.

Van Schaack Papers, Columbia University.

Benjamin Hawkins to James Madison
3 July 1789

I am anxious to know the fate of your attempt to mend the constitution, and whether anything can, with certainty, be done that will conciliate its opponents. If it should appear in the investigation that there are difficulties greater than you seem to apprehend, I wish that the subject could be postponed 'till after the meeting of our Convention.[1]

The opponents here will, I expect, avail themselves of every thing to strengthen their party.

James Madison Papers, DLC.

---

[1]The second North Carolina ratification convention met from 16 to 23 November 1789.

John Fenno to Joseph Ward
5 July 1789

I think this business of amendments a very unpropitious affair, just at this juncture—Mr. M[*adison*]. is universally acknowledged a man of the first rate abilities: but there appears to be a mixture of timidity in his disposition, which, as he is so influential a character, I some times fear will be productive of effects, not salutary, to say the least—every movement of this kind, unhinges the public mind, gives an opening to the artful, unprincipled, & disaffected—who are waiting with burning impatience for an opportunity to embroil & embarrass public affairs.

Joseph Ward Papers, Chicago Historical Society.

James Madison to James Madison, Sr.
5 July 1789

The subject of amendments will not be resumed til the revenue matters are over. I hope it will then be duly attended to, and will end in such a recommendation as will satisfy moderate opponents. This however is but opinion, nothing having passed from which any conclusion can be drawn with regard to the Sentiments of the two Houses, particularly the Senate.

James Madison Papers, DLC.

Richard Peters to James Madison
5 July 1789

I see you have been offering Amendments to the Machine before it is known whether it wants any. After these shall be added the Ingenuity of those who wish to embarrass its Motions will find out some Things that it wants & so after making it as complicated as a Combination of Dutch Stocking Looms they will alledge it to be too intricate for Use. I was glad on one Account to observe you were not joined by these great Artists who offer Repairs before a Thing is worn, but I was mortified on the other Hand that you were in a Situation to put it in their Power to neglect you. You must not be hurt at these clodhopping Sentiments of mine for I love you so truly that I dislike your mixing with so many Parts of your Conduct that command my Approbation, any one I cannot praise. You see into what a Scrape you have brought yourself by being kind to me. Yet it is more than possible I am wrong in all this Business as you know more of the Necessity of such Accomodations than I do—If Chips must be put into the Porridge however, I think I would let the bad Cooks put them into the Pot, nor should any throw out Tubs but those who were afraid of the Whale.

James Madison Papers, DLC.

Richard Parker to Richard Henry Lee
6 July 1789

I observe the slip of the newspaper sent me and know the design, but still I think a Bill of rights not necessary here tho in france absolutely so and twas proper for the Duke of Orleans to recommend it for France[1] the King claims all power here the States claim & have all power but what they have given away—However I have no objection to such a bill of Rights as has been proposed by Mr. Maddison because we declare that we do not abridge our Rights by the reservation but that we retain all we have not specifically given—I have not been able to consider the Amendments proposed to be made to the Constitution but think some of the objections made to it will if they are adopted be taken away, I wish not they should be too minute lest greater inconveniencies arise.

Lee Family Papers, ViU.

[1] In the winter of 1788–89, Louis-Phillipe, duc d'Orleans, published his *Instructions à ses bailliages*, seventeen articles that recommended to the Estates-General guarantees of certain individual liberties.

Samuel Johnston to James Madison
8 July 1789

. . . I should be sorry to see any material Alterations take place in the Constitution, yet the addition of a little Flourish & Dressing without injuring the substantial part or adding much to its intrinsic value, such as a pompous Declaration of Rights, may have a happy effect in complimenting the Judgment of those who have themselves up in Opposition to it and afford a *Salvo* to some well disposed men, who were unwarily drawn into these measures, for changing an Opinion which they had too hastily adopted.

James Madison Papers, DLC.

Samuel Nasson to George Thatcher
9 July 1789

I find that Ammendments are once again on the Carpet. I hope that such may take place as will be for the Best Interest of the whole A Bill of rights well secured that we the people may know how far we may Proceade in Every Department then their will be no Dispute Between the people and rulers in that may be secured the right to keep arms for Common and Extraordinary Occations such as to secure ourselves against the wild Beast and also to amuse us by fowling and for our Defence against a Common Enemy you know to learn the Use of arms is all that can Save us from a forighn foe that may attempt to subdue us for if we keep up the Use of arms and become well acquainted with them we Shall allway be able to look them in the face that arise up against us for it is impossible to Support a Standing armey large Enough to Guard our Lengthy Sea Coast and now Spare me on the subject of Standing armeys in a time of Peace they allway was first or last the downfall of all free Governments it was by their help Caesar made proud Rome Own a Tyrant and a Traytor for a Master.

only think how fatale they ware to the peace of this Countery in 1770 what Confeusion they Brought on the fatal 5 of March[1] I think the remembrance of that Night is enough to make us Carefull how we Introduce them in a free republican Government—I therefore hope they will be Discouraged for I think the man that Enters as a Soldier in a time of peace only for a living is only a fit tool to inslave his fellows for this purpos was a Standing Army first introduced in the World anoather that I hope will be Established in the bill is tryals by Juryes in all Causes Excepting where the parties agree to be without I never wish to be in the power of any Sett of Men let them be Never so good but hope to be left in the hands of my Countery and if any Enemey means to bribe he must have money anough to settle it with the Country.

George Thatcher Papers, MSaE.

[1]On 5 March 1770 British troops stationed in Boston fired on a crowd of civilians who were harrassing them. The event became immortalized as the Boston Massacre.

Elbridge Gerry to John Wendell
10 July 1789

I never was for rejecting the constitution, but for suspending the ratification untill it could be amended, as may be seen by my letter to the legislature of our state soon after the dissolution of the federal Convention[1]—indeed as objectionable as the constitution was in my mind I

[1]Gerry's influential and widely published letter of 18 October 1787 contained his objections to the Constitution. It can be found in *DHROC* 13:546–50.

should have preferred an adoption of it, to an hazard of a dissolution of the Union, but, being very apprehensive that the necessary amendments would never be obtained unless previously to a ratification I tho't good policy directed a suspension, & time must determine whether or not I was mistaken, untill the effects of the efforts of the states for amendments could be ascertained. I shall chearfully submit to any form of government which my fellow citizens may choose, reserving always a right to remove from oppression should it ever prevail in my native country which I pray God may never be the case; but at the same time, I shall always exercise the natural right of withholding my assent to any system which I think dangerous, whilst its adoption is a question of political discussion. Whether the present constitution will preserve the ballance, or change to an aristocracy or monarchy, must depend on the alterations that shall be made in the constitution & on the administration thereof: should there be no amendments I am of opinion it will verge to a monarchy & verging to it that such a form of government upon hereditary establishment will soon be found more safe & advantageous than a system altogether elective & participating of principles both republican & monarchical, but the field widens & obliges me to quit it.

Gratz Collection, PHi.

William Ellery to Benjamin Huntington
13 July 1789

After you have completed the act for collecting the Impost, and have established the Judiciary, amendments to the Constitution will, I suppose, be brought upon the tapis. If any amendments are to be proposed to the legislatures of the States the sooner they are offered the better. An early decision either way on that subject would, I believe, be beneficial; for so long as there is any expectation of amendments, that expectation may be assigned as a reason—by the non acceding States for their not acceding, and they who have acceded may not be so perfectly easy as they would otherwise be.

It is true, that an expectation of amendments is a feeble reason for their not embracing the Union; because by the addition of their force they might be more likely to obtain them, than by standing out—and they *must* sooner or later accede, whether the Constitution is amended or not. But a bad excuse with some characters is better than none. Take away this false ground, and if they then stand out, they will stand, as the Hibernians did, upon nothing. They will be fools indeed, and without even the shadow of an excuse.

Benjamin Huntington Papers, R-Ar.

Henry Gibbs to Roger Sherman
16 July 1789

Your favor of the 1rst. Ult. came seasonably to hand as has also that of the 7th. Inst. the former inclosed the pieces under the signature of "a Citizen of New Haven" which I immediately handed to our Printers & which were publish'd in their papers of June 30th. & July 7th. I am far from wishing that the Beauty of our new System should be marred by the many preposterous Alterations which have been propos'd, but as it was adopted by some of the States in full Confidence that the subject of Amendments would be soon constitutionally enter'd upon, I hope Congress will not delay canvassing the matter any longer than their more important Business renders necessary. All Ambiguity of Expression certainly ought to be remov'd; Liberty of Conscience in religious matters, right of trial by Jury, Liberty of the Press &c. may perhaps be more explicitly secur'd to the Subject & a general reservation made to the States respectively of all the powers not expressly delegated to the general Government. These indeed may be tho't by most to be the spirit of the Constitution, but there are some who have their fears that the loose manner of expression in some instances will not sufficiently guard the rights of the Subject from the invasion of corrupt Rulers hereafter. Some such explanatory & reserving Clauses may therefore without giving umbrage to the friends of the new plan of Government tend greatly to conciliate the minds of many of it's Opponents. As to any essential Alterations neither time nor Capacity will allow of my forming an Opinion respecting them.

Roger Sherman Collection, CtY.

Theodore Sedgwick to Benjamin Lincoln
19 July 1789

Mr. Madison's talents, respectable as they are will for some time be lost to the public, from his timidity. He is constantly haunted with the gohst of Patrick Henry. No man, in my opinion, in this country has more fair and honorable intentions, or more ardently wishes the prosperity of the public, but unfortunately he has not that strength of nerves which will enable him to set at defiance popular and factious clamors. His system of amendments we must fairly meet, and must adopt them in every instance in which they will not shackle the operations of the government. It is a water gruel business, and I hope will be so managed as only to produce a more temperate habit in the body politic. Those substantial amendments which would have a tendency to produce a more compleat and natural arrangement of the national union we must despair of attaining at present.

Benjamin Lincoln Papers, MHi.

Benjamin Goodhue to Cotton Tufts
20 July 1789

I am at a loss whether we shall have time to take up the subject of amendments the present session—I believe it will be thought to be good policy to propose such as will not injure the constitution and which may serve to quiet the honest part of the dissatisfied.

Miscellaneous Mss., NHi.

Richard Peters to James Madison
20 July 1789

It is but within a Day or two that I recieved yours of the 14th. in which you very properly leave me as you found me on the Subject I rambled into. But I will revenge myself by sending you a Copy of an old Fable which I have in a curious Collection by me entitled "*Aunciente connynge Balladdes*." I am chained to my Chair by my old Tormentor the Piles & I maliciously wish not that all my Friends should be entirely at Ease. But I let you off gently by only obliging you to read some bad Verses which I know not that you are any wise concerned in save that had you lived in the Days of these Cooks your Easiness of Temper (for which I do not like you a Jot the worse) would have prompted you to indulge the Anti Soupites in some of their Whims of an innocent Nature especially if they had been some of your Neighbours. . . . .

The Wise Cooks & foolish Guests
A Fable

Eleven Cooks assembled once
To make a Treat of Soup
All knowing—not a Dunce
Among the skilful Group.
The Soup was made—delicious! good!
Exclaim'd each *grateful* Guest,
But some who would not taste the Food,
Declar'd it wanted Zest.
Among those Malcontents were found
Some faulting each Ingredient
While others eager search'd around
To find out some Expedient
With which at once to damn the whole
Not take it in Detail.
They would not sup a single Bowl
Lest more they dare not rail.
At Length the Grumblers all fell out
In Nothing could agree
Not e'en while making of a Rout
of what the Soup *should be*.
They curse the Cooks & hungry rave
For those of better Skill—
Another Mess some swear they'l have
On which they'l freely swill.
"Pray taste the Soup" requir'd the Cooks
"We'll yield if we're outreason'd."
—We know 'tis bad—"by what?"—its Looks
'Tis rich & highly season'd—
We wish for Soup in th'Maigre Stile
That's thin—to save Expences—
(The Cooks exclaim & archly smile
"Good Sirs you've lost your Senses!")
We know you Cooks who've learnt your Trade
Will think we talk like Asses—
But we'll have Broth tha's cheaply made
No Salt—*not much* Molasses.
Instead of Dumplins we'll have Chips
Instead of Gravy—Vapour—
And e'er it goes between our Lips

We'll fine it down with—Paper—
And that all Palates we may please
And on your Plan refine
We'll add some scrap'd Rh: Island Cheese
Warm'd up with Knotts of Pine.
We'll tender this to all we meet
And if their Tastes forsake 'em
So that our Fare they will not eat
By—with Force we'll make 'em—
If we can't have our proper Broth
We'll join & spoil your Mess.
No Master Cook we'll have—In Troth
We wish for Nothing less—
We'll make a *Bargain with ourselves*
That one sha'n't poison t'other
We are such wise suspicious elves
That none will trust his brother.
We'll watch our Pot with sleepless Care,
O'er all we'll keep a tight Hand,
For Honesty *we feel*'s so rare
Our left will cheat our right Hand—
"Our Comprehensions" cry the Cooks
"With yours are not on Level.
"To us your Mixture really looks
"A Pottage for the Devil.
"At us, good Sirs, then cease to rave
"You're surely touch'd with Mania
"We'll eat our Soup—do you go shave—
"Lord help your Pericrania!"

Moral

To mend is truly always right
But then the Way to do it
Is not so facile to the Wight
Who undertakes to shew it.

James Madison Papers, DLC.

Roger Sherman's Proposed Committee Report
21–28 July 1789

Report as their Opinion, that the following articles be proposed by Congress to the legislatures of the Several States to be adopted by them as amendments of the Constitution of the united States, and when ratified by the legislatures of three fourths (at least) of the Said States in the union, to become a part of the Constitution of the United States, pursuant to the fifth Article of the Said Constitution.

1 The powers of government being derived from the people, ought to be exercised for their benefit, and they have an inherent and unalienable right, to change or amend their political constitution, when ever they judge such change will advance their interest & happiness.

2 The people have certain natural rights which are retained by them when they enter into society, Such are the rights of conscience in matters of religion; of acquiring property, and of pursuing happiness & safety; of Speaking, writing and publishing their Sentiments with decency and freedom; of peaceably Assembling to consult their common good, and of applying to Government by petition or remonstrance for redress of grievances. Of these rights therefore they Shall not be deprived by the government of the united States.

3 No person shall be tried for any crime whereby he may incur loss of life or any infamous punishment, without Indictment by a grand Jury, nor be convicted but by the unanimous verdict of a Petit Jury of good and lawful men Freeholders of the vicinage or district where the trial shall be had.

4 After a census Shall be taken, each State Shall be allowed one representative for every thirty thousand Inhabitants of the description in the Second Section of the first Article of the Constitution, until the whole number of representatives Shall amount to but never to exceed

5 The Militia shall be under the government of the laws of the respective States, when not in the actual Service of the united States, but Such rules as may be prescribed by Congress for their uniform organisation & discipline shall be observed in officering and training them. but military Service Shall not be required of persons religiously Scrupulous of bearing arms.

6 No Soldier Shall be quartered in any private house, in time of Peace, nor at any time, but by authority of law.

7 Excessive bail shall not be required, nor excessive fines imposed, nor cruel & unusual punishments be inflicted in any case.

8 Congress shall not have power to grant any monopoly or exclusive advantages of Commerce to any person or Company; nor to restrain the liberty of the Press.

9 In Suits at common law in courts acting under the authority of the united States, issues of fact Shall be tried by a Jury if either party, request it.

10 No law that Shall be passed for fixing a compensation for the members of Congress except the first Shall take effect until after the next election of representatives *posterior* to the passing Such law.

11 The legislative, executive and judiciary powers vested by the Constitution in the respective branches of the government of the united States, shall be exercised according to the distribution therein made, so that neither of said branches shall assume or exercise any of the powers peculiar to either of the other branches.

And the powers not delegated to the government of the united States by the Constitution, nor prohibited by it to the particular States, are retained by the States respectively. nor Shall any the exercise of power by the government of the united States the particular instances here in enumerated by way of caution be construed to imply the contrary.

James Madison Papers, DLC. This document is apparently Sherman's proposal to the House select committee, showing how Madison's amendments could be revised and placed at the end of the Constitution.

Lambert Cadwalader to George Mitchell
22 July 1789

A Committee is appointed to report on the Amendments proposed by Madison to the Constitution—& those proposed by the State Conventions—the Committee is composed of Federalists & the Report will be such as we may adopt with Safety—& tho of little or no Consequences it will calm the Turbulence of the Opposition, in Virg[*ini*]a, & some of the other States, and certainly bring N. Carolina into the Union.

Charles Roberts Autograph Collection, PHC.

Peter Muhlenberg to Benjamin Rush
22 July 1789

Yesterday Mr. Maddison brought in his propositions for amending The Constitution, the whole day was taken up in debating, whether they should be refer'd to a Committee of the whole House, or a select Committee. I was not sorry to find the latter prevail, as I conceive no one good purpose can be answer'd by discussing this subject before Crouded Galleries, circumstanced as we are at present. The Committee are directed to report generally.

Gratz Collection, PHi.

Fisher Ames to George R. Minot
23 July 1789

We have had the amendments on the *tapis*, and referred them to a committee of one from a State. I hope much debate will be avoided by this mode, and that the amendments will be more rational, and less *ad populum*, than Madison's. It is necessary to conciliate, and I would have amendments. But they should not be trash, such as would dishonor the Constitution, without pleasing its enemies. Should we propose them, North Carolina would accede.

Seth Ames, ed., *The Works of Fisher Ames*, 2 vols. (Boston, 1854), 1:65–66.

John Wendell to Elbridge Gerry
23 July 1789

I perfectly agree in Sentiment with you, that unless some necessary Amendments take Place, (and there are so many offered as I fear will perplex & confound & perhaps entirely prevent the whole) the present Constitution will become Aristocratical to a high Degree, and that being too obnoxious to the People, will naturally bring on another Revolution in favr. of Monarchy; and could we be sure of a Race or Races of Washingtons to the End of Time, I should not care how soon it was established.

Formerly on deposit, Southern Illinois University.

Benjamin Goodhue to Michael Hodge
30 July 1789

inclosed I send you such amendments as a Committee of one from each State have reported, they are such as the Committee conceived might quiet the minds of the dissatisfied without injuring the Constitution, and as far as I can judge of the prevailing sentiments of the members they appear to be impressed with the policy of proposing such amendments, provided there is a probibility of giving quiet by so cheap a purchase—other amendments of an injurious nature will be likely to be moved for, but will be rejected.

Eben F. Stone Papers, MSaE.

Archibald Stuart to James Madison
31 July 1789

I am happy to inform you that throughout the Whole of My Circuit (which is not small) Party spirit & Political dissentions are now no more— We all wish to come in under the Cloak of a few amendments should they even be inadequate to a compleat Justification of our former Opinions: for this purpose if no Other reasons could be offered I hope some of your amendments will go down.

James Madison Papers, DLC.

August 1789

James Madison to Wilson Cary Nicholas
2 August 1789

The proposed amendments of which I sent you a copy have since been in the hands of a committee composed of a member from each State. Their report is inclosed. [*Some*] of the changes are perhaps for the better, others for the worse. From the concord of the Com[*mitte*]e. and the language used in the House on the last discussion, I indulge a confidence that something will be affected. For the Senate I can less answer, but I have no reason for distrust in case the plan be kept within its present limits.

Pierpont Morgan Library, New York City.

Edward Carrington to Henry Knox
3 August 1789

The People in this state are generally well reconciled to the New Government—Madison is becoming popular with the Antis, who say they believe he is to be the most depended upon for procuring amendments.

Miscellaneous Manuscripts, NHi.

Roger Sherman to Henry Gibbs
4 August 1789

You have doubtless before this seen the amendments to the Constitution reported by the Committee—they will probably be harmless & Satisfactory to those who are fond of Bills of rights, I don't like the form in which they are reported to be incorporated in the Constitution, that Instrument being the Act of the people, ought to be kept intire—and amendments made by the Legislatures Should be in addition by way of Supplement.

Gibbs Family Collection, CtY.

Richard Henry Lee to Samuel Adams
8 August 1789

But so wonderfully are mens minds now changed upon the subject of liberty, that it would seem as if the sentiments which universally prevailed in 1774 were antediluvian visions, and not the solid reason of fifteen years ago! Among the many striking instances that daily occur, take the following, communicated to me by an honble. member of the H. of R. here. You well know our former respected, republican friend, old Mr. R–g–r–Sh–n [*Roger Sherman*] of Con. whose person, manners, and every sentiment appeared formerly to be perfectly republican. This very gentleman, our old republican friend opposed a motion for introducing into a bill of rights, an idea that the Military should be subordinate to the Civil power. His reason as stated was "*that it would make the people insolent*!" This was in a committee of the H. of R. for reporting amendments to the Constitution. The subject of Amendments is now under consideration of the same house—how they will terminate I cannot say—But my wishes are stronger than my expectations.

Samuel Adams Papers, NN.

Robert Morris to Richard Peters
9 August 1789

I do not think you are in any danger of having the next Session of Assembly prolonged by propositions of Amendments to the Federal Constitution because we seem to have sufficient business on our hands that must be first got through, to employ us untill the period of your Adjournment, it is possible however that in this respect I may be mistaken.

Richard Peters Papers, PHi.

William L. Smith to Edward Rutledge
9 August 1789

The Committee on amendmts. have reported some, which are thought inoffensive to the federalists & may do some good on the other side; N. Car[*olin*]a. only wants some pretext to come into the Union, & we may afford that pretext by recommending a few amendments.

There appears to be a disposition in our house to agree to some, which will more effectually secure private rights, without affecting the structure of the Govt.

William Loughton Smith Papers, ScHi. This letter was written on 9, 10, and 15 August. The respective parts are printed under headings for those dates.

Thomas B. Wait to George Thatcher
9 August 1789

The amendments to the National Constitution are generally good; but my friend there is an essential omission; and which I wish you to attend to when the Committee's report comes before the house—It is this: "That Congress shall have power to appoint the times, and places of elections." &c. *whenever any State shall neglect or refuse* &c. The addition of this last clause, if it does no good, can never do an injury to the Constitution; and you may rest assured that it will have a salutary effect on the minds of the people.

Thomas B. Wait Papers, MHi.

William L. Smith to Edward Rutledge
10 August 1789

I shall support the Amendmts. proposed to the Constitution that any exception to the powers of Congress shall not be so construed as to give it any powers not *expressly* given, & the enumeration of certain rights shall not be so construed as to deny others retained by the people—& the powers not delegated by this Constn. nor prohibited by it to the States, are reserved to the States respectively; if these amendts. are adopted, they will go a great way in preventing Congress from interfering with our negroes after 20 years or prohibiting the importation of them. Otherwise, they may even within the 20 years by a strained construction of some power embarass us very much. I had this in contemplation not a little, in my opposition to the Legislature's giving judicial constructions on the Constitutn.

William Loughton Smith Papers, ScHi.

Pierce Butler to James Iredell
11 August 1789

If you wait for substantial amendments, you will wait longer than I wish you to do, speaking *interestedly*. A few *milk-and-water* amendments have been proposed by Mr. M[*adison*]., such as liberty of conscience, a free press, and one or two general things already well secured. I suppose it was done to keep his promise with his constituents, to move for alterations; but, if I am not greatly mistaken, he is not hearty in the cause of amendments.

Griffith J. McRee, *Life and Correspondence of James Iredell*, 2 vols. (New York, 1857), 2:263–65.

Benjamin Goodhue to Samuel Phillips
11 August 1789

The subject of amendments will come under consideration tomorrow, and the principal part of those reported will probably be accepted, but I confess I feel but a small encouragement to endeavour to reconsile the people to the Government by proposing amendments if the revenues of the public are to be squandered in enabling hungry mendicants to riot in luxury and profusion.

Phillips Family Papers, MHi.

Fisher Ames to George R. Minot
12 August 1789

We are beginning the amendments in a committee of the whole. We have voted to take up the subject, in preference to the Judiciary, to incorporate them into the Constitution, and not to require, in committee, two thirds to a vote. This cost us the day. To-morrow we shall proceed. Some General, before engaging, said to his soldiers, "Think of your ancestors, and think of your posterity." [1] We shall make a dozen or two of rights and privileges for our posterity. If I am to be guided by your advice, to marry

[1] Perhaps Shakespeare's Henry V at Agincourt.

and live in Boston, it behooves me to interest myself in the affair. It will consume a good deal of time, and renew the party struggles of the States. It will set Deacon Smead and many others to constitution-making, a trade which requires little stock, and often thrives without much custom. The workman is often satisfied to be the sole consumer. Our State is remarkable for it. We made several frames of government, which did not pass. The timber was so green, the vessels rotted on the stocks. However, I am persuaded it is proper to propose amendments, without delay, and if the *antis* affect to say that they are of no consequence, they may be reproached with their opposition to the government, because they protested that the principles were important.

Seth Ames, ed., *The Works of Fisher Ames*, 2 vols. (Boston, 1854), 1:66–68.

"Pacificus" [*Noah Webster*] to James Madison 14 August 1789

IN a debate upon the Impost Bill, you declared yourself an enemy to local attachments, and said you considered yourself not merely the representative of *Virginia*, but of the *United States*. This declaration was liberal, and the sentiment just. But Sir, does this accord with the interest you take in amending the constitution? You now hold out in justification of the part you take in forwarding amendments, that you have pledged yourself in some measure to your *constituents*. But, Sir, who are your *constituents?* Are they the electors of a small district in Virginia? These indeed gave you a place in the federal legislature; but the moment you were declared to be elected, you became the representative of three millions of people, and you are bound, by the principles of representation and by your own declaration, to promote the general good of the United States. You had no right to declare that you would act upon the sentiments and wishes of your immediate constituents, unless you should be convinced that the measures you advocate coincide with the wishes and interest of the whole Union. If I have any just ideas of legislation, this doctrine is incontrovertible; and if I know your opinions, you believe it to be so.

Permit me then, with great respect to ask, Sir, how you can justify yourself, in the eyes of the world, for espousing the cause of amendments with so much earnestness? Do you, Sir, believe, that the people you represent generally wish for amendments? If you do Sir, you are more egregiously mistaken than you ever were before. I know from the unanimous declaration of men in several states, through which I have lately travelled, that amendments are not generally wished for; on the other hand, amendments are not mentioned but with the most pointed disapprobation.

The people, Sir, admit what the advocates of amendments in Congress, generally allow, that the alterations proposed can do very little good or hurt, as to the merits of the constitution; but for this very reason they reprobate any attempt to introduce them. They say, and with great justice, that, at the moment when an excellent government is going into operation; when the hopes of millions are revived, and their minds disposed to acquiesce peaceably in the federal laws; when the demagogues of faction have ceased to clamor, and their adherents are reconciled to the constitution—Congress are taking a step which will revive the spirit of party, spread the causes of contention through all the states, call up jealousies which have no real foundation, and weaken the operations of government, when the people themselves are wishing to give it energy. We see, in the debates, it is frequently asserted, that some amendments will satisfy the opposition and give stability to the government.

The people, Sir, in the northern and middle states do not believe a word of this—they do not see any opposition—they find information and experience every where operating to remove objections, and they believe that these causes will, though slowly, produce a change of conduct in North-Carolina and Rhode-Island. Is it not better to wait for this event, than risk the tumults that must grow out of another debate upon the constitution in every one of the United States.

It seems to be agreed on all hands that paper declarations of rights are trifling things and no real security to liberty. In general they are a subject of ridicule. In England, it has been necessary for parliament to ascertain and declare what rights the nation possesses, in order to limit the powers and claims of the crown; but for a sovereign free people, whose power is always equal, to declare, with the solemnity of a constitutional act, *We are all born free, and have a few particular rights which are dear to us, and of which we will not deprive ourselves, altho' we leave ourselves at full liberty to abridge any of our other rights*, is a farce in government as novel as it is ludicrous.

I am not disposed to treat you, Sir, with disrespect; many years acquaintance has taught me to esteem your virtues and respect your abilities. No man stands higher in my opinion, and people are every where willing to place you among the most able, active and useful representatives of the United States. But they regret that Congress should spend their time in throwing out an empty tub to catch people, either factious or uninformed, who might be taken more honorably by reason and equitable laws. They regret particularly that Mr. Madison's talents should be employed to bring forward amendments, which, at best can have little effect upon the merits of the constitution, and may sow the seeds of discord from New-Hampshire to Georgia.

NYDA, 17 August 1789. For identification of Webster as "Pacificus," see Kenneth R. Bowling, "Tub to the Whale," *Journal of the Early Republic* 8:225n.

Rev. James Madison to James Madison 15 August 1789

That the Business of Amendments has been entered upon in so dispassionate a Manner must afford real Satisfaction to every Friend to the Union. Some of those proposed appear to be important, at least in removing the Objections of many of the Opponents to the Constitution; tho' I do not observe that the Comm[*itt*]ee. has proposed such as appear of the first Magnitude. Would it not be adviseable to seize the present Moment to render the Constitution more perfect in the most essential Parts; or to do away those Defects, wh. it's warmest Friends admit, must eventually if continued, render the Govt. less prosperous. Suppose, for Instance, that the Union of the Legislative & Executive Powers was entirely done away—& that the Executive, or cheif Magistrate, had his Council with whom he shd. always consult & not with a Branch of the Legislature. Let the Senate be entirely confined to the Object of Legislation, let not one of it's Members be styled Vice-Presidt. But let the Senior Councillor transact the necessary Business in Case of Inability—or Absence of a President. I wd. not wish to weaken the Hands of the Executive, or diminish aught of the Powers assigned by the Constitution, but I think they might be modelled anew in a Manner, wh. wd. promise more Stability & Prosperity to the Genl. Govt. Other Improvements of perhaps a more important Nature may have occurred to you, who have so long & so deeply reflected upon the Subject; and if it were not presumptuous to advise one who will always be directed by the most enlightened & patriotic Views, I wd. recommend the present Moment as the most proper to attempt the Introduction of them.

Defects themselves gain Strength & Respect by Time. Wd. it not then be better to expose fully, & in the Manner of wh. you are so capable, those Alterations wh. are necessary, or wch. wd. in Theory render the Govt. more perfect. The first Object shd. be to render the Theory as perfect as possible: if the Theory be such, the Practice will be correspondent. Principles wh. are true in Theory, cannot fail in the Execution of them. Besides such an Exposition of those Alterations wh. wd. *really render* the Govt. more perfect, if they were not adopted at present, wd. at least have this important Effect: it wd. fix the public Mind upon those great &

necessary Improv[*em*]ents; it wd. thus be gradually prepared for them, & Time might bring about, what the Spirit of Faction may now prevent. I hope then, as you have begun, you will compleat, or attempt to compleat the arduous Task.

James Madison Papers, DLC.

Robert Morris to Francis Hopkinson
15 August 1789

The House of Representatives . . . are now playing with *Amendments*, but if they make *one* truely *so* I'll hang. poor Madison got so Cursedly frightened in Virginia, that I believe he has dreamed of amendments ever since. This however is, ad Captandum.[1]

Francis Hopkinson Papers, PHi.

[1]To play the crowd.

William L. Smith to Edward Rutledge
15 August 1789

We have been these three days on amendmts.—a motion of Tucker's this morning respecting the right of the people to [*illegible*] *instruct* their represents. occasioned some warmth [*page torn*] rudeness of Mr. Gerry, & some reflexions of Burke's [*on the*] Committee who brought in the Amendmts. & particularly on Madison: he said these Amendmts. were a mere *tub to the whale* & similar observations which were taken up warmly by Madison & others: Tucker's motion was voted for by 8 or 9 antifedls.—It is worthy of observation that the antifederals in our House have thrown difficulties in the way of these Amendmts. merely because they can't carry alterations which wd. overturn the Governmt.—there has been more ill-humour & rudeness displayed today than has existed since the meeting of Congress—allowing to Gerry & one or two more—& to make it worse, the weather is intensely hot.[1]

William Loughton Smith Papers, ScHi.

[1]Elbridge Gerry may have been referring to this debate when he wrote his brother Samuel on 30 June 1790:

> The report respecting a duel is misrepresented in part: last session debates ran very high in the House & a Gentleman from the southward who was a friend

of mine & in the same side as myself of a question respecting the amendments proposed by the States to the Constitution, took affront at Mr. Ames who was in the other side of the question & hinted an intention to call him out: but Mr. Ames made an apology in the House & finished the dispute; immediately on this another gentlemen who was also on Mr. Ames's side of the question, said if Gentlemen talked of calling out, he had reason to be offended at something I had said & should use the same freedom with me. I instantly informed him, I had not the least objection & should meet any proposition which he might think proper to make out of the House: but he never tho't it advisable to make any & so the matter ended—This part of the letter you will consider as confidential. (Samuel R. Gerry Papers, MHi)

Thomas Hartley to Jasper Yeates
16 August 1789

We had Yesterday warm debates about amendments—and what is very curious the Antis do not want any at this Time—we are obliged in Fact to force them upon them. I am sorry that Business was brought forward this session—but we must pay attention to it for a Day or two more.

Yeates Papers, PHi.

George Leonard to Sylvanus Bourne
16 August 1789

For three days past the proposed amendments have been under Consideration, the Political Thermometer high Each day.

Bourne Papers, MH.

John Brown to William Irvine
17 August 1789

The three days last past have been spent in considering the Amendments reported by the Committee as yet we have made very little progress. The Antis viz. Gerry Tucker &c. appear determined to obstruct & embarrass the Business as much as possible. Is it not surprising that the opposition should come from that quarter.

Caryl Roberts Autograph Collection, PHi.

William Smith to Otho H. Williams
17 August 1789

The hot weather & the Subject of amendments which was discussed the last week Kept the house in bad temper, The Antis have opposed their being brot. forward in every Stage & I am inclined to believe the proposed amendments will fail, for although they are approved by the federalists & a majority will no dou[*b*]t vote for the whole of them, I woud. question if two thirds will concur. A small party are opposed to all amendments, And others who do not think they go far enough, are making every exertion to put off the consideration of that business untill the Next Session—this day will I expect determine the issue of that question.

Otho Holland Williams Papers, MdHi.

Frederick A. Muhlenberg to Benjamin Rush
18 August 1789

But this Day has at length terminated the Subject of Amendments in the Comittee of the whole House, & tomorow we shall take up the Report & probably agree to the Amendments proposed, & which are nearly the same as the special Comittee of eleven had reported them. I have no Doubt but there will be two thirds as required by the Constitution in our House, but cannot say what Reception they will meet with in the Senate. Mr. Gerry & Mr. Tucker had each of them a long string of Amendts. which were not comprised in the Report of the special Comittee, & which they stiled Amendments proposed by the several States. There was a curious medley of them, and such as even our Minority in Pennsylvania would rather have pronounced dangerous Alterations than Amendments—these they offered in separate Resolutions to the House in Order to get them referred to a Comittee of the whole, but both Attempts faild—the previous question having been ruled against Gerrys Motion, & carried, and Mr. Tuckers was negatived by a very large Majority. Thus far I hope this disagreeable Business is finished, & no other Amendments will I think take place for the present. Altho' I am sorry that so much Time has been spent in this Business, and would much rather have had it postponed to the next Session, yet as it now is done I hope it will be satisfactory to our State, and as it takes in the principal Amendments which our Minority had so much at Heart, I hope it may restore Harmony & unanimity amongst our fellow Citizens & perhaps be the Means of producing the much wished for Alterations & Amendments in our State

Constitution. It is a strange yet certain Fact, that those who have heretofore been & still profess to be the greatest Sticklers for Amendments to the Constitution of the U.S. have hitherto thrown every Obstacle they could in their way & by lengthy Debates & numberless Amendts. which they know full well neither ⅔ds of Congress nor 3 fourth of the different Legislatures would ever adopt, have endeavoured to mar their progress, but it is obvious their Design was to favour their darling Question for calling a Convention—which however I think is also determined for some Time to come. The Debates in our House have hitherto gone on with much Candor firmness and good Humor, but this Day some Gentlemen got into great warmth—more so indeed than ever since our first meeting, so that a frequent call to Order became absolutely necessary—& from this Day forward I expect, especially as we have sat so long and are about to close the session—that the Debates will be high. Such I think is the present Temper of the House, that I think the sooner we close the Session the better. I am happy however to find that our Delegation have kept cool and moderate & unanimous.

Society Autograph Collection, PHi.

Edmund Randolph to James Madison
18 August 1789

Mr. H[*enry*]., (As Colo. Leven Powell tells me) is pleased with some of the proposed amendments; but still asks for the great desideratum, the destruction of direct taxation.

James Madison Papers, DLC.

James Madison to Richard Peters
19 August 1789

The papers inclosed will shew that the nauseous project[1] of amendments has not yet been either dismissed or despatched. We are so deep in them now, that right or wrong some thing must be done. I say this not by way of apology, for to be sincere I think no apology requisite. 1. because a constitutional provision in favr. of essential rights is a thing not

[1]Madison is referring to Peters' poem of 20 July, which compared the process of amending the Constitution to cooks spoiling a fine soup.

improper in itself and was always viewed in that light by myself. It may be less necessary in a republic, than a Monarchy, & in a fedl. Govt. than the former, but it is in some degree rational in every Govt., since in every Govt. power may oppress, and declarations on paper, tho' not an effectual restraint, are not without some influence. 2. In many States the Constn. was adopted under a tacit compact in favr. of some subsequent provisions on this head. In Virg[*ini*]a. It would have been *certainly* rejected, had no assurances been given by its advocates that such provisions would be pursued. As an honest man *I feel* my self bound by this consideration. 3. If the Candidates in Virga. for the House of Reps. had not taken this conciliary ground at the election, that State would have [*been*] represented almost wholly by disaffected characters, instead of the *federal* reps. now in Congs. 4. If amendts. had not been proposed from the federal side of the House, the proposition would have come *within three days*, from the adverse side. It is certainly best that they should appear to be the free gift of the friends of the Constitution rather than to be extorted by the address & weight of its enemies. 5. It will kill the opposition every where, and by putting an end to the disaffection to the Govt. itself, enable the administration to venture on measures not otherwise safe. Those who hate the Govt. will always join the party disaffected to measures of the administration, and such a party will be created by every important measure. 6. If no amendts. be proposed the language of antifedl. leaders to the people will be, we advised you not to adopt the Constn. witht. previous amendts. you listened to those who told you that subsequent securities for your rights would be most easily obtained—we urged you to insist on a Convention as the only effectual mode of obtaing. these—You yielded to the assurances of those who told you that a Convention was unnecessary, that Congs. wd. be the proper channel for getting what was wanted, &c. &c. Here are fine texts for popular declaimers who wish to revive the antifedl. cause, and at the fall session of the Legisla[*tu*]res. to blow the Trumpet for a second Convention. In Virga. a majority of the Legislature last elected, is bitterly opposed to the govt. and will be joined, if no amendts. be proposed, by great nos. of the other side who will complain of being deceived. 7. Some amendts. are necssy. for N. Carol[*in*]a. I am so informed by the best authorities in that State.

James Madison Papers, DLC.

Benjamin Goodhue to Michael Hodge
20 August 1789

We have been for some time past and still are upon the boundless field of amendments, and whether we shall bring any thing to issue or not is uncertain, for the opinions are almost as various as there are members, a few antis are perplexing the House and taking up their precious moments in propositions which are of such an inadmissable a nature as invariably to meet a rejection which they so justly merit, they say the propositions reported by the committee of eleven are only calculated to amuse without materialy affecting those parts of the Constitution which were particularly objectionable and therefore unavailing—its true they do not answer their unwarrantable purposes of weakening the constitution which they are aiming at, but I presume they go as far towards quieting the honest part of the dissatisfied, as any friend of an energetic national government can go. I am sorry the subject has been taken up at this time since its likely to be of so long a continuance. the reasons urged for it were that a few simple amendments would probably give general satisfaction and accelerate the adoption of the Constitution by the States of N. Carolina and R. Island. The fact is it has always lain on my mind, and what I sincerely believe is founded in truth is, that so far from the State Governments being in hazzard from the National Government, the danger is wholy on the other side, and the latter wants an acquisition of strength rather than a diminution.

Eben F. Stone Papers, MSaE.

Theodore Sedgwick to Pamela Sedgwick
20 August 1789

We are still engaged about the unpromising subject of amendments. The introduction of it at this period, of the existence of our government was in my opinion unwise and will not produce those beneficial effects which its advocates predicted. Before we could be said to have a government to attempt to amend the constitution argues a frivolity of character very inconsistant with national dignity.

Sedgwick Papers, MHi.

James Madison to Edmund Pendleton
21 August 1789

The last 8 or 10 days have been spent on the subject of amendts. The work has been extremely difficult and fatiguing, as well on account of the dilatory artifices of which some of the antifederal members are suspected, as of the diversity of opinions & fancies inseparable from such an Assembly as Congress. At present there is a prospect of finishing to day, the plan so far as it lies with the H. of Reps. It does not differ much from the original propositions offered on that subject.

The Judiciary bill was postponed to consider the preceding subject.

James Madison Papers, DLC.

James Madison to Edmund Randolph
21 August 1789

For a week past the subject of Amendts. has exclusively occupied the H. of Reps. Its progress has been exceedingly wearisome not only on account of the diversity of opinions that was to be apprehended, but of the apparent views of some to defeat by delaying a plan short of their wishes, but likely to satisfy a great part of their companions in opposition throughout the Union. It has been absolutely necessary in order to effect any thing to abbreviate debate, and exclude every proposition of a doubtful & unimportant nature. Had it been my wish to have comprehended every amendt. recommended by Virg[*ini*]a. I should have acted from prudence the very part to which I have been led by choice. Two or three contentious additions would even now frustrate the whole project.

James Madison Papers, DLC.

Samuel Adams to Elbridge Gerry
22 August 1789

I hope Congress, before they adjourn, will take into very serious Consideration the necessary Amendments of the Constitution. Those whom I call the best—the most judicious & disinterested Federalists, who wish for the perpetual Union, Liberty & Happiness of the States and their respective Citizens many of them, if not all are anxiously expecting them—They wish to see a Line drawn as clearly as may be, between the federal Powers vested in Congress and the distinct Sovereignty of the several States upon which the private and personal Rights of the Citizens depend. Without such Distinction there will be Danger of the Constitution issuing imperceptibly, and gradually into a Consolidated Government over all the States, which, altho it may be wished for by some, was reprobated in the Idea by the highest Advocates for the Constitution as it stood without amendmts. I am fully persuaded that the People of the United States being in different Climates—of different Education and Manners, and possest of different Habits & Feelings under one consolidated Governmt. can not long remain free, or indeed under any Kind of Governmt. but Despotism.

Beinecke Library, CtY.

William Smith to Otho H. Williams
22 August 1789

Our house will I expect this day finish the Amendments, so far as in their power, *after considerable debate & altercation*, the greatest objections arose from those opposed to the constitution, very high words passed in the house on this occasion, & what nearly amounted to direct chalenges, the weather was excessive hot, & the blood warm. on the change in the Air the heat of Debate Subsided, & all are now in good humour.

Otho H. Williams, MdHi.

Benjamin Goodhue to the Salem Insurance Offices
23 August 1789

We have at last so far got through the wearisome business of amendments to the great joy of I believe every member of the House that nothing is left but for a committee so to put the amendments in order that they may stand properly arranged, they are materialy the same which you have seen publishd in the papers as reported by the Committee of 11 with this difference that instead of their being incorporated into the Constitution as was proposed they are to go forth as seperate propositions by the way of supplement to be laid before the several legislatures for their adoption either in whole or in part as to them may seem proper—what the Senate will do with them is uncertain but I rather think they will refer them to the next session—Those who were not friendly to the Constitution made every effort with their most persevering diligence to introduce a variety of propositions which a large majority of the House deemed totally inadmissable at length after exhausting themselves as well as the patience of their brethren they appear tolerably satisfied with the issue of the business, God grant it may have the effects which are desired and that We may never hear any more of it.

Benjamin Goodhue Papers, New York Society Library.

Thomas Hartley to Tench Coxe
23 August 1789

We have nearly done with the Business of Amendments—I imagine those we shall offer will give you and our Friends satisfaction—the great Principles of the Constitution are preserved and the Declarations and Explanations will be acceptable to the People.

Coxe Papers, PHi.

Samuel Adams to Richard Henry Lee
24 August 1789

I mean, my friend, to let you know how deeply I am impressed with a sense of the Importance of Amendments; that the good People may clearly see the distinction, for there is a distinction, between the *federal* Powers vested in Congress, and the *sovereign* Authority belonging to the several States, which is the Palladium of the private, and personal rights of the Citizens. I freely protest to you that I earnestly wish some Amendments may be judiciously, and deliberately made without partial or local considerations—that there may be no uncomfortable Jarrings among the several Powers; that the whole People may in every State contemplate their own safety on solid grounds, and the Union of the States be perpetual. . . . Your Letter requires a further Consideration—I will at present only express my astonishment at the strange, and absurd opinion of our former *republican Connecticut* friend—Tempora mutantur, et hic mutatur in illis.[1]

Richard Henry Lee Correspondence, PPAmP.

---

[1]The times are changed, and we are changed with them.

William Ellery to Benjamin Huntington
24 August 1789

Pacificus has [*animadverted*] pretty severely on Mr. Maddison. What the real sentiments of the latter are with respect to amendments I don't know; but he is certainly very sensible; a good federalist, and I don't doubt an honest man. I remember to have seen a printed letter, written by him, in which it was suggested that some amendments or explanations might be necessary.[1] This, his instructions, and a paragraph in the President's speech might perhaps justify his bringing forward and supporting those which have been published. Whether amendments should be interwoven with the Constitution, or stand by themselves is I believe not a question of magnitude. Those proposed are indeed very innocent, and the admission of them might gratify the pride of some opposers of the New Government, and facilitate their embracing it. But the allowance of them might induce States to propose others, and the expectations of further amendments might unsettle the minds of the people, and invalidate the force of the present government. It has always been my opinion that it would be best to try on the Constitution first, and see how it would fit, before any amendments should be made. Try all things and *hold fast* that which is *good* says an authority with which you are well acquainted.[2]

Huntington Autograph Letterbook, Jervis Public Library, Rome, N.Y.

---

[1]See the Introduction, n. 5.
[2]I Thessalonians 5:21.

James Madison to Alexander White
24 August 1789

The week past has been devoted to the subject of amendments, all that remains is a formal vote on a fair transcript which will be taken this morning; and without debate I hope as each of the propositions has been agreed to by two thirds of the House. The substance of the report of the Committee of eleven has not been much varied. It became an unavoidable sacrifice to *a few* who knew their concurrence to be necessary, to the despatch if not the success of the business, to give up the form by which the amendts. when ratified would have fallen into the body of the Constitution, in favor of the project of adding them by way of appendix to it. it is already apparent I think that some ambiguities will be produced by this change, as the question will often arise and sometimes be not easily solved, how far the original text is or is not necessarily superceded, by the supplemental act. A middle way will be taken between the two modes, of proposing all the amendts. as a single act to be adopted or rejected in the gross, and of proposing them as independent amendts. each of which shall take place or not, as it may be individually decided on. The several propositions will be *classed* according to their affinity to each other, which will reduce them to the number of 5 or 6 in the whole, to go forth as so many amendts. unconnected with one another.

James Madison Papers, DLC.

Robert Morris to Richard Peters
24 August 1789

Poor Madison took one wrong step in Virginia by publishing a letter, respecting *Amendments* and you, who know every thing, must know What a Cursed Thing it is to write *a Book*.[1] He in consequence has been obliged to bring on the proposition for making Amendments; The Waste of precious time is what has vexed me the most, for as to the Nonesense they call Amendments I never expect that any part of it will go through the various Trials which it must pass before it can become a part of the Constitution, By calling the whole Nonesense I may expose myself to a charge of wanting Sense especially as I candidly own that I have not considered any of the propositions made, but Condemn the attempt by the Lump, I am however strengthened in pronouncing this Sentence, by the opinions of our Friends Clymer & Fitzsimmons who said Yesterday that the business of Amendments was now done with in their House & advised that the Senate should adopt the whole of them by the Lump as containing neither good or Harm being perfectly innocent. I expect they will lie on our Table for some time, but I may be mistaken having had but little conversation with any of the Senators on this Subject.

Richard Peters Papers, PHi.

[1]See the Introduction, n. 5.

Richard Peters to James Madison
24 August 1789

I am obliged by your Information & acknowledge that some of your Reasons are the best that can be given. They are such therefore as I knew you could give. But many of them are founded on Apprehensions which forgive me for saying I think too highly wrought. I believe that a Firmness in adhering to our Constitution 'till at least it had a longer Trial would have silenced Antifederalists sooner than magnifying their Importance by Acknowledgments on our Part & of ourselves holding up a Banner for them to rally to. All you offer comes not up to their Desires & as long as they have one unreasonable Wish ungratified the Clamour will be the same. I know there are among them good Characters, but many of those who lead do it not from other Motives than to make or keep themselves Heads of a Party. Our Character abroad will never acquire Consistency while Foreigners see us wavering even in our Government about the very Instrument under which that Government acts. In short I fear worse Consequences from the good Disposition of the Conciliators (especially now when some Things done by Congress have startled even many Federalists) than I apprehend from an Adherence to the System. But I have agreed with myself not to enter far into a Subject which you have so long considered.

James Madison Papers, DLC.

The Diary of William Maclay
25 August 1789

after this the Amendments. they were treated contemptuously by Z [*Izard*], Langdon and Mr. Morris. Z moved they should be postponed to next Session Langdon seconded & Mr. Morris got up and spoke angrily but not well. they however lost their Motion and Monday was assigned. for the taking them up. I could not help observing the Six Year Class hung together on this business or the most of them.

DHFFC 9:133.

Patrick Henry to Richard Henry Lee
28 August 1789

As to my opinion of the Amendments, I think they will tend to injure rather than to serve the Cause of Liberty—provided they go no further than is proposed as Ideas—For what good End can be answered by [*page torn*] Rights, the Tenure of which must be during Pleasure—For Right without her Power & Might is but a Shadow—Now it seems that it is not proposed to add this Force to the Right by any Amendment—It can therefore answer no purpose but to lull Suspicion totally on the Subject—While Impediments are cast in the Way of those who wish to retrench the exorbitancy of Power granted away by the Constitution from the People, a fresh grant from them is made in the first Moment of Opportunity, & of a Nature & extent too which full Success in the Business of Amendments would scarcely compensate—I mean the uncontrouled Power of the President over the Officers.

Patrick Henry Papers, DLC.

Richard Henry Lee to Charles Lee
28 August 1789

The enclosed paper will shew you the amendments passed the H. of R. to the Constitution—They are short of some essentials, as Election interference & Standing Army &c. I was surprised to find in the Senate that it was proposed we should postpone the consideration of Amendments until Experience had shewn the necessity of any—As if experience was more necessary to prove the propriety of those great principles of Civil liberty which the wisdom of Ages has found to be necessary barriers against the encroachments of power in the hands of frail Men! My Colleague was sick & absent. The laboring oar was with me. A Majority of 2 thirds however agreed to take the Amendments under consideration next Monday—I hope that if we cannot gain the whole loaf, we shall at least have some bread.

Washburn Papers, MHi.

September–October 1789

Edmund Pendleton to James Madison
2 September 1789

I congratulate you upon having got through the Amendments to the Constitution, as I was very anxious that it should be done before y'r adjournment, since it will have a good effect in quieting the minds of many well meaning Citizens, tho' I am of opinion that nothing was further from the wish of some, who covered their Opposition to the Government under the masque of uncommon zeal for amendments, & to whom a rejection or a delay as a new ground of clamour, would have been more agreeable. I own also that I feel some degree of pleasure, in discovering obviously from the whole progress, that the public are indebted for the measure to the friends of Government, whose Elections were opposed under pretense of their being averse to amendments. . . .

PJM 12:368–69.

William Ellery to Benjamin Huntington
8 September 1789

I don't think the amendments will do any hurt, and they may do some good, and therefore I don't consider them as of much importance. I am glad that the gentleman who talks so much from his stick,[1] was disappointed in all his efforts to procure amendments. He is a restless creature, and if he don't take care, he will injure weaken the reputation for honesty to which I used to think he was justly entitled.

Benjamin Huntington Papers, R-Ar.

---

[1] Probably Gerry.

George Mason to Samuel Griffin
8 September 1789

I have received much Satisfaction from the Amendments to the federal Constitution, which have lately passed the House of Representatives; I hope they will also pass the Senate. With two or three further Amendments such as confining the federal Judiciary to Admiralty & Maritime Jurisdiction, and to Subjects merely federal—fixing the Mode of Elections either in the Constitution itself (which I think would be preferable) or securing the Regulation of them to the respective States—Requiring more than a bare Majority to make Navigation & Commercial Laws, and appointing a constitutional amenable Council to the President, & lodging with them most of the Executive Powers now rested in the Senate—I cou'd chearfully put my Hand & Heart to the new Government.

Mason Papers, DLC.

Edward Carrington to James Madison
9 September 1789

The people enquire with composure what Congress is doing and discover no apparent apprehension for the fate of the proposed amendments—I mention these things to you, because reports may reach you of a different nature. Stories have been brought to this City by a few weak, as well as wicked, men that the magistrates in the southern Counties would generally refuse the oath. A very considerable change has taken place amongst the Antis as to yourself, they consider you as the patron of amendments, and it is no uncommon thing to hear confessions that they had been formerly imposed on, by representations that you were fixed against any alteration whatever. the subject of direct taxation is viewed in its proper light by many who were clamorous against it sometime ago, but the generality of the people seldom appear to think of it at all. indeed I see no appearance of any thing but acquiescence in whatever may be agreed on by those whom they have deputed to take care of their affairs.

I have observed with some little attention the amendments which have been agreed on in the Hs. of Rs. One of them which seems at present to be much approved of & was indeed made a considerable object of by all the States, will not I apprehend, be found good in practice—I mean the excessive enlargement of the representation; and what is still worse it will produce its inconveniences very unequally by their falling principally on the distant States: the greater the representation, the more difficult will it be to find proper characters whose convenience will admit of punctual attendance and this difficulty will be encreased in proportion to the distance from the Seat of Government—small as the Representation now is, compared with what is proposed, disadvantages of this kind would be felt by the distant States as soon as the novelty of the service might have in some degree worn off. But independently of these considerations, I would prefer a small representation. Numerous Assemblies deliberate but badly even when composed, and it is almost impossible to keep them so.

James Madison Papers, DLC.

Theodorick Bland Randolph to St. George Tucker 9 September 1789

The house of Representatives have been for some time past engaged on the subject of amendments to the constitution, though in my opinion they have not made one single material one. The senate are at present engaged on that subject; Mr. Richd. H. Lee told me that he proposed to strike out the standing army in time of peace but could not carry it. He also sais that it has been proposed, and warmly favoured that, liberty of Speach and of the press may be stricken out, as they only tend to promote licenciousness. If this takes place god knows what will follow.

Brock Collection, Henry E. Huntington Library, San Marino, Calif.

John Randolph to St. George Tucker 11 September 1789

A majority of the Senate were for not allowing the militia arms & if two thirds had agreed it would have been an amendment to the Constitution. They are afraid that the Citizens will stop their full Career to Tyranny & Oppression.

St. George Tucker Papers, DLC.

James Sullivan to John Langdon 12 September 1789

The two houses have proposed more amendments than I wished to see because some of them I think are rather alterations than amendments.

Langdon-Elwyn Family Papers, New Hampshire Historical Society.

Benjamin Goodhue to Samuel Phillips
13 September 1789

The Amendments have come from the Senate with amendments, such as striking out the word *vicinage* as applied to Jurors, and have struck out the limitation of sums for an appeal to the federal Court &c. Those two have been the darling objects with the Virginians who have been the great movers in amendments, and I am suspicious, it may mar the whole business, at least so far as to refer it to the next session.

Phillips Family Papers, MHi.

Richard Henry Lee to Francis Lightfoot Lee
13 September 1789

Your letter of the 8th Ulto. has lain long unanswered because I have been absorbed about the Amendments to the Constitution. They have at length passed the Senate, with difficulty, after being much mutilated and enfeebled—It is too much the fashion now to look at the rights of the People, as a Miser inspects a Security, to find out a flaw—What with design in some, and fear of Anarchy in others, it is very clear, I think, that a government very different from a free one will take place eer many years are passed.

Morristown National Historical Park, New Jersey.

Elbridge Gerry to John Wendell
14 September 1789

Whether the present constitution will preserve its theoretical ballance, for I consider it altogether as a political experiment, if it should, what will be the effect, or if it should not, to what system it will verge, are secrets that can only be unfolded by time: as to the amendments proposed by Congress, they will not affect those questions or serve any other purposes than to reconcile those who had no adequate idea of the essential defects of the Constitution. I shall however console myself with the reflection, that should the consequences be injurious or ruinous, nothing has been wanting on my part in Convention or Congress to prevent them.

Fogg Autograph Collection, Maine Historical Society.

Richard Henry Lee to Patrick Henry
14 September 1789

[*I have*] since waited to see the issue of the proposed amendts. to the Constitution, that I might give you the most [*exact*] account of that business. As they came from the H. of R. they were very far short of the wishes of our Convention, but as they are returned by the Senate they are certainly much weakened. You may be assured that nothing on my part was left undone to prevent this, and every possible effort was used to give success to all the Amendments proposed by our Country—We might as well have attempted to move Mount Atlas upon our shoulders—In fact, the idea of subsequent Amendments was delusion altogether, and so intended by the greater part of those who arrogated to themselves the name of Federalists. I am grieved to see that too many look at the Rights of the people as a Miser examines a Security to find a flaw in it! The great points of free election, Jury trial in criminal cases much loosened, the unlimited right of Taxation, and Standing Armies in peace, remain as they were. Some valuable Rights are indeed *declared*, but the powers that remain are very sufficient to render them nugatory at pleasure.

The most essential danger from the present System arises, [*in my*] opinion, from its tendency to a Consolidated government, instead of a Union of Confederated States—The history of the world and reason concurs in proving that so extensive a Territory [*as the*] U. States comprehend never was, or can be governed in freed[*om*] under the former idea—Under the latter it is abundantly m[*ore*] practicable, because extended representation, know[*ledge of*] character, and confidence in consequence, [*are wanting to sway the*] opinion of Rulers, without which, *fear* the offspri[*ng of Tyranny*] can alone answer. Hence Standing Armies, and des[*potism*] follows. I take this reasoning to be unrefutable, a[*nd*] therefore it becomes the friends of liberty to guard [*with*] perfect vigilance every right that belongs to the Sta[*tes*] and to protest against every invasion of them—taking care always to procure as many protesting States as possible—This kind of vigilance will create caution and probably establish such a mode of conduct as will create a system of precedent that will prevent a Consolidating effect from taking place by slow, but sure degrees. And also not to cease in renewing their efforts for so amending the federal Constitution as to prevent a Consolidation by securing the due Authority of the States. At present perhaps a sufficient number of Legislatures cannot be got to agree in demanding a Convention—But I shall be much mistaken if a great sufficiency will not e'er long concur in this measure. The preamble to the Amendments is realy curious—A careless reader would be apt to suppose that the amendments desired by the States had been graciously granted. But when the thing done is compared with that desired, nothing can be more unlike. . . .

By comparing the Senate amendments with [*those*] from below by carefully attending to the m[*atter*] the former will appear well calculated to enfeeble [*and*] produce ambiguity—for instance—Rights res[*erved*] to the States or the *People*—The people here is evidently designed fo[*r the*] People of the *United States*, not of the Individual States [*page torn*] the former is the Constitutional idea of the people—We *the People* &c. It was affirmed the Rights reserved by the States bills of rights did not belong to the States—I observed that then they belonged to the people of the States, but that this mode of expressing was evidently *calculated* to give the Residuum to the people of the U. States, which was the Constitutional language, and to deny it to the people of the Indiv. State—At least that it left room for cavil & false construction—They would not insert after people thereof—altho it was moved.

Patrick Henry Papers, DLC. Words in brackets are taken from historian Charles Campbell's pre-Civil War transcript in the Hugh Blair Grigsby Papers, Virginia Historical Society.

James Madison to Edmund Pendleton
14 September 1789

The Senate have sent back the plan of amendments with some alterations which strike in my opinion at the most salutary articles. in many of the States juries even in criminal cases are taken from the State at large—in others from districts of consider[*able*] extent—in very few from the County alone—Hence a [*dis*]like to the restraint with respect to *vicinage*, which has produced a negative on that clause. A fear of inconvenience from a constitutional bar to appeals below a certain value, and a confidence that such a limitation is not *necessary*, have had the same effect on another article. Several others have had a similar fate. The difficulty of uniting the minds of men accustomed to think and act differently can only be conceived by those who have witnessed it.

James Madison Papers, DLC.

Fisher Ames to Caleb Strong
15 September 1789

The Amendments too have been amended by the Senate, & many in our house, Mr. Madison, in particular, thinks, that they have lost much of their sedative Virtue by the alteration. A contest on this subject between the two houses would be very disagreeable.

Thompson Autograph Collection, Hartford Seminary Foundation.

Roger Sherman to Samuel Huntington
17 September 1789

Your Excellency has doubtless Seen the amendments proposed to be made to the Constitution as passed by the House of Representatives, enclosed is a copy of them as amended by the Senate, wherein they are considerably abridged & I think altered for the Better.

William Griswold Lane Memorial Collection, CtY.

Paine Wingate to John Langdon
17 September 1789

As to amendments to the Constitution Madison says he had rather have none than those agreed to by the Senate.

Dreer Collection, PHi.

James Madison to Edmund Pendleton
23 September 1789

The pressure of unfinished business has suspended the adjournment of Congs. till saturday next. Among the articles which required it was the plan of amendments, on which the two Houses so far disagreed as to require conferences. It will be impossible I find to prevail on the Senate to concur in the limitation on the *value* of appeals to the Supreme Court, which they say is unnecessary, and might be embarrassing in questions of national or constitutional importance in their principle, tho' of small pecuniary amount. They are equally inflexible in opposing a definition of the *locality* of Juries. The vicinage they contend is either too vague or too strict a term, too vague if depending on limits to be fixed by the pleasure of the law, too strict if limited to the County. It was proposed to insert after the word juries—"with the accustomed requisites"—leaving the definition to be construed according to the judgment of professional men. Even this could not be obtained. The truth is that in most of the States the practice is different and hence the irreconciliable difference of ideas on the subject. In some States jurors are drawn from the whole body of the community indiscriminately; In others from large districts comprehending a number of Counties; and in a few only from a single County. The Senate suppose also that the provision for vicinage in the Judiciary bill, will sufficiently quiet the fears which called for an amendment on this point. on a few other points in the plan the Senate refuse to join the House of Reps.

James Madison Papers, DLC.

Rhode Island Governor John Collins to the President and Congress 26 September 1789

The People of this State [*Rhode Island*] . . . have apprehended danger by way of precedent—can it be thought strange then that with these impressions they should wait to see the proposed system organised and in operation? to see what further checks and securities would be agreed to, and established by way of amendments before they could adopt it as a constitution of government for themselves and posterity?

These amendments we believe have already afforded some relief and satisfaction to the minds of the People of this State. And we earnestly look for the time when they may with clearness and safety be again united with their sister States . . . .

Record Group 59, National Archives.

Richard Henry Lee to Patrick Henry 27 September 1789

My third letter to you on the 14th. inst. will satisfy you how little is to be expected from Congress that shall be any ways satisfactory on the subject of Amendments. Your observation is perfectly just, that right without power to protect it, is of little avail. Yet small as it is, how wonderfully scrupulous have they been in stating Rights? The english language has been carefully culled to find words feeble in their Nature or doubtful in their meaning! . . .

By an Address, received two days ago from the Assembly of R. Island, copy of which I will sent you by my brother, to the federal government, it appears to me as if they intended to keep out of this Union until effectual Amendments were made—We ought in common prudence to have done the same—Does N.C. design to act in the same manner.

Miscellaneous Manuscripts, DLC.

Richard Henry Lee and William Grayson to the Speaker of the Virginia House of Delegates 28 September 1789

We have now the honor of enclosing the propositions of Amendments to the Constitution of the United States that has been finally agreed upon by Congress. We can assure you Sir that nothing on our part has been omitted to procure the success of those Radical Amendments proposed by the Convention and approved by the Legislature of our Country, which as our Constituent, we shall always deem it our duty with respect and reverence to obey. The Journal of the Senate herewith transmitted will at once shew how exact and how unfortunate we have been in this business. It is impossible for us not to see the necessary tendency to consolidate Empire in the natural operation of the Constitution if no further Amended than now proposed. And it is equally impossible for us not to be apprehensive for Civil Liberty when we know no instance in the Records of history that shew a people ruled in freedom when subject to an undivided Government and inhabiting a Territory so extensive as that of the United States, and when, as it seems to us, the nature of Man and things join to prevent it. The impracticability in such case of carrying representation sufficiently near to the people for procuring their confidence and consequent obedience compels a resort to fear resulting from great force and excessive power in Government. Confederated Republics when the federal hand is not possessed of absorbing power, may permit the existance of freedom, whilst it preserves Union, strength, and safety. Such amendments therefore as may secure against the annihilation of the State Government we devoutly wish to see adopted.

If a persevering application to Congress from the States that have desired such Amendments should fail of its object we are disposed to think, reasoning from Causes to effects, that unless a dangerous apathy should invade the public mind, it will not be many years before a constitutional number of Legislatures will be found to demand a Convention for the purpose.[1]

Peter Force Collection, DLC.

[1]On this same day, Virginia's two senators sent a similar but shorter notification of the proposed amendments to Virginia's Governor, attesting to their vain efforts to promote Virginia's proposed amendments and their "grief that we now send forward propositions inadequate to the purpose of real and substantial Amendments." The critical tone of the letters conflicted with the generally favorable attitude of most Virginians, and the Virginia legislature refused officially to publish the letters. Both were eventually leaked to the *Virginia Gazette and Public Advertiser*, where they were printed on 10 December 1789, and subsequently reprinted in many newspapers throughout the country.

William Grayson to Patrick Henry
29 September 1789

With respect to amendments matters have turned out exactly as I apprehended from the extraordy. doctrine of playing the after game: the lower house sent up amendments which held out a safeguard to personal liberty in a great many instances, but this disgusted the Senate, and though we made every exertion to save them, they are so mutilated & gutted that in fact they are good for nothing, & I believe as many others do, that they will do more harm than benefit: The Virginia amendments were all brought into view, and regularly rejected Perhaps they may think differently on the subject the next session, as Rhode Island has refused for the present acceeding to the constitution. . . .

Patrick Henry Papers, DLC.

Thomas Tudor Tucker to St. George Tucker
2 October 1789

You will find our Amendments to the Constitution calculated merely to amuse, or rather to deceive.

Roberts Autograph Collection, PHC.

Biographical Gazetteer

Adams, John (1735–1826), a signer of the Declaration of Independence from Braintree, Massachusetts, was a Harvard educated lawyer who served in the Continental Congress and, later, in a number of diplomatic posts. He actively promoted the Federalist position from abroad, and, upon returning to the United States in 1788, was elected vice president, in which capacity he presided over the Senate.

Adams, Samuel (1722–1803), a signer of the Declaration of Independence, was elected lieutenant governor of Massachusetts in 1789. An Antifederalist spokesman of national importance, he voted in favor of the Constitution at the state ratification convention because of pressure from his Boston constituents and the convention's decision to propose amendments. Fisher Ames defeated him in the first congressional election.

Ames, Fisher, Rep. (1758–1808), Harvard-educated lawyer from Dedham, Massachusetts, served in the Massachusetts House of Representatives before being elected as a Federalist to the First Congress. As a member of the Massachusetts convention, he ardently supported ratification.

Avery, John, Jr. (1739–1806), a merchant and Federalist from Boston, had been Massachusetts secretary of state since 1780.

Baldwin, Abraham, Rep. (1754–1807), a New England-born and Yale educated lawyer from Augusta, Georgia, attended the Confederation Congress and the Federal Convention, where he signed the Constitution.

Barlow, Joel (1754–1812), European agent for the Scioto Land Company and brother-in-law of Abraham Baldwin, was a teacher, poet, and Federalist from Hartford, Connecticut. He was in Paris in 1789.

Beckley, John (1757–1807), a Federalist from Richmond, Virginia, was clerk in a number of state political bodies, including the Virginia ratification convention, before being selected as the first clerk of the U.S. House of Representatives.

Belknap, Jeremy (1744–98), historian and pastor of a Congregational church at Boston, corresponded widely with intellectuals and Federalist political leaders.

Benson, Egbert, Rep. (1746–1833), a Federalist from Dutchess County, New York, studied law at Kings (Columbia) College, and was a frequent representative in the state assembly and the Confederation Congress.

Bland, Theodorick, Rep. (1742–90), an Antifederalist, was a doctor from Prince George County, Virginia, who served in both the Confederation Congress and the Virginia House of Delegates. In the Virginia convention he voted against ratification of the Constitution. There and elsewhere he often opposed positions held by James Madison.

Boudinot, Elias, Rep. (1740–1821), a Federalist lawyer from Elizabethtown, New Jersey, held many offices at the state and national level, including presidency of the Confederation Congress.

Bourne, Sylvanus (1756–1817), a Federalist and merchant from Barnstable, Massachusetts, was chosen by Congress to inform John Adams of his election as vice president.

Brown, John, Rep. (1757–1837), settled in Frankfort and became a prominent lawyer active in the Kentucky statehood movement. He represented the district of Kentucky in the Virginia Senate and also served as a delegate to Congress before being elected as a Federalist.

Burke, Aedanus, Rep. (1743–1802), an Antifederalist, was born in Ireland and settled in Charleston, South Carolina, where he served as a judge of the state courts and a state representative. He voted against ratification in South Carolina's convention.

Butler, Pierce, Sen. (1744–1822), an Irish born British army officer before he settled in Prince William Parish, South Carolina, served as a state officeholder and representative to the Confederation Congress and the Constitutional Convention. He advocated ratification at the state convention.

Cadwalader, Lambert, Rep. (1743–1823), a Federalist, was a Philadelphia merchant who settled in Trenton, New Jersey, and represented that state in the Confederation Congress.

Campbell, Arthur (1743–1811), of Washington County, Virginia (Kentucky), was an Antifederalist and leader in the Kentucky statehood movement.

Carrington, Edward (1749–1810), a Federalist, represented Powhatan County in the Virginia House of Delegates, 1788–90. He had been a member of the Confederation Congress, 1786–88.

Carroll, Charles, Sen. (1737–1832), and *Daniel Carroll, Rep.* (1730–96), cousins and members of one of Maryland's preeminent merchant and land-owning families, were educated abroad and began their public service as state officeholders following the emancipation of Catholics in 1776. Charles served in the Continental Congress and signed the Declaration of Independence, Daniel served in the Confederation Congress, and both were elected as delegates to the Constitutional Convention. Charles declined to serve, although he was a leading advocate of ratification at the state convention.

Chambers, Stephen (ca. 1750–89), of Lancaster, a lawyer and unsuccessful candidate in the first congressional election, voted to ratify the Constitution at the Pennsylvania ratification convention.

Chase, Samuel (1741–1811), signer of the Declaration of Independence and a lawyer and merchant from Baltimore, declined to serve in the Federal Convention. An Antifederalist leader in Maryland, he voted against the Constitution at the ratification convention.

Clymer, George, Rep. (1739–1813), signer of the Declaration of Independence, was a prosperous Philadelphia merchant and former member of the Pennsylvania Assembly. He represented that state at the Federal Convention and signed the Constitution.

Collins, John (1717–95), was governor of Rhode Island from 1786 to 1790. He was not nominated for office in 1790 because he had cast the deciding vote in favor of calling a ratification convention in 1790.

Contee, Benjamin, Rep. (1755–1815), a Federalist, was a merchant and lawyer from Charles County, Maryland, who served briefly in the Confederation Congress.

Coxe, Tench (1755–1824), Philadelphia merchant and political economist, was one of the most prolific Federalist writers. Tainted by active loyalism until 1778, his political career had been limited to the Annapolis Convention and the last months of the Confederation Congress.

Dane, Nathan (1752–1835), a lawyer from Beverly, Massachusetts, had served in the Confederation Congress in 1786–88. Originally an Antifederalist, he changed parties in July 1788 and ran unsuccessfully as a Federalist for the U.S. House and Senate.

Davie, William R. (1756–1820), a lawyer and Federalist, represented North Carolina at the Federal Convention and the town of Halifax at both state ratification conventions.

Dawson, John (1762–1814), a resident of Madison's congressional district, represented Spotsylvania County in the Virginia House of Delegates, 1786–89, and Virginia in the Confederation Congress, 1788–89. An Antifederalist member of the state ratification convention, he voted against the Constitution.

Dwight, Thomas (1758–1819), a lawyer from Springfield, Massachusetts, was a Federalist. His wife and Pamela Sedgwick were cousins.

Ellery, William (1727–1820), chief justice of Rhode Island, signer of the Declaration of Independence, and a Federalist from Newport, served in Congress for almost a decade beginning in 1776.

Ellsworth, Oliver, Sen. (1745–1807), a jurist from Hartford, Connecticut, who was educated at Yale and Princeton, served in the state legislature and the Confederation Congress. A member of the Federal Convention, he promoted ratification in the press and at the state convention.

Fenno, John (1751–98), moved from Boston to New York in 1789 to establish the *Gazette of the United States*, a Federalist newspaper. The Senate employed him to print its official documents.

Fitzsimons, Thomas, Rep. (1741–1811), a Federalist, was born in Ireland and settled in Philadelphia, where he became a wealthy merchant. He served in the Pennsylvania Assembly and in the Confederation Congress.

Gale, George, Rep. (1756–1815) represented Somerset County, Maryland, in a number of state offices. He voted to ratify the Constitution at the state convention.

Gerry, Elbridge, Rep. (1744–1814), an Antifederalist, was a merchant and officeholder from Cambridge, Massachusetts. He attended the Continental Congress, where he signed the Declaration of Independence, and the Confederation Congress. A delegate to the Federal Convention, he refused to sign the Constitution and actively protested its ratification in the press and at the state convention, which he attended as an unofficial observer.

Gibbs, Henry (1749–94), was a merchant from Salem, Massachusetts.

Goodhue, Benjamin, Rep. (1748–1814), a Federalist, was a Harvard educated merchant from Salem, Massachusetts, who held a number of state and county offices.

Gore, Christopher (1758–1827), was an attorney who represented Boston in the Massachusetts House of Representatives. At the state convention, he voted to ratify the Constitution.

Grayson, William, Sen. (ca. 1736–90), an Antifederalist, was a lawyer from Prince William County, Virginia. He served in the Virginia House of Delegates, the Confederation Congress, and the state ratification convention.

Griffin, Samuel, Rep. (1746–1810), was a lawyer and planter who represented Williamsburg, Virginia, in the state legislature before being elected as a Federalist to the First Congress.

Hall, Stephen (1743–94), of Portland, was active in the movement to separate Maine from Massachusetts.

Hampton, Richard (1752–92), represented the Saxe-Gotha District in the South Carolina Senate, 1784–92, and at the ratification convention, where he voted against ratification.

Hartley, Thomas, Rep. (1748–1800), developed a lucrative law practice in York County, Pennsylvania, before serving in a number of state offices. He voted to ratify the Constitution at the state convention.

Hawkins, Benjamin, Sen. (1745–1816), a planter from Halifax, North Carolina, served in the state House of Commons, the Confederation Congress, and the state's second ratifying convention in 1789. He was elected as a Federalist after the first session of the First Congress.

Henry, Patrick (1736–99), of Prince Edward County, Virginia, a longtime political enemy of James Madison, declined to represent Virginia in the Federal Convention and became one of the most prominent Antifederalists in the United States. At the ratification convention he led the Antifederalist opposition and voted against the Constitution. A powerful force in the legislature, he prevented the election of James Madison to the U.S. Senate and then supported legislation creating a decidedly antifederal congressional district around Madison's home county of Orange, and requiring that candidates reside in the district they sought to represent.

Henshaw, Samuel (1744–1809), a Federalist who represented Northampton in the Massachusetts House of Representatives in 1788–90, acted as Theodore Sedgwick's "campaign manager" during the first congressional election.

Hiester, Daniel, Rep. (1747–1804), of Montgomery County, Pennsylvania, was a farmer like his German immigrant father. He was a member of the

Supreme Executive Council before being elected as a Federalist to the First Congress.

Hodge, Michael (1743–1816), a merchant and town clerk of Newburyport, Massachusetts, was a Federalist.

Hopkinson, Francis (1737–91), who had signed the Declaration of Independence for New Jersey, was a Philadelphia judge and prominent Federalist propagandist. He directed the huge parade in Philadelphia in 1788 that celebrated ratification of the Constitution by ten states.

Howard, John Eager (1752–1827), a Federalist, was a Baltimore planter and land developer. In 1789 he was governor of Maryland.

Humphreys, David (1752–1818), a Federalist, merchant, and poet from Derby, Connecticut, was a presidential aide. In 1785–86 he served as secretary to Thomas Jefferson, American minister to France.

Huntington, Benjamin, Rep. (1736–1800), a Yale educated lawyer from Norwich, Connecticut, was an active municipal and state officeholder. He served in the Confederation Congress and was elected as a Federalist to the First Congress.

Iredell, James (1751–99), a lawyer from Edenton, North Carolina, led the unsuccessful attempt to ratify the Constitution at the state convention in 1788.

Izard, Ralph, Sen. (1742–1804), a Federalist, was probably the wealthiest planter in South Carolina. He spent many years abroad on diplomatic missions before serving in the Confederation Congress and the South Carolina legislature.

Jackson, James, Rep. (1757–1806) was a British immigrant who practiced law in Savannah, Georgia. He served in the state assembly and was elected as a Federalist to the First Congress.

Jefferson, Thomas (1743–1826), author of the Declaration of Independence and American minister to France, 1785–89, had worked closely with his friend James Madison to secure adoption of the Virginia statute of religious freedom in 1786. His letters to Madison during the winter of 1788–89 helped to convince Madison that amendments guaranteeing civil liberties should be added to the Constitution. Although he claimed to be more of a Federalist than an Antifederalist, his widely circulated suggestion that once nine states had ratified the Constitution, the others should withhold their consent, made him a moderate Federalist at best.

Johnson, William Samuel, Sen. (1727–1819), the son of an Anglican minister and educator, was trained at Yale and practiced law in Stratford, Connecticut, holding various legislative and judicial offices at the state level before serving in the Confederation Congress and in the Philadelphia convention. He voted for ratification at the state convention.

Johnston, Samuel, Sen. (1733–1816), a planter from Edenton and governor of North Carolina, represented that state in the Confederation Congress. He supported ratification at the state's second convention in 1789 and then served in the U.S. Senate.

Jones, Joseph (1727–1805), Fredericksburg lawyer, member of Congress in 1780–83, and member of the Virginia Council of State in 1789, was a Federalist.

King, Miles (1747–1814), of Hampton, Virginia, represented Elizabeth City County in the House of Delegates, 1784–89, and in the ratification convention where he voted in favor of the Constitution.

King, Rufus, Sen. (1755–1827), a Harvard educated lawyer and officeholder in Massachusetts, represented that state in the Confederation Congress and the Constitutional Convention, voting to ratify the Constitution at the state convention the next year. Failing to win election to national office in his native state, he moved to New York and was elected as a senator to the First Congress.

Knox, Henry (1750–1806), of Boston, secretary of war from 1785 to 1794, was an active Federalist who acted as a clearing house for information about national politics during 1787–88.

Langdon, John, Sen. (1741–1819), was a prosperous merchant from Portsmouth, New Hampshire, who held various state offices and served in the Continental and Confederation Congresses. He attended the Constitutional Convention and voted to ratify the Constitution at the state convention.

Laurance, John, Rep. (1750–1810), a Federalist, immigrated from England and settled in New York City, where he practiced law. He served in a number of local and state offices, as well as the Confederation Congress.

Lee, Charles (1758–1815), brother of Rep. Richard Bland Lee and cousin of Sen. Richard Henry Lee, was a Federalist and state naval officer in Alexandria, Virginia.

Lee, Francis Lightfoot (1734–97), signer of the Declaration of Independence and brother of Sen. Richard Henry Lee, was a Federalist.

Lee, Richard Bland, Rep. (1761–1827), a large landowner and planter in Loudoun County, belonged to the politically prominent Virginia dynasty that included his brothers Henry Lee and Charles Lee, and cousins Richard Henry Lee and Francis Lightfoot Lee. He served in the Virginia legislature and as a Federalist in the First Congress.

Lee, Richard Henry, Sen. (1732–94), an Antifederalist of national prominence, was a landowner and planter from Westmoreland County, Virginia, who served in a number of local and state offices. He attended the Continental Congress, where he signed the Declaration of Independence, and the Confederation Congress. Elected as a delegate to the Federal Convention, he declined to serve.

Leonard, George, Rep. (1729–1819), a Harvard trained Federalist lawyer from Norton, Massachusetts, served in a number of local and state legislative and judicial posts.

Lincoln, Benjamin (1733–1810), of Hingham, Massachusetts, was a Federalist delegate to the state ratification convention. He was elected lieutenant governor in 1788, but lost in 1789 to Antifederalist Samuel Adams.

Livermore, Samuel, Rep. (1732–1803), of Holderness, New Hampshire, graduated from Princeton and practiced law while serving in various legislative and judicial positions. As a member of the state convention, he voted for ratification.

Maclay, William, Sen. (1737–1804), son of Scotch-Irish immigrants, settled in Sunbury, Pennsylvania, where he was a surveyor and officeholder in county and state government. A Federalist, he was elected to the First Congress as a compromise candidate representing the western and agricultural interest, which was predominantly Antifederal.

Madison, James, Jr., Rep. (1751–1836), was a Princeton-trained lawyer who settled in Orange County, Virginia, and represented it in Virginia revolutionary and legislative bodies. He represented Virginia in the Confederation Congress and at the Federal Convention. He promoted ratification of the Constitution in the press and as a delegate to the state convention. See also the Introduction.

Madison, James, Sr. (1723–1801), father of the Representative, was a planter in Orange County, Virginia.

Madison, Rev. James (1749–1812), president of the College of William and Mary, was a cousin of the Virginia Representative.

Mason, George (1725–92), principal author of the Virginia Declaration of Rights and state constitution in 1776, refused to sign the Constitution at the Federal Convention in 1787. Because he was an Antifederalist writer of national importance, his predominantly Federalist home county of Fairfax refused to send him to the ratification convention. He represented Stafford instead and voted against the Constitution.

Minot, George Richards (1758–1802), a Boston Federalist, was clerk of the Massachusetts House of Representatives and the state ratification convention. He and Fisher Ames formed a close friendship when they studied in the same law office.

Mitchell, George (died ca. 1799), a Sussex County Federalist and speaker of the Delaware Legislative Council, served as a presidential elector.

Moore, Andrew, Rep. (1752–1821), was a lawyer from Rockbridge County, Virginia, which he represented in the state legislature. A delegate to the state convention, he voted to ratify the Constitution.

Morris, Robert, Sen. (1734–1806), born in England and trained as a merchant in Philadelphia, served in the Continental Congress during the war, and as Congress's superintendent of finance from 1781 to 1784. He signed the Declaration of Independence and the Federal Constitution.

Muhlenberg, Frederick A., Speaker (1750–1801), was a pastor of German Lutheran churches before settling permanently in Montgomery County, Pennsylvania. A popular officeholder in county and state government, he was elected president of the state's ratifying convention and served as a Federalist in the First Congress.

Muhlenberg, Peter, Rep. (1746–1807), trained, like his brother, for the Lutheran ministry, served as a pastor in Virginia before moving to Montgomery County, Pennsylvania, where he became active in the state government. A delegate to the state convention, he voted for ratification.

Nasson, Samuel (1744–1800), represented Sanford, Maine, in the Massachusetts ratification convention, where he voted against the Constitution.

Nicholas, Wilson Cary (1761–1820), a Federalist constituent of Madison's, represented Albemarle County in the Virginia house of delegates and at the state ratification convention.

Otis, Samuel Allyne (1740–1814), educated at Harvard, was a bankrupt Boston merchant active in local politics who served in the state legislature and the Confederation Congress. He ran unsuccessfully as a Federalist candidate in the first congressional election, thereafter using his connections with prominent New England and Southern political leaders to secure appointment as the first secretary of the Senate.

Page, John, Rep. (1744–1808), was the son of a wealthy planter of Gloucester County, Virginia, which he represented in numerous state offices before being elected as a Federalist to the First Congress.

Parker, Richard (1729–1813), of Westmoreland County, was a judge of the general court of Virginia.

Partridge, George, Rep. (1740–1828), studied at Harvard and taught school in Duxbury, Massachusetts, before being elected to various county and state offices. A delegate to the Continental and Confederation Congresses, he voted to ratify the Constitution at the state convention.

Pendleton, Edmund (1721–1803), a prominent jurist and elder statesman from Caroline County, Virginia, presided over the state supreme court of appeals and the state ratification convention. He voted to ratify the Constitution.

Peters, Richard (1744–1828), a lawyer and Federalist from Philadelphia, was speaker of the Pennsylvania Assembly, 1788–90. He had been a leading member of the Board of War, 1777–81, and a member of Congress, 1782–83.

Phillips, Samuel, Jr. (1752–1802), a Federalist and manufacturer from Andover, represented Essex County in the Massachusetts Senate from 1780 to 1800.

Pickering, Timothy (1745–1829), moved to Luzerne County, Pennsylvania, from Massachusetts in 1787. He voted for ratification at the Pennsylvania convention.

Pinckney, Charles (1757–1824), governor of South Carolina, was a lawyer from Charleston. He attended the Confederation Congress and the Federal Convention.

Powell, Leven (1737–1810), represented Loudoun County in the Virginia ratification convention and voted for the Constitution.

Randolph, Edmund (1753–1813), governor of Virginia, 1786–88, refused to sign the Constitution at the Federal Convention but voted for it at the state ratification convention.

Randolph, John (1773–1833), and *Randolph, Theodorick Bland* (1771–92), were brothers and students at Columbia College. They were the wards of

St. George Tucker, who had married their mother, and the nephews of Rep. Theodorick Bland.

Randolph, Thomas Mann, Sr. (1741–93), a Goochland County planter who had grown up with Thomas Jefferson, was a prominent resident of Madison's congressional district.

Rush, Benjamin (1745–1813), Philadelphia physician, reformer, and signer of the Declaration of Independence, began as early as 1776 to write newspaper articles in favor of a strong central government. He voted for the Constitution at the state ratification convention.

Rutledge, Edward (1749–1800), a signer of the Declaration of Independence from Charleston, South Carolina, voted in favor of the Constitution at the state ratification convention.

Scott, Thomas, Rep. (1739–96), a county and state officeholder from Washington County, Pennsylvania, voted in favor of the Constitution at the state ratification convention.

Sedgwick, Pamela (ca. 1753–1807), of Great Barrington, Massachusetts, married Rep. Theodore Sedgwick in 1774. Their correspondence is filled with important details about politics.

Sedgwick, Theodore, Rep. (1746–1813), studied at Yale and practiced law in Berkshire County, Massachusetts, which he represented in the state legislature. He attended the Confederation Congress and the Massachusetts state convention, where he voted for ratification.

Seney, Joshua, Rep. (1756–98), a Federalist, was a lawyer and farmer from Queen Annes County, Maryland, who served in the state legislature and in the Confederation Congress.

Sherman, Roger, Rep. (1721–93), a publisher, lawyer, merchant, judge, and municipal and state officeholder from New Haven, Connecticut, served for many years in both the Continental Congress, where he signed the Declaration of Independence, and the Confederation Congress. He assumed an important role at the Federal Convention and actively supported ratification in both the press and the state convention.

Silvester, Peter, Rep. (1734–1808), a Federalist, practiced law in Albany, New York. He represented that town in the state legislature and in the First Congress.

Sinnickson, Thomas, Rep. (1744–1817), a wealthy merchant from Salem, New Jersey, served in various county and state offices before being elected as a Federalist to the First Congress.

Smith, William, Rep. (1728–1814), a Federalist, was a prominent merchant from Baltimore. He represented Maryland briefly in the Continental Congress.

Smith, William Loughton, Rep. (1758?–1812), the son of a wealthy merchant of Charleston, South Carolina, studied law in London during the Revolutionary War. Upon his return to South Carolina, with the support of several influential friends and patrons, including his father-in-law, Ralph Izard, he enjoyed a rapid rise in state politics before being elected as a Federalist to the First Congress.

Stevens, Edward (1745–1820), a Federalist, planter, and constituent of Madison's, represented Culpeper, Spotsylvania, and Orange counties in the state senate, 1779–90.

Stiles, Ezra (1727–95), president of Yale College at New Haven, Connecticut, was a Federalist.

Stone, Michael Jenifer, Rep. (1747–1812) of Port Tobacco, Maryland, was trained in the law and served briefly in the Maryland legislature before attending the state convention, where he voted for ratification.

Strong, Caleb, Sen. (1745–1819), a lawyer and officeholder from Northampton, Massachusetts, was a delegate to the Federal Convention. He became an important leader of the ratification forces at the state convention and was later elected as a Federalist to the First Congress.

Stuart, Archibald (1757–1832), a lawyer from Staunton, Virginia, represented Augusta County in the House of Delegates, 1786–88, and the state convention, where he voted to ratify the Constitution.

Stuart, David (1753–ca. 1814), represented Fairfax County, Virginia, in the House of Delegates and the state convention, where he voted to ratify the Constitution. He married the widow of Martha Washington's son Jack Custis and became a close friend of George Washington, who attempted to persuade him to run for the U.S. House of Representatives in 1789.

Sullivan, James (1744–1808), a lawyer and jurist from Boston, was an Antifederalist.

Sumter, Thomas, Rep. (1734–1832), an Antifederalist, came from a poor background in the Virginia Piedmont and settled in Statesburg, South Carolina, which he represented in the state legislature. He voted against ratification at the state convention.

Thatcher, George, Rep. (1754–1824), Harvard educated, settled in the Massachusetts province of Maine where he practiced law. He served briefly in the last year of the Confederation Congress, and thereafter was elected as a Federalist to the First Congress.

Tilghman, William (1756–1827), a loyalist during the war and a lawyer, represented Kent County, Maryland, in the House of Delegates, 1788–90, and the state convention, where he voted for ratification.

Trumbull, Jonathan, Jr., Rep. (1740–1809), born into a politically prominent family, served in the Connecticut legislature before representing his state as a Federalist in the First Congress.

Tucker, St. George (1752–1827), a Virginia jurist, attended the Annapolis Convention in 1786. He was the brother of Rep. Thomas Tudor Tucker.

Tucker, Thomas Tudor, Rep. (1745–1828), an Antifederalist, was born in Bermuda and settled in Charleston, South Carolina, where he practiced medicine. He was a delegate to the state legislature and, briefly, to the Confederation Congress.

Tufts, Cotton (1737–99), a doctor from Weymouth, Massachusetts, represented Suffolk County in the state Senate and voted in favor of ratification at the convention.

Turberville, George Lee (1760–98), a planter, represented Richmond County in the Virginia House of Delegates, 1785–90. He ran for election to the state ratification convention as a Federalist but lost.

Van Schaack, Peter (1747–1832), a loyalist from Kinderhook in Columbia County, returned to New York in 1785 and was readmitted to the state bar a year later. A Federalist, he was defeated for election to the state ratification convention. Rep. Peter Silvester was his brother-in-law.

Vining, John, Rep. (1758–1802), a Federalist, praticed law in his native Dover, Delaware. He served in the state legislature and the Confederation Congress.

Wait, Thomas B. (1762–1824), was the publisher of the Portland *Cumberland Gazette*, the first newspaper in Maine.

Ward, Joseph (ca. 1737–1812), a Boston land developer and business promoter, was a Federalist.

Washington, George (1732–99), president of the Federal Convention and first President of the United States, was a planter and politician in Fairfax County, Virginia, before the Revolutionary War.

Webster, Noah (1758–1843), a Connecticut native residing in Philadelphia, was an editor who wrote tracts advocating a strong central government.

Wendell, John (1731–1808), a Federalist, was a merchant in Portsmouth, New Hampshire.

White, Alexander, Rep. (1739–1804), studied law in England and had a successful practice in his native Frederick County, Virginia, which he represented in the state legislature. He was a member of the state convention and voted for ratification.

Williams, Otho Holland (1749–94), naval officer for the port of Baltimore, Maryland, since 1783, was a Federalist and the son-in-law of Rep. William Smith.

Wingate, Paine, Sen. (1739–1838), studied at Harvard and settled as a farmer in Stratham, New Hampshire, which he represented in the state legislature. He served briefly in the Confederation Congress before being elected as a Federalist to the First Congress.

Wolcott, Oliver, Sr. (1726–97), lieutenant governor of Connecticut, represented Litchfield at the state convention and voted to ratify the Constitution.

Yeates, Jasper (1745–1817), an attorney from Lancaster, voted for ratification at the Pennsylvania convention.

Index

An asterisk denotes a member of Congress. Biographical data appear on pages 301–14.

Printed in the United States
133030LV00001B/415-417/A